MY MOTHER'S GHOST

MY MOTHER'S GHOST
FERGUS M. BORDEWICH

DOUBLEDAY

New York   London   Toronto

Sydney   Auckland

PUBLISHED BY DOUBLEDAY
a division of Random House, Inc.
1540 Broadway, New York, New York, 10036

DOUBLEDAY and the portrayal of an anchor with a dolphin are
trademarks of Doubleday, a division of Random House, Inc.

Book design by Paul Randall Mize

Excerpt from "Little Gidding" in FOUR QUARTETS,
copyright 1942 by T.S. Eliot and renewed 1970 by Esme Valerie Eliot,
reprinted by permission of Harcourt, Inc.

Library of Congress Cataloging-in-Publication Data

Bordewich, Fergus M.
My mother's ghost / Fergus M. Bordewich.—1st ed.
p.   cm.
1. Bordewich, Fergus M.   2. Bordewich, Fergus M.—Family.   3. Journalists—
United States—Biography.   4. Madigan, LaVerne, d. 1962—Death and burial.
I. Title.
PN4874.B6246   A3   2001
070'.92—dc21
[B]   00-029710

ISBN 0-385-49129-8
Copyright © 2001 by Fergus M. Bordewich
All Rights Reserved
Printed in the United States of America
First Edition: January 2001

1 3 5 7 9 10 8 6 4 2

For Jean and Chloe

Part One

ઝ

Ghost

We never think that what we think hides us from what we are.

—PAUL VALERY,
Monsieur Teste

W<small>E GOT OFF</small> to a bad start that summer, the summer of my fourteenth year. Even now, remembering what happened is like watching a continuous film strip that turns back upon itself and is always the same, always curiously comforting in its familiarity, except for its last catastrophic scene, which changed everything.

In 1962 it was a ten-hour drive to the lake from our home in Yonkers, just north of New York City. We had only been on the road a couple of hours when my mother's Buick began to overheat. She let the engine cool off and then started up again and drove for a while before the same thing happened again. Not one to give in easily, least of all to a machine, she toughed it out as long as she could, until we could all see that we weren't going to make it all the way to northern Vermont like that. By the middle of the afternoon she was so snappish that even Maddy, my grandmother, fell silent and the two dogs crouched on the floor of the back seat with their snouts in their paws. Finally she stopped at a repair shop somewhere on Route 22. When the mechanic came out from under the hood, he said it was the thermostat and that he'd have to get a new one from somewhere too far away to put it in that day. When my mother protested, he said that she could go ahead and burn out the engine if she wanted, he didn't care, or we could stay the night in the motel across the road.

Not that I blamed my mother. She hadn't counted on driving all the way herself. As I watched her pacing the concrete apron in front of the garage and lighting Winstons one after the other, sucking hard on them, ignoring the N<small>O</small> S<small>MOKING</small> signs posted all around, I felt only sympathy. She didn't know how to be helpless and couldn't bear it at all. If I blamed anyone, it was my father, who always drove us to Vermont. He was supposed to join us at the lake in a week. The company he worked for, which had hired him just a few months before and where he planned heating systems for housing developments and plants, had asked him to stay on an extra week. I still couldn't forgive him, even though I knew that he hadn't been free to refuse. I stared furiously over the panorama of hills as green and neat as ones in a kid's storybook, thinking about how we couldn't go riding the next day and worrying that if the car wasn't fixed we'd miss the day after that too, and that maybe we'd never even get to the lake at all, and our whole vacation would be ruined.

That night in the motel I lay with my eyes closed listening to my grandmother's mad voice going on about how she had to get down to Fort Hamilton to roll bandages for the troops. "Which troops?" my mother asked, already knowing the answer, and Maddy said, "Teddy Roosevelt's." My mother answered back with barely suppressed irritation, "That was the Spanish-American War." Then Maddy asked if there was any news in the paper about Mrs. Astor, and then she said that she wanted to go see Nell Hogan as soon as we got back from New Orleans, and my mother said we were going to Vermont not New Orleans and that Nell Hogan was dead and Mrs. Astor was too, and please try to get to sleep now, because we all needed sleep, lots of sleep.

I was not a very observant boy, but I couldn't help seeing that my grandmother was odd. Some days she wore a hairpiece that didn't match her hair, or wore it on the side of her head and insisted that it was a style. She appeared in peculiar combinations of clothing or reported conversations that she said she'd had with one of the dogs. She put strange things on our dinner plates. Sometimes I found her cooking dirt on the stove and saying that she was making stew. Over the past year her memory had become steadily more unpredictable. People and places, entire eras fused and splintered and recombined in ways that increasingly unnerved me.

NEXT MORNING, to everyone's relief, the Buick was repaired and ready to go.

My mother rolled the top down and the dogs climbed onto

Maddy's lap, and as the car gathered speed their pink tongues flapped like pennants in the wind. The air smelled sweet, and I knew that we'd be crossing the state line into Vermont any time and that now the weeks would unfurl after all into endless days when there would be time enough for everything. We went from farmland to forest and then followed the Green Mountains north until we reached the towns we knew, Hardwick and Glover and Barton, where we always shopped for groceries and bought the *New York Times,* and where I already felt within the lake's grasp.

The lake lay a few miles east of Barton. It was a dark, ungentle landscape, and it made me uneasy when I was small, before I got to know it and made it my own. The lake—large for the region, nearly seven miles long from end to end—was so deep that on any but the brightest days the deep glacial trough that cradled it swallowed the sunlight entirely, leaving the black surface with a chilly, vestigial glint. The naked cliffs that towered over the lake's southern end and the scree of shattered rock beneath them suggested cataclysm and rupture, a memoir in granite of the primeval violence from which it sprang. Most of the summer cottages, however—usually shingled affairs painted in muted greens and browns and grays—lay in sunnier settings at the northern end of the lake and had cute names like Nod-Away, Wayward Winds, and Brookadoon. And, of course, the Lyndon.

In later years, I vividly "remembered" having spent many seasons in the Lyndon. But this isn't true. In years past we had rented a succession of cottages; my mother had discovered the Lyndon only the year before and been enchanted by its rambling verandas and old yellow planked walls and the huge wood-fired stove that she liked to think of as a dragon that dwelled in the kitchen. I didn't understand then that she craved its space, space into which she could flee from Maddy's nattering drone, space into which she could retreat with her alps of notes from her trips to Alaska and Mississippi and Florida and for the Northern Plains book that was supposed to get written that year.

My mother had had an extraordinary life for a woman of her

generation. For most of the last decade she had led the Association on American Indian Affairs, then the only important national organization concerned with the rights of Native Americans. As its executive director, she introduced community activism to Indian country at a time when reservations were governed like colonial satrapies by the Bureau of Indian Affairs and when Washington had committed itself as a matter of policy to the systematic dismantling of the tribes. She charmed even those who opposed her with her vibrant and earthy Irish humor and with an erudition that sometimes daunted even good friends. If she feared anything, it was only boredom and ineffectuality. A stylish dresser, an epitome of Manhattan chic, she nonetheless never seemed more at home than on a busted sofa in some prairie cabin, her arm flung back, and laughing with a Winston dangling jauntily from her lips, surrounded by her Indian friends. Lakotas who adopted her into their family gave her the name Tokeya Icaga Win, or Eldest Child; Omahas called her We-hae-tunga, or Big Sister, and Miccosukees, Knee Hat Kee, or White Day. She never changed her name when she married and was known to everyone she worked with as Miss LaVerne Madigan.

She worked ten and twelve hours a day most days, sometimes six or even seven days a week. When I went to bed, I would often see her scribbling on pad after pad of yellow foolscap, chain-smoking and drinking strong coffee. Sometimes she would still be writing when I woke in the morning, and then she would drink more coffee and then get into the Buick and drive to her office in Manhattan. It was Alaska that was absorbing most of her energy that year. The past November she had brought Inupiat leaders from across the Alaskan Arctic face-to-face with each other for the first time in history, in the town of Barrow, to make them aware that they would soon have to deal with an onrush of legislation intended to forestall future native claims on the new state's land and mineral wealth. She had gone to Alaska again in the spring, and then a third time in June, taking me with her, as she would often do, for two or three weeks at a time, lifting me out of the predictable cycle of suburban life and transforming me, as

I imagined, from being just a son, her only child, into a colleague and partner, her best friend.

On this trip she took me to Tanana on the Yukon River, where at her instigation Indians from the lower part of the state were coming together, also for the first time, as the Inupiat had the previous November. Since there were no roads, we flew into Tanana in a small plane over a green tumult of forest so vast and forbidding that as we descended into it I felt as if we were about to sink away in a fathomless green sea. My mother refused any special accommodations for us, and for two days we slept with strangers in someone's home, on floors that were covered with mattresses, sleeping bags, and piles of clothing that did for pillows, and dined on peanut-butter sandwiches and coffee.

The meeting took place in a shingled hall on the edge of the forest. Although much that was said went over my head, I was old enough by now to see how masterful my mother was in the play of debate. She was always at the center of things, yet unobtrusive, never calling attention to herself, always ready to let others take credit for what she had done. And she was afraid of nothing. At fourteen, I was shy and tentative by nature, and her fearlessness amazed me. Mostly, she listened as native people spoke, answering their questions about what she thought Washington meant to do and what kind of help she could give them if they challenged the politicians in Juneau. At one point a Catholic priest stood up, a white man, who said that he was speaking for the villages in his parish. He said he knew that they, *his* people, not to mention most of the people in that very room, didn't want to get mixed up in politics and that they were sure to suffer for it in the end if they paid attention to outsiders like my mother, who were only filling them with dreams of power that they wouldn't know how to use for many years yet.

I can see them: my mother, a head shorter than anyone else in the place, with her pale Irish skin, her blue eyes clear and penetrating, her pale hair swept back in its vivid natural wave, and then the red-faced priest, scowling down at her, not realizing what he was in for.

Standing up, she asked the priest how he had been elected. When he said that he hadn't, but that he didn't need to be because everyone trusted him to speak for them, she asked him, never raising her voice, whether he had ever asked himself whether native people were capable of speaking for themselves. It was obvious that he was unaccustomed to being challenged, because he started to tell her in front of everyone to sit down and be quiet. But she pressed on, gently smiling, telling him that when she was a girl at Sacred Heart School any little boy who spoke to a girl like that would be swatted but good by the nuns. There was silence for a while, maybe even shock at the sight of my mother standing up to the kind of bullying white man they all recognized, and then the Indians began snickering and then laughing as she asked him, didn't he think it was time for native people to make their own decisions and for white people to get out of their way?

As I watched her, I thought fiercely that I wanted to be her more than anything in the world.

We had only been home a week when she flew off again to Washington to testify before a congressional committee on the situation in Alaska, and then to Mississippi to confer with the Choctaws. By the time we left for Vermont, even she admitted that she was ready for a rest.

THERE WAS PLENTY TO DO at the lake while we waited for my father to arrive. My mother and I went riding every morning on horses that we rented from Wally Hunt, a farmer who lived a little north of the lake on the Barton road. I loved the feel of the animal beneath me and the sense of power that came with it. But far stronger was the knowledge that it was something that belonged to my mother and me alone. It was something we had done together every summer morning in Vermont since Wally had taught me to ride years before. I can now see that I was never much of a rider, never really skilled at anything much more than staying on and avoiding mistakes, and that I mistook obedience and the willingness to follow directions for skill and strength. But I was proud of what I could do then, and I rode with a poise and a self-confidence that I felt almost nowhere else in my life.

In the afternoon we usually swam from the tiny beach below the Lyndon. Later I would sit for hours on the veranda, my chair tilted back against the wall and my feet on the railing, reading Bruce Catton's history of the Army of the Potomac, trying to ignore Maddy's incessant chatter.

One night at dinner Maddy turned to my mother and said, "Wouldn't it be nice if LaVerne was here? That's all we need to be happy!"

My mother looked at her with an expression as close to terror as I ever saw on her face and said, "Mother, I am here."

After my grandmother went to bed, my mother and I sat reading in front of the fire, which we built on chilly evenings and kept stoked with pine logs from a bin on the veranda. I was aware for some time that she was watching me, waiting for me to speak. When I didn't, she told me how we would go together to Nebraska next year and that we'd drive across the sand hills to South Dakota and see the Badlands again, and the Black Hills. And then, smiling at me conspiratorially, she promised that before we left Vermont this year she would teach me to drive, license or no, though I was only fourteen, since plenty of Indian boys began driving when they were even younger than that, so why shouldn't I.

FINALLY MY FATHER ARRIVED in his Rambler with a stack of whodunits and a bottle of rye. I was glad to see him, happy that we were all together the way we were supposed to be, but at the same time I was uneasy around him in a way that I couldn't explain to myself at all. Were he a hard man, I might have understood my feelings better. But he was amiable and soft-spoken, and with people he liked he was gregarious in a modest, unoffending way, a popular man on the next barstool. Secretly, however, I wished for a different father. I was ashamed of this, of course, but I couldn't control it, like something illicit and disgraceful. When I put my parents' images next to each other in my mind they simply would not match up, as if I had gotten a photo from a stranger's collection mixed up with my own.

A couple of days later my mother and I and four or five other riders rode with Wally over the hills to Brownington. My father brought Maddy to meet us there by car, and when we arrived they already had picnic baskets open on the bank of a stream. We climbed down and ate sandwiches and drank lemonade, and I wished that I could ride every day and lie spread-eagled on the grass with the sun hot on my face and my bare feet dangling in the icy stream, surrounded by the smell of horses and new-mown grass and the voices of my parents close by. They were talking about how tomorrow night we would go to the movies, and on the weekend to Quebec City, where we would hear French and eat croissants.

This would be the last scene in which I was to see us all together, in a single frame, so to speak. Examining it all now, it seems like something out of another century, or out of an old Hollywood film, polished by the passage of too much time and by the wish to see things as simpler than they were. Even the landscape evoked myth: the New England village with its austere clapboard homes and white steeples suggesting an eternal America in which all things have their allotted and immutable place. For years I would return to this image as if I could believe that we would go on forever as we were.

MY MEMORY of what happened is cold and crystalline and hard, compacted by time. It always begins the same way. As soon as my eyes are open I am instantly aware of the pale green of the room and of the damp chill seeping through the old walls and that we are already late. We are due at Wally's in ten minutes to ride and we will never make it. I run past my grandmother's room to my parents' and see that my mother is still fast asleep. I tug at the sheets. She rolls away from me and pulls the covers over her head. When I tell her she's got to hurry she murmurs, "Please let me sleep."

It's drizzling outside and sheets of clouds lie over the lake, cloaking the peaks of Mount Pisgah and Mount Hor and darkening the water. We are already so late that there's hardly any point in going now, but our morning ride is what I look forward to most and we already missed yesterday because of the rain and I won't miss another.

I beg her to get up.

Finally she forces herself awake. She looks out the window at the rain and says, raw-nerved from tobacco and not enough sleep, "Let's not go today."

The day is about to be spoiled even before it has begun but I am determined to save it.

"No," I say. "Let's go." It is going to clear. I can see cracks in the clouds and pale streaks of light that bode good weather. I tell her, "Just look," and then that Wally is expecting us and, knowing that it's not true, that he'll be sore at us if we don't show up.

I know that I can make her get up. She hardly ever refuses me anything.

Through all this my father never stirs.

Finally she reaches over and takes a Winston from the night table and lights it, and then one or two more until she has smoked herself awake. She sends me downstairs, and a few minutes later comes down herself dressed in rust-colored trousers and a white blouse, a favorite outfit, and carrying a purse made of reindeer hide that she brought back from Alaska.

Driving north in silence in the Buick I can tell that she's annoyed at me but determined to keep it to herself, that she doesn't want to spoil my ride. The road skirts the east shore of the lake, then hooks around the small beach at the lake's northern end, then turns north again past stony, hardscrabble fields and stands of pine. Just short of the Hunts' place we see Wally driving a tractor alongside the road. He is a short, prodigiously muscular man baked the color of old bricks from years in the sun. He has given up waiting for us and gone back to work and now leans down from the tractor and asks if we still mean to ride, pointing out that it's drizzling again and that it might start raining for real any time, and saying we didn't still want to ride, did we, what with the weather.

My mother asks me, What shall we do?

The easiest thing would be to go back to the cottage.

But if we do that, I say, we'll have gotten up for nothing. The day will be spoiled for no reason, because anyone can see that it's going to clear up. So let's ride, that's what we planned, so let's go.

My mother says, I don't think Wally wants to. I can see that Wally is planning to bale hay.

My mother wants to go back to bed.

I want to ride.

Finally my mother says that's what we'll do then, and she restarts the Buick and Wally pushes the tractor into gear and turns back toward his house.

The Hunts' place is a couple of hundred yards off the Barton road at the end of a dirt lane. Under a large oak in front of the farmhouse there are some wooden lawn chairs and a metal table. We wipe them off and sit there while we wait for Wally to come back and saddle the horses. Wally's wife Gertrude brings out coffee and my mother drinks cup after cup of it black. The clouds at last begin to blow away, and with them the rain. I'm happy now. I want her to cheer up and forgive me for dragging her out of bed, and chatter about going to Newport to the movies and about Quebec.

By now it is ten thirty. Two women from New Jersey have turned up wanting horses too, and will ride along with us. My mother tells Wally that she'll ride Pepper, who requires a firmer hand than most of the other horses. She likes him just for that, because he's tough and proud and unresigned to the bit, what she admires in people and what people will someday tell me they admired in her. I'll ride old General, who's more compliant, less difficult, less provocative.

We ride off together—my mother and I, and Wally, and the two New Jersey women—back to the Barton road and turn north on it and then after a few hundred feet we turn into one of the Hunts' fields, where we trot three or four times around the edge of it, warming up the horses, and then ride north again to Fiske Road and turn east, a route that we have taken many times.

My mother and I are already some distance ahead of the others.

After a while, saying let's go now, she nudges Pepper into a brisk trot, then a canter, finally a gallop. I keep up as best I can. For the first time I see that my mother is happy as she turns in the saddle and beckons me to catch up as the close woods unfurl into a panorama of forested hills that dip and roll away to the south, where granite crags bulge against the lightening sky.

I am close enough to my mother to see the taut smile on her face and, when she turns, her blue eyes brilliant and wide in the wind. She seems fused with the horse's rippling muscles and poised and powerful and splendid. By now we have left Wally and the others far behind. We are alone together in the scrubbed air, hurtling gloriously past fields freighted with guernseys. Some days we stop and call to them like friends but today we are racing and there is no time.

Nearing the four corners where we will turn onto Spiller Road, Pepper inexplicably gathers speed. Perhaps he senses that we've reached the halfway point of our ride and that from here on we're heading back to the barn, or is testing my mother, measuring her strength, hinting that she rides only at his sufferance. We are galloping faster, now, then faster still, faster than I like, but even so I am falling behind, watching my mother pull away from me up the road. For what seems a long while she gallops in silence, her small torso straining at the reins.

Then—what an effort it must have cost her to admit it—she cries out that she can't stop him, can't rein him in at all, and for the first time in my life I am frightened for her. I have never thought of her as too weak for anything. What she lacks in size she more than makes up in grit and intellect, a tool of wonderful construction that I know is capable of solving any problem. But suddenly she looks small and in control of nothing at all. She is shouting my name now, calling to me for help, begging me to tell her what to do.

I will save my mother, I think. I'm thrilled at the idea.

I know what to do. I've seen it done in a hundred Western movies. I will gallop next to my mother, lean from my horse, seize her bridle, and pull Pepper to a halt. I kick General forward. "I'm catching up," I cry. But this is fantasy, because I am not catching up at all, because the faster I gallop the faster Pepper goes, steadily widening the gap between us, not saving my mother but panicking her more.

She is calling my name over and over in a voice that I have never heard before and that terrifies me like nothing I have ever known.

We ride on like this for what seems like many long minutes but which cannot possibly be more than a few seconds.

Is my mother swinging her leg over Pepper's back? Is she really doing this? Can this possibly be what I see?

From this point on I seem to be watching everything with a strange detachment, as if a piece of my psyche has swung loose from its moorings and flung itself up above the scene before my eyes. I think: *Yes, my mother is getting off the horse. That is the wrong thing. You are not supposed to get off a galloping horse. It is a mistake, a mistake. Please get back on the horse.*

Time, which only a moment ago seemed so strangely expansive, now suddenly compresses into an atom, hard and dense with import.

In that atom of time my mother's hands let go of the reins, her other foot comes out of the stirrup and, perhaps in the monstrous belief that she can simply step down onto the road, she drops away from the horse. But her foot never even touches the ground.

Everything speeds up again. My small, blond, terrified mother goes over backward toward the road, toward me. I am a length behind her, less than that. She goes over backward under General's hooves. Then she is on the road.

I pull General to a halt a few lengths beyond where she has fallen. I slide off and run back to her. Her eyes are closed. There is a vivid trickle of blood seeping from her forehead, and another from her mouth. Her head has cracked open on the road. Or General has kicked it open.

Wally and the others are still out of sight behind us. I call to her. There was never a single moment in my life when she had not responded to my voice.

· · ·

NOTHING WAS MORE CERTAIN in my mind than that my mother was all right. She would open her eyes any second, pull herself to her feet. "What a fall!" she would say. We would round up Pepper, she would scold him, and we would walk back toward the Hunts', leading the horses until my mother felt steady enough to remount. I knew all this immediately. It was what would happen.

But it didn't. I stood on the road staring at the trickle of blood seeping over my mother's face and onto the road. I pleaded with her to get up.

Then I began to run. I left my horse like a talisman because it was the only thing I could leave to reassure her that I had not abandoned her on the road. I ran back to the four corners and across the road to the nearest farmhouse. I pounded on the door. A gaunt woman appeared. She stared at me through the screen door.

I knew that I couldn't make sense. I gasped. I pointed up the road from which I had come, not realizing that it was impossible to see my mother from where we stood. The woman listened in silence for a short while and then closed the door in my face.

I ran back into the road. I could now see Wally and the others in the distance. I began to run toward them, shouting.

By the time they reached my mother the blood had made a dark pool on the hard-packed earth.

I stared at her and said, "Mom?"

It was difficult for me to speak.

Wally galloped back to the gaunt woman's house and telephoned Gertrude, phoned to Newport for an ambulance and called my father at the Lyndon.

It was twenty-five miles to Newport. It would take the ambulance half an hour to arrive. But I knew that my mother would be all right. The ambulance was coming. Maybe we could still go to the movies.

Wally told me to go back to the farm with the other riders while he waited for the ambulance. There was no need for me to stay. My mother was going to be all right. I would drive to Newport with my father. There was no need for me to go in the ambulance. Did Wally tell me that, or did I merely think it? By this time I couldn't tell the difference any longer between what I saw and thought, wanted and feared.

It seems incomprehensible to me now that I could have believed this. But it was perfectly clear at the time as I stood there on the hard-packed road in the sunlight. It seemed bizarrely reasonable and necessary that I should leave my mother on the road in a pool of blood, that I should leave without speaking to her, or calling to her, or cradling her head, or begging her to stay with me.

Instead I got onto General and rode back to the Hunts' with the people from New Jersey. I made sure to maintain proper posture in the saddle, the way my mother had taught me, as if that were still what mattered. By the time I got to the Hunts' my father had already arrived. I told him that the ambulance had been sent from Newport, that she would be all right. We drove to the four corners. The ambulance had already been there. Only a dark stain in the dust remained.

It took half an hour to drive to Newport. My father and I sat for what seemed a long time on plastic chairs in the emergency room of the hospital. My father began complaining about the wait. He intensely disliked hospitals. They reminded him of the flu epidemic of 1918, when he was a boy. Friends who went into hospitals then never came out again. I could tell that my father wanted a drink.

When a doctor finally arrived, my father asked, "How soon will she be able to leave?"

"Your wife is dead," he said.

The doctor was much taller than my father and wore glasses. Perhaps he said something more. And perhaps he said what he had to say more gently than the single shockingly blunt sentence that I remember. Perhaps he put his hand on my father's shoulder, or on mine. But I don't remember it.

She was dead on arrival.

We drove back to the lake through Coventry, Irasburg and Barton. Neither of us spoke. *She'll be at the Lyndon*, I thought. I knew it absolutely. Relief flooded through me. Then I thought, *We won't be able to go to the movies tonight*. Then I thought, *I won't be able to ride tomorrow*. When we got to the Lyndon, my father sat down at the wooden dining table and cried. It was the first and only time in my life that I ever saw him cry. I felt ashamed for him and went outside into the ripe air. The sky had cleared, and it had become a splendid day. I had been right about that. I could hear motorboats on the lake and the shouts of water-skiers. I listened to my father and thought, *I am not going to cry*. And I didn't.

It was only later that I thought, *I've killed my mother*.

2

MY FATHER drove us back to Yonkers in the Rambler. Beforehand he told me, Don't tell Maddy your mother's dead or it will kill her. So we lied to her all the way home, and kept on lying.

When she asked, "Where's LaVernie?" my father would say, "She's in Washington. Don't you remember?" and Maddy would say, "Of course, then everything is all right."

And then, after a while she would say, "Where's LaVernie?"

Had anyone asked me, I would have said that nothing happened on the trip home, that it was just blank space between our shattered vacation and the funeral that would have to be put together as soon as we got home. But I can see that I was already learning to be silent and to think of silence as a kind of courage, the one thing that I could still give my mother. I kept telling myself the story that she often told me when I was small and making a fuss over something that hurt, the story about the Spartan boy who had taken a vow of silence, and when someone asked him what he had under his cloak said nothing even though it was a fox cub that was tearing away his innards with its claws. I thought, that's the way I will be. And I was.

When we got home, we found telegrams from all over the country. A political ally of hers from Montana wrote, "Montana Indians mourn the loss of LaVerne Madigan, whose indefatigable work for their advancement cannot be forgotten nor can her knowledge, zeal, and interest be replaced." Her Cheyenne friend John Woodenlegs wrote, "We weep for the loss of our great friend LaVerne Madigan. The Northern Cheyenne tribe will never forget what she did for them." "Deeply shocked," wrote William Whirlwind Horse, the chairman of the Pine Ridge Sioux tribe of South Dakota. "We shall always remember Miss Madigan as a friend and champion of the Oglala Sioux people." An Alaskan native rights advocate wrote that he considered her "one of the greatest Americans I have ever known." There was even a telegram from her adversaries at the Bureau of Indian Affairs that praised her "vigorous leadership" in focusing national attention on problems involving Indians: "Her contributions to their welfare will be long enduring and remembered."

My mother's body had meanwhile been sent home by train from Newport. The funeral was a hurriedly organized affair. For a day my father and I sat on metal chairs facing the corpse where it lay exposed in a coffin at a funeral home in White Plains. Most of the people who showed up were our neighbors from Yonkers and rough-cut men my father knew, who installed boilers and air conditioners for a living and had worked with him before he got the job with GE. His pal Big John showed up drunk and loud. He swayed over us and tried to talk my father into taking a drink from the bottle he had brought. Someone finally took him outside, but he kept coming back weeping, saying "It's all shit, Harry, it's all shit." A woman who had once been a beauty and whom I had known since childhood squeezed my thigh and told me to come and see her some afternoon after school, alone. "We could be lonely together," she said. But I knew that I would not be lonely, because even staring hour after hour at her corpse, even standing next to it and peering down into its face, I refused to believe that my mother was dead. My mother was still in Vermont. Or she had gone to Nebraska, or Mississippi, or New Mexico. There was no reason for all the fuss. She would come home when she was ready.

My mother's face was crusted with powder where the undertaker had made an effort to hide the damage. But it was still easy to see the jagged line where her skull had cracked open on the road. I couldn't keep my eyes off the scar. I was so absorbed with it that I didn't hear what people said to me. They thought I was overcome with grief, but they were wrong. I was thinking how my mother was flawed forever now. I imagined her walking in the door of the funeral home and signing the guest book next to the Francks and the Liebowitzes and Feeleys and then standing over the coffin and looking at the cracked and powdered thing inside it. I wondered what she would do when she saw it. Would she burst into tears? Would she be angry? Ashamed? The question seemed to have a terrible urgency. Whatever she felt, now I would know how to comfort her. I would tell her that the scar didn't matter and that I would love her forever in spite of it. Then I thought that she would also tell me what she thought about it, and how I could think about it so that it wouldn't upset me, and that when we had talked it over everything would be okay and we could go home. I spent so much of the day thinking about this that when it was finally time to leave, I thought, feeling suddenly stricken with anxiety in a way that I had not all day, why hasn't my mother come?

Hundreds of people came to the service the following day. There were Indians from Nebraska and the Dakotas, and Montana, and an Eskimo from Barrow, Alaska, sweating ferociously in the August heat. A Miccosukee came from Florida, dazzlingly dressed in feathers. There were political people from Washington, and the Jewish women from my mother's office in the city, one or two childhood friends from her youth in Mount Vernon, and a few friends from our block, looking shy and out of place in the cosmopolitan crowd. The mass was said by my mother's aged friend Father John LaFarge, one of the most influential liberal Catholic theologians of his generation. That there was a mass at all was a mistake. In the confusion following her death someone had told the funeral home that my mother was Catholic. Although she was raised piously enough, she had been an atheist most of her life. In the end, in a travesty of her convictions, she went into the Westchester earth as a Catholic anyway. She would probably have been amused by the irony.

The temperature that day was so hot that it squeezed moisture from the air like sap. Stupidly I had chosen a woolen suit to wear to the funeral, and by the time we reached the cemetery I was bathed in sweat. Father LaFarge, a large man who would himself die a few months later, shuffled around the grave with ponderous, unsteady dignity, murmuring Latin. In the frozen center of my being I felt a flame of rage. I looked at my father, and the Omahas and Lakotas and Cheyennes, and the Washington people, and the women from the city in their veils and high heels, and as I watched the coffin being lowered I knew that I would never forgive them for abandoning her. I felt a fierce vengefulness in my heart, as if what was taking place on that sunny hillside in White Plains was not a burial but a murder carried out before my own eyes, and as I watched the coffin sink into the ground, I thought, I will never let you go. I knew even then that this was foolish, but also that it was true.

The next day I was washing the Rambler in front of our house when a boy I played football with came down the street and tried to shake my hand.

"I'm sorry," he said.

I said, "For what?"

"About your mother."

"What about her?" I wasn't going to give anything away.

I watched him squirm. I saw that he couldn't bring himself to say that he knew she was dead. I just watched him. He looked at me strangely. "I'm sorry," he said again and went away.

I felt a strange ease in my silence, a deepening numbness, as if parts of myself, like a failing machine, were shutting down one after another. It was a frightening sensation at first. But then fear shut down too, and I felt nothing at all.

Probably no more than a few minutes elapsed from the time my mother and I began to gallop until the moment of her fall. But that moment would never stop reverberating, radiating its meaning outward through my life and everything that I touched. It would become an eternal moment, ever occurring, like something in a Hindu myth, unhindered by the laws of time and space. In a sense it would become my home, a place always to return to, familiar, necessary, and awful. I could enter it any time. It was always terrifying. I would never stop hoping that it would turn out differently.

My mother's death would become the benchmark against which I reflexively measured the depth and authenticity of all experience. It marked the end of my childhood and the beginning of all that came after. It taught me about terror, despair, guilt and self-pity. It taught me that my worst fears could be realized without any warning. It taught me that life is short and urgent and that even when they are done well, with conviction and faith and competence, the things that matter most can be undone in an instant. It taught me that love is powerless to save the people I love. It taught me to be afraid.

AFTER MY MOTHER'S DEATH the fragility of our life quickly became clear. My mother's salary had accounted for most of the family income. With her gone, we went suddenly from a life of relative affluence to one that was only marginally middle-class. My father saw to it that there was food in the refrigerator and that I had whatever clothes I wanted for starting high school that year. But there was an increasing sense that money had to be watched closely, that there was a limit to things. Life dulled. There were no more trips out West, or lunches, just my mother and I, at fashionable city restaurants, no more telephone calls from senators and congressmen, no more picturesque men from Kotzebue, or Lame Deer, or Pine Ridge turning up for dinner at our home. My father gave away my mother's clothing and jewelry, everything but her books. He asked Wally Hunt to sell the Buick in Vermont. The sumptuous rose garden that my mother had cultivated for as long as I could remember was allowed to run to seed.

Strangely, my father is virtually invisible in my recollection of the period immediately after her death. Possibly he was working longer hours now, or perhaps he felt freer to spend time in his favorite gin mills. But Maddy and I could not really have been as alone as I seem to remember. My friends must have come and taken me away to hit flies in the field at the end of Mayfair Road. We must have ridden our bicycles to the Sprain Brook reservoir and eaten peanut-butter-and-jelly sandwiches on top of the boulder alongside Jackson Avenue. I know that these things must have happened. Many of those nights, my father must have brought us dinner—pizza, take-out Chinese, cold cuts from the German deli on Tuckahoe Road—must have sat in his black leather armchair watching TV and drinking alexanders. But only my grandmother and I exist in my memory, alone in the house, as if the rest of the world had completely melted away. I can see now that in that autumn of 1962 we were a part of each other's wreckage, debris in the backwash of my mother's death, equally unable to survive without her. Our living room, with its blue walls and the leggy Danish modern furniture with the blue cushions—the blue that my mother loved—became her theater, a stage upon which she played out her unraveling history, blurring me kaleidoscopically hour after hour into the shape of her father or her husband, dead twenty-five years, or her dead brother Jack, or into some suitor she had known in Brooklyn in the 1890s, or into a son she never had, or into my father, whom, it now became clear in her charging, chaotic monologues, she had long held in contempt.

IN MY MEMORY of these weeks I see Maddy and myself as if we were figures in a frieze, frozen in postures that never change, speaking the same words over and over, still almost unbearable to hear.

My grandmother sits on the couch, bent almost double, caved into the blue cushions. I am curled up in the black leather chair beneath the dark cliffs of my mother's books. Night after night we are locked together in her madness, players in a masque, playing to the ghosts that hover around us in the air.

The room is bathed in the flickering light of the old Philco TV. We watch quiz shows one after another. I love the bright sets, the smiling emcees, the commercials, the glistening predictability. I want it to go on forever. The dim blue light of the screen plays weirdly across my grandmother's terrified face as memory and history and fantasy conflate and disintegrate. Whole decades and lifetimes turn to liquid and melt into others and flood around us like a swollen river in a storm.

Sometimes we are on the boardwalk at Coney Island or on our

way to a mountain house in the Catskills that Maddy knew in her girlhood, or somewhere in Mount Vernon in my mother's youth, or on Wall Street in the halcyon days of the twenties. Coquettish inflections rasp eerily from her eighty-year-old throat: "Let's go for a swim!" I am Maddy's suitor Neil Boynton, or the dental surgeon (always "the doctor") she married, or her brother Jack who promoted Buffalo Bill's Wild West Show, or my father, or even myself, or the infant that I once was, in need of pablum or changing, or her own father, the man with the walrus mustache whom I know only from pictures and who has just been to a banquet at Delmonico's, or has just died, or has just gone to New Orleans.

Then she says, "Where's LaVernie?"

The innocence of the question has a relentless ferocity. I hate her for this. I feel it as an attack, an attempt to destroy me. Her innocence is a subterfuge, a trick to get me to tell her the truth. I ignore her as long as I can. But there is no point in pretending that the question hasn't been asked, because I know that she will ask it over and over again until she gets an answer.

"She went to Nebraska," I tell her finally. Sometimes I say Washington, or South Dakota, or Florida, or Maine.

"When is she coming home?"

Sometimes, in Maddy's monologues, there is a small child in danger, a girl, herself perhaps, little Georgiana Farrell long ago in Brooklyn, tyrannized by one or another of the seven brothers she said she had, or perhaps my mother, ghostly time traveler that she has now become, floating out of her own childhood and into my grandmother's, where her life has been rekindled as a sister or friend.

My grandmother is sniffling like a child. "What have they done to LaVernie?"

"Nothing," I say. "LaVernie is fine."

"What have they done to her?" she whimpers.

I want to crawl into the TV and live there forever.

The heat is almost insupportable. Every window has been thrown open. Still, sweat is pouring over me. My clothes are stuck to my skin. Nothing moves except the flickering light of the TV.

Sometimes, when I could bear this no longer, I would go to my room and wage war with lead soldiers. I had amassed thousands of them from the armies of the Napoleonic wars: fusiliers, grenadiers, tirailleurs, hussars, Polish lancers, kilted Highlanders, Bavarians, Russians, red-jacketed English, Frenchmen with tall black shakos. I had painted them by hand down to their cuffs, buttons, and eyeballs. With them I now waged vast battles across hills that I built with wood and forests of wire trees everywhere across the floor of my room, and that always ended in a slaughter to the last man.

I read compulsively far into the night, as if my life depended on it, as perhaps it did. I read hour after hour about worlds I wished I could flee into, all of them violent. I read histories of the Civil War and the First World War, stories of cataclysmic battles, of senseless butchery, of martyrdom in sacred causes. I immersed myself in abstruse corners of history: the reigns of the lesser Plantagenet kings, "Fighting Joe" Hooker's failures at Chancellorsville, the eccentricities of certain later Roman emperors. I invented numerologies of reading, plotting what time it would be when I turned the next thirty pages, the next fifty, the next hundred, how many pages I could read in a day, a week, a year.

Finally my father put Maddy in a nursing home. I came home one day from school and she was gone. She left nothing behind except a handful of worthless shares in the Mount Vernon Trust Company, the last vestige of the fortune that she had lost after the stock-market crash of 1929. I never saw her again. We never even spoke on the phone. It was as if she had simply ceased to exist.

I would have sworn that Maddy's dementia went on for years after my mother's death. Recently I came across her death certificate in a file and was startled to discover that my father had signed her into a nursing home in Poughkeepsie, New York, on December 22, 1962 (three days before Christmas!), only four months after my mother's death. She died there from "generalized arteriosclerosis" on February 9, 1965, at the age of eighty-two. The discrepancy between my memory and this irreproachable document, stamped with the embossed seal of Dutchess County and signed personally by one H. R.

Chase, the county's deputy registrar, is unnerving. I want to disbelieve this, to discard it as faulty and implausible evidence. But it is, of course, my own duplicitous memory that has betrayed me, seducing me with its self-certainty, begging for my trust, and in the end capable of amazing deceit. My grandmother's madness worked like a chemical on time, dilating and distorting it. Then, when she "went away"—as I always thought of it, crediting her with a degree of will and intent that was long gone—leaving my father and me alone together for the first time in our lives, time shriveled up like something utterly wasted and spent, and for years it seemed that it never moved again.

AFTER MADDY'S DEPARTURE only my father was left. At fifty-five, though starting to paunch, he was still well-built and strong in the hands. He was a nuts-and-bolts man, self-educated as an engineer, more at ease with blueprints and circuitry and ductwork than with the uncertainties of human emotion; he had a knack for sliding frictionlessly around people, leaving no trace, taking pride, I think, in his lack of affect. Since my mother's death I had come to think of him almost exclusively in terms of negation, a falling short, not-my-mother. How much he understood that, and how much it may have hurt him, I don't know. I didn't know myself well enough then to know that I never forgave him for being the one who had lived.

Anyone could see that we were headed for trouble.

AFTER MADDY WAS GONE, my father hired a woman named Phyllis to clean the house once or twice a week. Sometimes I would come home from school and find her passed out on the couch in front of the TV with a glass of rye still in her hand. She also stole things. Cash disappeared from table tops. The ancient Roman coins, the sestercii and denarii, that my mother had given me one or two at a time on birthdays and at Christmas disappeared. So did the savings that I kept in a tin can in my room. Strange though it seems to me now, I never told my father about any of this. Phyllis's thievery just seemed like part of the way things were supposed to be now. I expected to lose things. It seemed natural that things should disappear, fall apart, be taken away.

I STARTED HIGH SCHOOL two weeks after my mother's funeral. Orientation for my class was led by the health teacher, an officious woman with hair the color of gunmetal. She told us about the dress code ("Skirts for girls, and slacks for boys—no blue jeans—and detention if you forget your tie"), and comportment in the halls and the lunchroom, and how we would be getting more homework and needed plenty of protein in our diet and more sleep at night than we were probably getting. After half an hour or so of this she paused. She said that now she had something very important to say. One of the new students had lost a parent over the summer and we should know without having to be told that this student was going to need a lot of special love and support. I felt a confusion of nakedness and shame and relief. *How does she know?* I was mortified at being singled out, but at least everyone would understand the strangeness that I felt must be printed on me like a brand on my face. Then she mentioned a name. It wasn't me at all. It was a girl in a row somewhere behind me.

I waited, expecting the teacher to mention me next. But after assuring the girl that we all cared about her and would stand by her, she was already talking about the lesson for next week. I wanted to raise my hand and shout, What about me? My mother died too! If she so much as glanced at me now, I was afraid that I'd fling myself down and grovel at her feet and beg her to say about me what she said about the girl in the back. I felt sick at myself for even imagining it, and I thought, *My mother would be so ashamed of me.* Then I thought, *If she knew about the girl, why didn't she know about me? If she did, why didn't she tell them?* And I knew—was utterly sure I knew—that she had known and said nothing because for what I had done, and for what I had failed to do that morning in Vermont, there could never be any sympathy or forgiveness.

Because of some anomaly of districting, only a handful of students from the junior high school I had attended went on to the same high school as I did. Nearly all of us found ourselves assigned to the low-end classes that were the catch basins for the school's cutups and delinquents. My refuge was Latin. I took it because my mother had loved it and because when I was very small I thought that it was a kind of secret language that we had, just the two of us. She had taught me a batch of phrases, and I would stand on a stack of cinder blocks in the backyard with my arm flung wide like an orator in the forum and shout, *"Omnia Gallia in partes tres divisa est!"* and *"Patres conscripti!"* and she would clap and cry *"Ave!"* We would share animal crackers and lemonade and I would climb onto the cinder blocks and do it again and again until, laughing, she begged me to stop. Now when I parsed the ancient sentences I could hear not only the voice of dead Rome but hers too, as if in the conjugations and declensions and old dead words she still lived and where, that raw and lonely year, she could always be found.

I did well in my classes. I kept out of trouble. I had friends, mostly boys I had known for years in my neighborhood; it was the friendship of things done together, of ball games and trading stamps and trick-or-treating together on Hallowe'en, the wordless intimacy of boys who have been small together and who have begun to grow up but not very much and who had no vocabulary for talking about what had happened to me and so did not try, any of us. We played baseball deep into the autumn, getting up teams when we could but mostly just hitting flies in the empty field off Bretton Road, and then later playing rough but friendly football with boys, some of them strangers to us, who lived on the far side of Dover Lane. One day, playing football, I accidentally tripped one of these boys and sent him face forward into the dirt. When he got up, he told me that I could go fuck my mother, and without thinking, I threw myself on him and pummeled him uncontrollably with both hands, choking with raw, uncontrollable rage. He was bigger than I was, and I was not much of a fighter, and he would probably have beaten me except that the other boys pulled us apart and told him that my mother was dead. I wanted to stuff what they said back down their throats. I felt exposed and helpless and shook off the hands that were holding me and stumbled home, knowing that I would never let anyone see me like that ever again. After that, when my friends came to call for me, sometimes I would just peer down at them from my room through the boughs of the maple tree that shaded the front yard and watch them, pretending that I wasn't there while they rang the bell and called my name, until they finally went away, and I would think, *This is the way I am now. I will never be like them again. I will never have a mother.*

There were nights when I lay awake for hours, imagining that my mother was not dead but just lost. I imagined the phone ringing, that it was her calling from the West, or hearing the Buick in the driveway and knowing that she was home from work. I scoured books that we had of old photographs of New York City, sure that I would find her there somewhere: in that station on the Ninth Avenue el on a frigid winter's day, among the bundled-up people warming their hands at a potbellied stove. Perhaps she was among the strollers in Washington Square Park on a spring day in 1936, or in one of the windows across the park at NYU, staring down into the very scene into which I peered, as if through a mirror in time, so many years later. Perhaps she was the woman walking the dog, or one of the NYU students striding north toward the marble arch. *I know you're there,* I would think. Perhaps she was there inside the S. Klein store on Union Square, foraging for a frock beneath the watchful eyes of the supervisors who sat on enormous stools high above the mob of shoppers, or in the dense crowd passing the Forty-second Street library on a balmy autumn day. Sometimes I almost choked with panic: *What if you're there and I miss you?*

One Saturday night, without any apparent reason, I suddenly began weeping uncontrollably in front of my father. Ashamed as I was, I couldn't control it myself, and I cried over and over, "I just want to be happy," until my father looked up from the TV, even more embarrassed than I was, and said, "Forget about it. No one's happy. You're not going to be any different from anybody else, so get used to it." Perhaps I got up and fled to my room. Or maybe I bucked up and cleaned my face and went back to watching TV. And I never let it happen again.

Of course I could always find her in the family albums: fuzzy but familiar in lopsided snapshots I had taken with my Brownie on trips in the West, helping an unsteady infant—*me!*—to take his first steps across the terrace behind the house, surrounded by books in my parents' Greenwich Village apartment during the war, mugging for the camera in Washington Square Park with her friends from NYU. I would pore over the pictures for hours, unpacking her life like a set of Chinese boxes, drawn back always to her childhood in Mount Vernon, not far from our home in Yonkers, to generous gardens and birthday parties and balmy afternoons, from which the tiny girl who became my mother gazed back at me with sunny insouciance. Sometimes, if I immersed myself in the pictures long enough, I began to feel that I really had overthrown time and death and that she still had an entire life spread out before her, and that she would never have to ride that road in Vermont at all. Other times I would talk to her. *I know a secret that you don't know*, I would whisper. *I know where you will die. I know the hour, the minute. I know what your last sight of the earth will be. I will see your face at the last extremity of life. I promise I will love you forever. I will live for you. I will never forget you a single day in my life.*

The great British historian Sir James Collingwood once wrote that a past that continued to exist would be a "limbo, where events which have finished happening still go on." It would imply "a world where Galileo's weight is still falling, where the smoke of Nero's Rome still fills the intelligible air, and where interglacial man is still laboriously learning to chip flints." My mother's death was like that for me, eternally present. Our horses were always gathering speed, my mother always rising in her saddle, always crying out to me, the bright blood always seeping from her skull. I could slip effortlessly and unexpectedly into that August morning at any time—in a classroom listening to a lecture on differential equations, on a baseball diamond waiting for a fly ball to descend over left field, or watching one of the TV shows that, in the absence of my mother's consuming contempt for television, now filled our evenings. When the memory came, it was as if a hole had suddenly opened in time and the present—the class, the ballgame—were but a transparent skin on the surface of a deeper and more permanent reality. I could feel the crisp morning air, smell the mown grass and cow manure, hear the clap of hooves on the hard-packed road. Sometimes this occurred once or twice a day, sometimes half a dozen times, sometimes not at all for days or weeks at a time. Each time it happened, it was accompanied by a wave of terror, guilt, and remorse. Yet, in truth, there was also something deeply pleasurable in these few minutes of galloping fear, because as long as they lasted my mother was still alive.

At the same time I used memory aggressively as a barrier—even a weapon—against the accumulating daily experience that threatened to engulf my mother and bury her forever. I knew that as long as I kept remembering, she would survive. I clung to the remembered sight of her beckoning me up my first flight of steps and folding her arms around me when I reached the top. And tucking a worm back into the ground in the garden behind the house, telling me never to forget to be gentle. And testifying before a congressional committee, at the center of things, like a gravitational force, or a heartbeat. And launching me, festooned with feathers, into a tribal dance. And eating peyote ceremonially with Cheyennes in a tepee on the Montana prairie. And walking along the Arctic shore in a landscape of gray sand and shattered ice and empty sky, in which no one at all existed but us. I tried to remember everything: the waves of her hair, the green pillbox hat that she wore the Hallowe'en that I was five years old, her hand on the caribou-hide purse that she bought one year in Alaska, the odor that followed her, of coffee, Shalimar perfume, and tobacco.

I kept this mnemonic obsession to myself, a private memory palace into which I welcomed no one. Meanwhile real life increasingly took on a temporary quality, like the atmosphere of a bus station or airport. I felt disembodied, as if I had no existence of my own

beyond what had already happened in the past and could never be repeated. I tried to recapture entire hours and days, reconstructing
every nuance of my mother's voice, every turn of her conversation,
her every gesture, down to the smallest detail, the glint of sunlight on
a windshield, the arabesques of smoke curling from her cigarette. So
much had already sunk away into oblivion. Meanings had already
eroded, leaving enigmatic images that were like mesas and pinnacles
in a once verdant but now empty landscape of time. I saw my mother
beside me in a small plane, descending toward upturned faces on a
runway. Where were we going? From where had we come? I saw myself standing terrified in front of a shabby clapboard house staring
down a road that cut through a sea of corn, willing my mother to appear, desperate for the sight of the cloud of red dust that would tell
me that she was returning. What did this mean? I remembered a
motel room. There was a man. He was familiar to me but I could not
make his face come clear. He and my mother were talking and talking about whether he would fly east with us the next day. While they
talked, I played with model airplanes that I had built from plastic
kits. I had a Messerschmitt and a Spitfire. I was fighting the Battle of
Britain over the twin beds, around my mother, around the man with
no face. Along with this image, I had an intense awareness of things
left unsaid. Why were they having such a hard time deciding whether
the man would come with us? What was the problem? Of all the non-
descript motel rooms that we stayed in across the West, I remembered
only this one. Years later, when I was old enough to understand such
things, I realized that what I was remembering was the way that
adults talk when they do not want children to know they are talking
about sex.

My father and I almost never talked about my mother or about
what happened in Vermont. When I think of us that year, after
Maddy had gone, I see us in the living room, myself curled on one of
the leggy Danish chairs, painting lead soldiers night after night, and
my father in the black leather chair, sipping alexanders, watching

"Gunsmoke" and "Bonanza" and "Have Gun Will Travel," separated by a space that neither of us had any idea how to bridge. Each of us had learned by now not to ask questions, to mind his own business, to maneuver around the other's silence.

Christmas that first year was strange and awful. My mother had always made a big thing of Christmas, festooning the house with ornaments and art that she had collected over the years and that she put out just for the holiday. Friends would come for dinner, and one or two of Maddy's old pals, and usually there would be an Indian from the West or an Eskimo from Alaska, and all around us an atmosphere of cheery bustle and gay talk and laughter. For dinner on Christmas Eve there would be a goose or a turkey and flotillas of elaborate dishes that my mother had prepared, and for dessert a mince pie and, finally, served always with a flourish and applause, the flaming plum pudding that she had made the previous Christmas and kept soaked in brandy in the basement all year.

How ridiculous it was to suppose that I could have preserved any of this. The hopelessness of it still makes me cringe with shame. Like so much else that disintegrated after my mother died, the Christmas that we knew had been held together like some glorious towering confection by her zeal and imagination, and without her it simply fell apart. My father and I should have gone out for Chinese food, or eaten TV dinners, or gone to the movies, anything. Maybe some rump end of trust might still have have been salvaged. But I had already brought down from the attic the splendid prints of Renaissance angels, and the tall antique candles, and the old Italian crèche, and the boxes of red and gold balls for the tree, and the European music boxes that we always put out only at Christmas. I decorated the tree and hung gilded garlands over the doors and arranged painted branches in intricate compositions on the mantelpiece and shelves the way my mother would. I ordered a turkey from the market and, following one of my mother's recipes, determined to cook it myself. I mashed potatoes and baked squash. I brought up the plum pudding from the basement. I put candles on the table and set the music boxes to playing all over the house. When my father and I sat down, alone together for Christmas for the first time, neither of us knew what to say. We tried to eat. But the turkey was undercooked and inedible, and I had bought the wrong kind of potatoes, and in the end neither of us had the heart to eat the plum pudding, the last that my mother made.

Leaving the wreck of the dinner on the table we went into the sunroom to open presents in front of the tree. I had done up mine carefully and labeled them, the way my mother used to for fun, "from Dinty" and "from Suzie," the dogs, and from the cat and "from Eric the Red," a teasing nickname that my mother gave me when I was small and that always made my father laugh. But he looked at me and asked what I had done all that for, and I could hear his annoyance not just at silly labels and the bad food but at the whole hopeless attempt to copy my mother. So I turned on the TV and we watched other people's Christmases. I imagined my mother all around me: the mother of my infancy, and the mother of Christmases and plum pudding, and the mother who took me out West, and the mother of her last morning, dressed to ride and about to die. They swarmed around me, straining to get my attention, drawing me to them, filling the silence with words that I couldn't quite hear but that I knew were meant for me alone. Looking across the room at my father, I saw a stranger, and I thought, *How will I ever survive?*

I TOOK MY MOTHER'S DEATH into me and loved it.

Her death made the past magical. The present seemed like an anticlimax to real life and living people only impostors for the one person who really mattered. I had no interest at all in the future. It was something that belonged to others, a foreign country in which I would be forever forced against my will to live. I loved death because my mother was there. I took my life over and over in my imagination. I put a gun down my throat and pulled the trigger. I put a gun to my forehead and pulled the trigger. I slit my wrists in the bathtub. I drove a car into a brick wall. I drove a car over a cliff. I drove a car into a river. I stepped in front of a speeding car. I lay in front of a train. I took an overdose of pills. I never imagined that I would meet my mother there, where she had gone, by killing myself. Rather, death had become part of my mother, like her intellectual brilliance, her stylishness, her conviction. My mother was now a dead person. I wanted to be like her. I wanted to be dead.

One night that winter I went into the bathroom and took down all the prescription drugs I saw and emptied them into my hand. I stared at them for a long time. I touched them with the tip of my tongue, then with my lips, feeling the shapes. Then I put down my hand. I stared at my face in the mirror. I put the pills to my lips again. I don't know how many times I did that. Perhaps I stood there an hour. Finally I threw the pills in the toilet and went back to my bed and lay there into the dawn, cursing myself for my lack of courage.

THE FOLLOWING YEAR I was assigned to college prep classes, where I felt more at home and made more friends. I also had the sense to recognize my shyness as an enemy that, if I surrendered to it, would condemn me to hopeless isolation. So I set out to join as many clubs as I could. I joined the debate team and the political science club and the United Nations club, and even the school chorus, although I had so much difficulty carrying a tune that during performances the director ordered me to just mouth the words. Saturday-afternoon football games, and parties where no one drank anything stronger than Coke, and we parsed the songs of Joan Baez and Bob Dylan, and talked earnestly about civil rights in the South, and as the year went on, about the departure of more and more American soldiers for the small and perplexing war in Vietnam. I wrote for the school newspaper, and in my senior year I became one of its editors. On the paper I met Rosalind, my first real girlfriend. I adored her. She had an eye-catching bohemian flair and wrote poetry and read books that no one else had heard of, and she knew how to make me laugh. I had the sense from the beginning that she had chosen me rather than I her, had plucked me from my self-absorption in spite of myself. Although the sexual revolution was gathering around us, it was no more than a haze on the distant horizon of our corner of suburbia. Even so, it

wasn't an easy situation. Her parents were Jews who, though nonob-
servant, loathed her seeing a boy who wasn't Jewish, and they made
it clear to both of us that I wasn't welcome.

When I look back now at this boy that I once was I am aghast at
his frailty, like something made of matchsticks that could be tipped
over with a breath. We usually made up the paper on Saturday afternoons at one of the editors' homes. Afterward Rosalind and I would
drive around, stopping somewhere for burgers or ice cream, and
then, if she was up to lying to her parents, we would park somewhere
in another neighborhood and make out with a heat made all the more
fierce by our self-imposed physical restraint. Perhaps all this—the
high boil of passion, even the innocence that I remember so fondly—
was just naïveté, the pathos of a boy who was all but helpless anywhere in the vicinity of affection. One of these afternoons not long
before graduation Rosalind seemed moody and skittish, and when it
was time to leave, she said, not looking me in the eye, that she was
going home with one of the other editors. He was a basketball player
and "fast" by the standards of the time, but I liked and trusted him.
Even now he was smiling at me as amiably as ever, as if nothing had
happened. I stood dopily gaping at the two of them. "Just go on
home," Rosalind said with a finality that went through me like a
razor. "Just go home."

I went out and got into my car and wheeled onto the Bronx River
Parkway and drove north, accelerating through Crestwood and
Scarsdale and White Plains. I felt a volcanic terror, what I had felt on
the road in Vermont and choked off then and would do anything to
kill so that I would never feel it again. Only this time I had a car that
I knew how to drive fast and deftly, the way my mother drove, and I
sped north, my foot on the floor, not thinking at all, crying, *What
have I done?* and having no answer.

Impulsively I shift from lane to lane, always accelerating, slicing
through the traffic like butter as far as Hawthorne Circle, where the
Bronx River Parkway meets the Saw Mill River Parkway and, because I can't think of anywhere else to go, I turn south on the Saw
Mill, toward home. There is no divider between the northbound and

southbound lanes. Impulsively I veer for a moment into the north-bound lane, testing for fear. I know what I am supposed to do. I think, *Now. Just do it!* As I approach a turn, I swing back across the line and close my eyes. My heart is pounding against my chest. I begin to count. When I reach ten, nothing has happened and I open my eyes. I'm still on the wrong side of the road, close to the curb. But there are no cars in sight. I turn back into the southbound lane. I let a few cars pass. *Just do it!* At the next bend I close my eyes again and veer back into northbound lane. I began to count. *Just do it! Four . . . five. Do it! Eight . . . nine*. When I get to ten again, I open my eyes. The road in front of me is empty.

Suddenly I feel drained and depressed and beaten. Suddenly I know that nothing I do will make any difference.

When I get home, my father is sitting in the black leather chair watching TV and drinking an alexander.

"How's the paper?" he asks.

I tell him it's fine, fine.

IN SEPTEMBER I went on to the City College of New York. I had always assumed that I would go to New York University, my mother's alma mater, had in fact dreamed of it for years when I was young, but when they admitted me I turned them down. City College was free then, and that mattered; but my father was not stingy with what money he had, and perhaps we could have found enough for NYU had I pressed him for it. But now that I was in a position to go, although I could not quite admit this to myself, I worried that I might never be able to match my mother's record: her magna cum laude and her phi beta kappa, her poetry, her translating papyri, and all that I knew, vaguely, that she had done there in the thirties and that to my seventeen-year-old mind seemed far beyond my reach. I think that I also knew somehow, with an instinct for self-preservation that was rare in me then, that I was likely to suffocate in a place where I would see her everywhere I turned, a ghostly presence in every hall, every classroom, inescapable.

As long as my mother lived, I had expected that I would work with her someday and that I would make my life in some way or other among the Indians. Now, when I thought about what I might do in the future I supposed without ever really thinking it through that I would make a career in archaeology. So as a student at City I mostly read history; I was no more than a second-rate student, bright enough but always more interested in the way I imagined the past, in the dream of it, than in real scholarship. What appealed to me, I think, was the sheer *pastness* of history, the feeling of it as a kind of foreign country that could be distantly glimpsed but never quite reached: I loved history just because it was gone.

The other thing I learned to love that first year was a drink. One day someone invited me along with a crowd to an Irish bar on Amsterdam Avenue a block or two from the campus. My father had taught me to drink, but I had hardly ever had more than a bottle or two of beer at a time, or a rum collins or brandy on special occasions. Now for the first time I was drinking as much as I wanted. I heard myself laughing for what seemed the first time in years. And I discovered that the more I had in me, the more I had to say and that I could say it with enough self-assurance and the odd clever turn of phrase for people to pay attention. I could have kept talking and drinking all day and half the night except that we had to get back to class. But I knew that I had found an ally against the shyness and feeling second-rate and the worry that I didn't really know anything except the fate of obscure Plantagenet kings and the history of the Army of the Potomac and the darkness that lay over my heart like a winter night.

Lots of things were easier with a drink.

I had made friends with a young woman who sat a few rows ahead of me in my European History class, and one day we were sitting in the cafeteria drinking coffee and talking about the French Revolution, which we were studying, when she suggested that we go to her friend's place in the Village, to which she had the key. We drove downtown still talking about this Estate and that Estate and the pre-Revolutionary French middle class, neither of us having the least interest in the subject anymore, and went to the friend's apartment, where we had a scotch, and suddenly we were in bed. Never having done this with any girl in Yonkers, or anywhere else for that matter, I didn't know what to think except that I wanted more of it and that the drinks we'd had were what had made it possible. Afterward, instead of going to dinner, we got in my car again and drove uptown to where she lived, and for the rest of the night I never for a minute thought about my mother or about what happened on the road in Vermont or how everything would have been different if I had been a different kind of a boy, who had known the right thing to do.

I threw myself into campus political activity. Academic concerns paled against the exigencies of the worsening war in Vietnam. The teeming South Campus cafeteria was a macédoine of pro-Soviet Marxists, Maoists, Young Socialists, anarchists, adherents of SDS and of Youth Against War and Fascism, and other small and strident groups that defended their tables and their ideological turf with Balkan ferocity. While I never shared the enthusiasm that many students I knew did for Karl Marx, after the monotony of suburbia I was thrilled by the atmosphere of engagement and the passionate polemics. Whenever I was asked, I marched in demonstrations against the war, and sometimes, always fighting shyness and the instinct to withdraw, I helped organize campus actions against military recruiters and defense contractors and the college's cooperation with the draft. No one had to talk me into engagement; I saw the Vietnamese through the same moral lens as Indians, beleaguered by the overwhelming might of the United States government, and opposing the war as a logical extension of the civil-rights struggle at home.

Several times on vacations I went south with other students from City College to help register black voters. Lying a rough sixty miles southwest of Richmond, Lunenberg County, Virginia, reminded me of the rural Mississippi that I had seen with my mother when she worked among the Choctaws: a thinly populated region of isolated farms, scrubby woodlands and scrabbling hamlets that still looked as if they had never recovered from the Great Depression or, for that matter, from the Civil War. For the past couple of years the local chapter of the NAACP had been laboring to enrol voters who for generations had been deterred from voting by literacy tests and, when those were overturned by the courts, by uncooperative county clerks and by their own fear, or just by the difficulty of getting to the courthouse in a place where for the poorest owning a car was beyond imagining.

Nathaniel Lee Hawthorne, the man who led the registration drive and without whose determination it would surely have stalled and died away, must have been only in his forties then, though he looked much older. He had been badly wounded in Italy during the Second World War and was on disability and in almost constant pain, and with his hollow body and jagged features he reminded me of a fierce warrior saint in some Byzantine fresco, ready to step out and whack you with his sword. In spite of that he was an easygoing and gracious man, patient beyond measure with young strangers who knew nothing about the customs or the opaque strata of mistrust and discontent of the insular community in which he had lived his entire life. The local police had stripped him of his driver's license on a fabricated charge of reckless driving, so I often drove him to meetings with political people in Richmond or to neighboring counties where there were other volunteers from the North, or from Victoria, where the Freedom House was and the only place in the county that passed for a town, to the small, neat brick house where he lived.

Mostly I spent day after day driving with the county map spread on the seat next to me to sagging cabins on dirt lanes and behind tobacco fields, where I would try to talk frightened people into coming with me to the courthouse to register. We already got the easy ones, Hawthorne told me at the start. It's the tough ones left now. You got to work at them.

Once in a while someone agreed to come with me, most often an elderly woman. She would put on her church-going clothes, a freshly laundered frock of some antique cut and white gloves if she owned them, and I would drive her to the court house and wait while she registered and then drive her home again, neither of us knowing what to say once it was over. But mostly it was frustrating work. People would tell me that the white lady up the road or in "that big house there" had already "done regis' " for them. I would explain that they couldn't do that, that no one could do it but you, and if someone said he had, well, he was telling a lie. And they would say, I never met you before but I know that lady. She done it for me, yes. I would walk away almost weeping with rage and frustration, not knowing what to say to make them understand, thinking of how effortlessly my mother seemed to touch people and how I couldn't do it at all. One day I followed a dirt track that soon became overgrown and without any trace that a car had passed down it in years, and then petered out in a streambed at the bottom of a crotch in the hills. Nevertheless I sensed the presence of people, faint but unmistakable. Eventually the woods broke away to a wide, ragged field with a falling-down farmhouse in the middle of it. I went up onto the veranda and knocked. I waited a while, knocked again, waited, then called hello and knocked again. Finally I walked around the side of the house. Far across the field I saw them: a man and a woman and two small children running as fast as they could in terror toward the trees. I felt sick in the pit of my stomach. Nobody had ever been scared of me in my life. I thought, *My mother would know how to bring them back.*

My mother was often in my mind. I thought almost daily of something that happened to her in Florida, a story that I remembered whenever I felt discouraged or afraid and wished that I could know what she would have done. She had driven out into the Everglades to introduce herself for the first time to the Miccosukees, then a reclusive people little known outside the great swamp, who had never signed a peace treaty with the United States and therefore had no legal standing, no claim to the cypress islets where most of them lived, and because of that were in danger of losing them to the encroachment of development and agriculture. Local people who were interested in the Miccosukees had called my mother in New York and begged her to come down and do something and see if she could overcome the suspicion of outsiders that kept them cut off from help. She parked in front of the only Miccosukee village anywhere near the road and walked in among the thatched, open-to-the-air homes called *chickees*, where the Miccosukees lived. Every person she approached, man and woman, silently turned their backs in her face. She kept trying until there was no one left who hadn't turned away. Finally, in the way that she spoke when she was talking with Indians, who respected quietness and disliked the blunt way that most white people talked, she said to the village headmen, "If you change your mind, if you want to talk to me, I'll be outside in my car." She sat in the car, in front of the village, hour after hour, all the rest of the morning and afternoon and into the evening. When night came, she was still there. Finally she locked the doors and curled up and tried to sleep. At dawn she was awakened by pounding on the car window. She opened her eyes to see that the car was surrounded by Miccosukee men peering in the windows. They stared at her expressionlessly for some while. Finally one of them tapped on the glass and said, "Well, I guess we might as well hear what you have to say." That day's conversation led, in time, to the Association becoming the Miccosukees' advocate to the federal government and the state of Florida and, thanks to my mother's relentless lobbying in Washington, to the tribe's recognition by the United States and to the creation of a reservation and the permanent protection of the Miccosukees' lands. When I recalled this story I loved the sight of the tiny, vulnerable woman alone in the midst of hostile men and how she knew just what it would take to get them to trust her, and that she did it all alone. And I loved it that a woman so bold and courageous and indefatigable was my mother.

If people like me were in any danger in Lunenberg County, it was nowhere near what it was for civil-rights workers in the deep South. Even so, in the months before I arrived, Hawthorne and two brothers who helped at the Freedom House and one or two others had been threatened and shot at. It was no secret that the Ku Klux Klan was recruiting in the county and the other counties roundabout. Crosses were being burned. And one moonless night a car followed me for miles, speeding up whenever I did, staying tight behind me, its lights on high so that I couldn't see what kind of car it was, and then abruptly swinging around and disappearing when I turned, my palms soaked with sweat, into the lane that led to the farm where I was staying.

Toward the end of the summer word went around that the Klan was going to hold a rally on the steps of the county courthouse. Word also went out that black people had better stay off the streets. The morning of the rally Hawthorne was sunk in gloom, pacing back and forth in the Freedom House, picking up things and putting them down, so prickly that no one could talk to him. Finally he said, I'm going to show them there's one black man in this county ain't afraid of them, and started for the door.

Three or four people were there. They tried to talk him out of it, saying what seemed obvious, that he was going to get hurt.

He said that if none of us was going to drive him he was going to walk then, and he went out. People stood around arguing how they shouldn't let him go. I thought, *He's going to die.*

I didn't think about what I did next. I only knew that the longer I stood there doing nothing the more I was going to be responsible for what happened to him. I got in my car and started driving, and when I came abreast of Hawthorne I stopped and said, I'll go with you.

Hawthorne said he appreciated it and got in.

A platform had been set up on the courthouse lawn. Someone had run the Stars and Bars up the flagpole on top of the United States flag, and from a loudspeaker a song was playing, twanging and tinny, too loud, at country-fair volume.

I parked, and Hawthorne and I walked down the road in plain view of everyone and sat down on the stoop of the general store across the street from the courthouse. People were coming up the road from the other end carrying rebel flags and little kids, some of them in jeans or overalls and some in their robes, shining white in the sun. Others were taking robes out of the trunks of their cars and putting them on there on the street, the wives smoothing them down like suits, picking off lint. Soon there were a couple of hundred people on the courthouse lawn and milling alongside the road.

Look at them in them sheets, Hawthorne said. Damn fools.

There was a state trooper's car parked on the road next to the store and Hawthorne said that as long as he was there we'd be all right. Nobody knew what we were really up to, and it was obvious from the way people looked at us and then up at the men in robes on the platform that they were waiting for something to happen.

Two or three Klansmen came up to the microphone and talked about how Christian civilization was going to hell in a handbasket because of the niggers and the communists. Then a man a head taller than the others and dressed in the scarlet robe of a Grand Dragon came up and once he got rolling you could almost see the steam rising around him. Every fourth word was "nigger-this" or "nigger-that": how the "nigger-loving outsiders" from "Nigger York" were coming where they weren't wanted, and why should Christian white folks have to take it.

All the while Hawthorne sat quiet and implacable, nothing on his face. I asked him if he thought we should go now. You can if you need to, he told me. My clothes were wet with sweat. No, I said, I don't need to.

Finally the man in the red robe leaned down close to the microphone and pointed his huge arm straight at Hawthorne and shouting at the top of his lungs said, See those two niggers over there? You see that black nigger? You see that other nigger? He was pointing at me now. He got white skin, but his heart's as black as that nigger next to him. What are they doing here? You happy about that? You going to do anything about it?

Nobody said anything, but you could feel what he meant going through the people gathered along the road like a breeze riffling a field of grass. Men started stepping out of the crowd. The state trooper got in his car and drove away. In a minute Hawthorne and I were surrounded. Ten or twelve men formed a ring around us, so that we couldn't see anything except their legs and couldn't be seen. They inched forward until their boots were against our backs.

Somebody started passing out empty Coke bottles from crates stacked against the wall. First they started tapping them against the railing. Then some of them started tapping Hawthorne and me on the back with the bottles, holding them around the necks like hammers.

I was tensed the way I was once when I was in a car that skidded in a snowstorm and was going to crash and I could do nothing about it.

I wondered, Will I be alive an hour from now? A half-hour from now? Fifteen minutes?

Then suddenly the man in the red robe turned back to Hawthorne. Do you know who that black nigger is? That's Nathaniel Lee Hawthorne, the head of the NAACP and you know what that stands for, yeah, the Nigger Association for the Advancement of Communists and Perverts, yeah. You know where he was at last week? Up to Richmond and talking to the governor! What was the governor doing with that nigger in his office?

He stopped for a moment to let that sink in.

In that moment the state trooper who had disappeared suddenly showed up again, and, maybe figuring that it might mean his job if a man the governor met only the day before got beaten to a pulp on his watch, gently began prying the men with the bottles away from us with a smile and a handshake. Then he turned to Hawthorne and me and said, You two get the hell out of here.

How you feel being a nigger? Hawthorne asked me.

He was chuckling as if nothing out of the ordinary had happened.

It feels real good, I said and meant it.

Well, he said, we sure showed them there's two black men ain't afraid of them.

I was proud of having stuck by Hawthorne, and of having done the right thing, and of having been braver than I had ever given myself credit for. But later when I thought more about what had happened I felt strangely let down, depressed. There was something that was hard for me to admit to myself and that I could tell no one: I wanted them to attack us. I wanted them to finish for me what I had failed to do myself. And it gnawed away at everything else, and spoiled it utterly.

Not long after that I went back to New York. I still thought that

I would go back to Virginia someday. But then Martin Luther King was killed in Memphis. In the last year of his life King was increasingly overshadowed by the kind of men—the Stokely Carmichaels and H. Rap Browns—who saw redemption mainly in violence, and when he was murdered in May 1968, everyone knew that it was the end of something hopeful and the beginning of something whose course was not yet clear but that would surely be far harsher than what he had preached. A friend of mine called me in tears and said that he was going to drive to Memphis for the memorial parade and did I want to come along. An hour or two later he picked me up at the apartment where I was living in the city. We saw the dawn somewhere in West Virginia and by the end of the day we were in Memphis. The procession was already well underway. We found a place in the long line of march and then, with nothing else to keep us there afterward, we drove back as far as Nashville, where we stayed the night in someone's friend's apartment while mobs of people, thoroughly liquored up and frenzied by King's death, were taking their feelings out on anything that caught their attention in the streets all around us. Looking out from our darkened room, I watched truckloads of soldiers racing past, and I heard shots in the night, and it seemed that history was boiling up around me, a frightening thing nothing like the history I knew from books, feral and confusing, a tidal wave that would leave none of us untouched.

There was a curfew, and when it was lifted the next day and we were on our way back to New York, my friend said this was the *beginning*, what everybody had been waiting for, the revolution. This was *it*. The more he talked, the more depressed I got. In a country that seemed to be disintegrating around us, the kind of patient work that my mother had done now seemed beside the point; it seemed to me that there was no longer a place for people like her, or me for that matter, with her essential confidence in democratic institutions and her faith that people in power were fundamentally honorable and, if it was made clear to them, would eventually do the right thing. I felt terribly young all of a sudden and with no clue to what was right anymore. You had to form an alliance with the Black Panthers, my friend was saying. You had to start buying guns. You had to start taking out policemen. But I didn't want a gun. I didn't want to shoot anybody. I wasn't sure that I wanted to be part of anybody's revolution. I wanted to go back to the way things were when I was a kid and in the West with my mother and what was right and who I would be seemed perfectly clear and the only enemies in sight were ones that I knew my mother would eventually vanquish. But of course there wasn't any going back.

When we got home to New York I dropped out of school. It was the very first thing I did. I knew that it made no sense. There was nothing wrong with my grades and the semester was almost over. But it was the only thing that was easy to do.

THAT SPRING my father remarried and moved upstate. He told me about it only after the date had been set and wedding plans made. Then he told me that he would rather I didn't come to the wedding, and then that, actually, I wasn't invited. He said that he hadn't yet told the woman he was marrying that he already had a son, and he didn't want to complicate matters now, at the last minute. He supposed it wouldn't matter to me.

Why should it matter, I said.

He said he'd tell her when the time came.

Tell her whenever, I said. Or don't tell her.

And that was that.

Years before, not long after my mother died, my father had warned me that he would probably marry again someday and that I ought to start thinking about that. I said then that I didn't need to and that if he did, I'd never forgive him. But I didn't hate him now. Only sometimes I felt an ache so sharp that I thought I would choke, and I would force it down until it was hard as a stone and I felt nothing at all. And I thought, *Now I have my mother all to myself.*

3

THAT SUMMER almost everyone I knew seemed to be going to California. I left New York in an old Rambler that I'd bought for two hundred and fifty dollars, stopping first in Washington to take part in the Poor People's March and then at the SDS convention in Michigan. In Minnesota the Rambler blew a valve and I left it by the roadside and set off hitchhiking west. The first person who picked me up was a traveling salesman who told me to sit in back and that he had a gun on the seat beside him and that he'd blow my head off if I tried anything funny. Then a carload of friendly students from Wisconsin on their way to Oregon drove me as far as Casper, Wyoming. Then a man who had gotten out of prison that morning—"Don't ask about what's none of your business"—carried me to Salt Lake City. I missed my car for a while, and then I didn't miss it at all as I watched the land open up and empty of people as I traveled further west, lulled for hours on end by the tidal roll of the prairie so that when I closed my eyes I would imagine that I was on a ship on the high seas bound for wherever, it didn't matter, and I didn't care if I got there at all.

I found a place to stay with some people I knew from City College who had an apartment in Berkeley. I had nothing special to do and I had money that I'd saved from working in the coat-check room at City College, and I felt a terrific excitement at first, a sense of being at the core of things, and that just by breathing the Berkeley air I was somehow in on something triumphant and special, that I was *plugged in*. But I felt increasingly uneasy and out of place. I ran into a young man I had envied at college for his irony and intellect and who was now dressed in beads and iridescent bell-bottoms and told me that he was on his way to join a commune in Arizona where, when I asked him what he planned to do there, said, "Nothing at all, just *be*." A black man I had never seen before came up to me on the street and grabbed hold of my shirt and put his face in mine and hissed, "Blue-eyed devil! You know what you are!" At an SDS rally I went to, speakers were talking about forming cells and going underground. One night I heard the radical psychologist R. D. Laing speak in an auditorium on the UC campus, telling us that sanity was a delusion and that those we thought mad might well be quite sane, in their own way—for who were the rest of us to judge them; too much insistence on our own sanity might well be evidence of our own madness.

I spent more and more time by myself, reading under the eucalyptus trees on the campus, and thinking and worrying. Was I sane? What if I wasn't? For a while when I was still a student at City College I had seen a therapist at the college's counseling center. The woman I was assigned to seemed nice and sympathetic, and I told her about my mother and what happened to her on the road, and about my life afterward, and how sometimes I felt that I was already dead, that I was the one who had died in Vermont. Then one day, by chance, I met this woman's son, who said, Oh, you're *Fergus*; he told me that she used to tell him over the dinner table what I had told her that day in her office, and she would warn him that if he didn't get his life together he'd wind up like me.

I wished now, sitting beneath the eucalyptus trees, that my mother were there to tell me what to do, what I was supposed to be, whether there was a place for me anywhere in the world, and where it was. I kept thinking about her, and about the horses and the road, until I was exhausted. The more I missed my mother, the more I thought about Alaska. Images kept floating into my mind. Everything I remembered—caribou flooding in vast herds across the tundra, the dark scratch of Siberia on the far shore of the Bering Sea, the blue glow in the heart of a glacier, upturned faces beneath us on an airstrip as we descended from the sky—seemed full of hope and renewal and of the future opening out before my mother and me like the Arctic horizon.

One morning I took my bag and walked to the northbound ramp onto I-5 and stuck out my thumb. It was slow going most of the day. Then in the afternoon I got a lift from two men who said first that they were going to Seattle but then, after we'd been riding and swapping stories for a couple of hours, confessed that they were on their way to Alaska too. We drove for five days straight without stopping except for gas and food, north through British Columbia and the Yukon. Time disintegrated into cycles of darkness and light as we sped through forests that spread out on all sides of us as far as I could see and beneath snow-capped peaks, spraying dust and gravel behind us like a wake. I felt that I had been sprung loose from civilization entirely, had left behind me everything that entangled and confused me, even memory.

When we got to Alaska, I planned to return to some of the native villages I had seen with my mother—maybe Shishmaref, or Barrow, or Kotzebue, or Point Hope, or Bethel—and to look up Tom Snapp, and Howard Rock the painter, and Frank Degnan, and Guy Okakok, who had believed in my mother before anyone else in Alaska and had walked with us along the shore of the Arctic Ocean among the half-wild sled dogs and the hacked-up carcases of seals. In Anchorage I found a few days' work with a carnival, unloading the semis that carried the rides and the midway and helping setting it all up. But the cost of traveling in Alaska soon put an end to the thought of flying to any bush villages, and when I tried to call any of the people we had known, I froze up. I'd look up a number and stand for long minutes at the phone, unable to dial, cursing myself for my fear. Finally, when the carnival had moved on and my money ran low and I saw that I would have to go home to New York, I telephoned a man, now a prominent politician, who as a young lawyer had worked closely with my mother. I remembered playing croquet with his daughter one summer evening in the soft endless light of the midnight sun, listening to the tap of the wooden mallets and balls and to my mother plotting political strategy in the background. I don't know what I expected, but I had become so used to reliving fragments of the past as if they still existed as unchanging pockets of time that I must have thought that after six years nothing had really changed and that I could go back to their home and to the croquet and to the sound of my mother's crisp voice driving forward across the lawn. I got the man's wife on the phone. I knew instantly that the call was a mistake. "Who are you?" she said. "Do we know you?" When I hesitated, she demanded to know what I wanted. I told her that I had dialed the wrong number and hung up. I could see now that there was no place for me in my mother's world without her.

That summer's journeys had changed me somehow. I came back from Alaska more self-confident, more sure that I could take care of myself among strangers, and with the feeling that was powerful and fierce if only half clear that if I could travel far enough, it might just be possible to leave the past behind. It would be the start of six years of almost constant traveling. Physical motion became an end in itself, a kind of drug, and arrival—in Phoenix, Billings, or Winnipeg that summer, on the hectic drive home in an old Chrysler that I'd bought for fifty dollars; and later, Cairo, Teheran, New Delhi, a score of other foreign cities—almost beside the point. It seems to me now, reading the journals that I began to keep at that time, and trying to make sense of the difficult and driven young person that I find in them, that it was only in travel—in the constant change and newness, in cities, states, whole landscapes, and later whole countries flickering past and falling away behind me—that I found release from the corrosive grip of nostalgia.

ONE OF THE LAST COURSES I took at City College was a survey of modern European literature. We read Proust, Mann, Gide, Joyce, Kafka, Sartre, Camus. I had always read, and before I was ten could recite the names of dozens of famous authors. The house in Yonkers was filled with my mother's books; they were everywhere, stacked on tables, propped open with empty drinking glasses and paperweights and packs of cigarettes, stuck in alcoves next to the beds, rising in lofty ranges and massifs up the walls of the living room. But apart from history my own reading was narrow, eccentric and, in truth, fairly juvenile. I had never encountered stuff like this before. The professor was a short, bullet-headed man who had known Albert Camus in Paris and spoke about the concerns of the novelists he taught, the Existentialists in particular, not as abstract problems of the intellect but as if they mattered to his own life. Like Hans Castorp, who in

Thomas Mann's *The Magic Mountain* went to visit an alpine sanito-
rium for three weeks and stayed for seven years, listening to the furious intellectual debates of a dying Europe, I didn't understand half of
what I was hearing, but I loved listening to it all the same. It was as
if a door I had never seen before had been flung open and I had
walked through it and found room after room inhabited by people
who welcomed me and who knew nothing about Vermont or what
had happened to my mother and who were endlessly entertaining,
and who wanted nothing from me, and who would never die. To a
mind so preoccupied with memory as mine was, this was the first
glimmer that fantasy might be put to productive use somehow. With
a growing sense that I had in some still tentative way come home, I
began to see that literature could be a way of coming to grips with
the stuff of one's own life and of transforming it into something of
value.

Not long after I returned to New York, I began to write. I
thought of writing then as something like stepping onto the highway
and putting my thumb out for a ride, destination unknown. During
the day I worked as a postman in lower Manhattan. At night I sat for
hours in cafés, drinking black coffee, filling sheaves of paper with stories, and sometimes writing the whole night through. I felt sometimes
as if the entire contents of my mind were boiling out with a furious
intensity. One of the first things I tried to write was what happened
on the road in Vermont, but I froze and after a few halting paragraphs couldn't write anything at all. Sometimes in the years that followed I would try again, but I could never succeed. The story refused
to be told, and the attempt would leave me feeling depressed and
drained and helpless, realizing that the thing that I needed most to
say I couldn't say at all. I fared better with stories that had nothing
to do with me. I can see easily enough now that this was at least in
part an attempt to create pasts that were not my own, in which I
might roam free from the gravitational pull of that Vermont road. Although I wrote with exuberance, the stories I produced almost always
ended in disaster and death. In one of them a man abandoned family
and career and took to the streets, proclaiming that the end of the

world was at hand. In another an elderly man suffocated to death amid the lifetime's memorabilia that he had packed into his room in a flophouse. In a third a commuter went mad on the morning train into Grand Central Station. Others were rogues' galleries of derelicts, drunks, and provocateurs. Thirty years later I find these stories callow and embarrassing, and occasionally frightening. But through them I taught myself to write. Language meant structure, order, control, and safety; I recognized that in language lay a kind of salvation.

The next summer I drove back to Alaska with a woman I had gotten to know, an off-and-on painter named Polly who for the several years before I met her had lived a nomadic life in the Middle East and Europe. I was attracted to her moody detachment, to her sullen rootlessness that somebody more farsighted than I would probably have recognized as unstable. There was still government land to be had free in Alaska then, and we went with the notion of homesteading there. But the homesteading idea was preposterous from the start, and we soon realized it. I did a few weeks' work loading planes flying freight to the oil fields on the north slope of the Brooks Range. Then in September we ran out of money. The only work I could find was in a drillers' camp five hundred miles north on the Arctic shore. No women were allowed there, so I sold the van and sent Polly to California, where she had friends. The drillers' camp was a colony of prefabricated trailers set out on the tundra a few miles from the Arctic Ocean. I made repairs, swept floors, helped out in the kitchen, whatever needed to be done, working twelve hours a day, seven days a week until, late in the autumn when, Polly having decided not to come back, I went home again to New York, intending to earn money and dreaming about the open road.

For the next four months I drove a taxicab ten or twelve hours a night, saving money, and then flew to Europe in the spring. I intended to stay only a few months, planning to spend most of that time in Greece. On the way there I stopped in Belfast, then still in the early throes of civil war, drawn there—the first in my family to return to Ireland—by a feeling of romantic affection for my great-grandfather James Patrick Farrell, who, Maddy often told me, had fled his native land for freedom in America just steps ahead of his British pursuers. Later I crossed to France and hitchhiked through Switzerland and south into Italy; a lucky lift from an Australian driving a London taxicab carried me the rest of the way to Athens.

Greece had always occupied a special place in my imagination. When I was small, my mother would sometimes show me a pair of old photographs of the Acropolis that she treasured and that had been given her by one of her classics professors at NYU. These buildings—the Parthenon, the Erectheion—were the most beautiful in the world, she would tell me. And she would say that if she could have one dream come true, it would be to take me there, to the fifth-century city, which I think was as close a thing to heaven as she conceived of, and we would listen to Socrates and Plato and Thucydides and Pericles, whose mysterious names rolled wonderfully off her tongue, and she would tell me that someday we would walk together beneath white marble columns in the Greek sun. Now, on my first day in Athens, standing in the shade of the Propyleia looking toward the Parthenon and the Erectheion, standing precisely where my mother's pictures had been taken perhaps half a century before, I hardly saw the real place at all but the old sepia images of it and myself on my mother's knees, and I tried until my head ached with the effort to see it through her eyes alone, as if the sight of it could somehow resuscitate her from the dead. And I thought, shading my eyes against the smog-saturated but still blinding light of modern Attica, *How much you would know, how much you would tell me.*

In the years to come I would often return to Greece with a kind of homing instinct. In time, of course, I learned to see past the skeletal remains of the classical past—even my mother's dream was peopled only by the men of the fifth century B.C.—and to love Greece for its own sake and not just because my mother had loved it. I felt nevertheless that my mother had led me there and had in a way taught me how to love it, that it was a gift from her, like books, and fascination with the written word, and openness to the foreign, and the hungry curiosity that as I got older I realized we shared. For a while, that first summer, I lived on a small island in the Cyclades in a white-washed cottage that I could reach only after a long hike on a mule trail that wound along a dry riverbed that in the summer was abloom with laurels. Fig trees and lemon trees perfumed the yard, and grapes dangled over the tiny terrace; I drew my water from a well, cooked in a clay oven, and slept with the smell of the sea. The local people were friendly and accommodating and would smilingly carry on a conversation for hours with the score of words we shared at first until, with the help of a local teacher and fisherman and a tavern-keeper I liked to drink with, I became passably fluent in Greek. Mornings I would swim and then sit at the stone table in front of my house and write—another novel, cribbing the style from Henry Miller—and in the evenings I would climb to the village that clung to a ridge on the spine of the island and drink resinated wine, and practice Greek, and then hike home, more than once falling off terraced fields that on dark nights I often mistook for the trail.

I had planned to fly back to New York at the end of the summer. Then one evening I fell into conversation with a sunburned young American togged out in gauzy, well-worn cotton garments that resembled pajamas, who told me that he had had just come back from India. He'd ridden local buses across Asia from Istanbul to Delhi, and told me that you didn't need to know the languages along the way, and you could easily get all the visas you needed, and sure it was safe, at least safe enough.

So, on impulse, I cashed in my airline ticket and went to India.

Following the American's instruction and scuttlebutt from other travelers I met along the way, I sailed to Turkey and started east and was soon seduced by the excitement of traveling fast on strange highways and by the magnetic tug of the unknown cities that lay ahead of me on the road: Erzurum, Tabriz, Mashhad, Kandahar, Kabul, names that evoked a jumbled fantasy of smoky bazaars, minarets and men in turbans, an East of the imagination about which I really knew pathetically little. Three weeks after I left Greece, I came down from Afghanistan through the Khyber Pass into Pakistan, peering through the grimy window of a wheezing minibus packed with gimlet-eyed Pathans and mesmerized by the flat green hazy expanse of the Indian subcontinent spread out before me. In India I traveled almost every-where by train, in the hard-seat third-class compartments that were what I could afford.

There were other young foreigners traveling the same way around India, and I would run into them again and again, in the same cheap hotels and train stations and bus depots. Some were searching for legendary varieties of hashish, others for gurus, and others were just traveling from habit, having spent years on the road. If I fit into any of these categories, it was the last. Having no interest in drugs or religion, what I wanted was to lose myself in the foreign, hoping that by this one heroic effort of immersion I might remake myself into somebody, anybody, else. Embarrassed by my ignorance, I read every-thing I could get my hands on: histories of the Sepoy Mutiny, tomes on the caste system and on Buddhist cave painting, Mughal poetry, exegeses of the Bhagavad Gita, communist screeds, old census re-ports, the hilarious novels of R. K. Narayan. I meticulously wrote down everything I saw. I described the taste of tea on railway plat-forms at dawn, the sight of a vast flooded landscape punctuated by men in breechcloths wading in water up to their knees, half-naked brahmins chanting the night away in the sanctum of a centuries-old temple, apes scampering over the roofs of decaying colonial bunga-lows. All the while I kept moving, north into the Himalayan foothills, then south to Delhi, down the Ganges to the holy city of Varanasi, then to Madras and the cities of the far south, finally north again through Kerala toward Bombay.

In a bus station in northern Kerala I met a Spanish woman who had spent too long in India. She was of indeterminate age and must have been attractive once; she was obviously well educated, though she didn't want to talk about that, saying that she had been another person then. She was dressed in ragged Indian garments and her hair was cropped so that from a distance it was impossible to tell her sex. We traveled together for a couple of days up the west coast, an ar-duous route then, involving many local buses, and roads that petered out onto riverbanks, and ferries with no posted departures. She had been traveling for years in search of the right spiritual guide and didn't know if she would ever go home to Spain. Right now she wasn't sure where she was going, but she said that she would know it when she got there. "That's the way it is in India, you just know." She frightened me because I could see something of her lostness in myself. Whoever she was, she had escaped her country, her family, her past, even her century. I wondered, was this what I would become? Then one day at an unmarked fork in the road she suddenly told the driver to stop and she climbed down down from the bus and walked away into the jungle. I had an impulse to go with her, thinking that to disappear that way would be a kind of solution. But something held me back, and the bus had already begun to move, and feeling like the worst coward, I watched until her small, scrubby figure was obscured by the jungle. That night I wrote, "India had sunk very deeply into us both and lay on us like a crust. Our own civilization lay somewhere beneath as a common disturbing memory, no longer reachable. I had been alone with my thoughts for so long that it was difficult even to speak to her—or she to me, for that matter." I added, "Language now seems a cumbersome, useless instrument."

4

I RETURNED TO NEW YORK briefly in 1971, out of money and having worked my way home as a deckhand on a Norwegian freighter. Driving a taxi at night, by day I wrote up my jottings into a narrative of my travels in India and sent it to the *New York Times*. The editor of the Sunday Travel Section saw something in what I had sent and published it in two very long parts on two succeeding weekends. He introduced the first installment with these words: "The travelogue cliché for a large and varied country like India is 'kaleidoscopic,' but like most clichés, it captures only part of the truth while it begs the rest. Tourists usually look through the kaleidoscope; Fergus M. Bordewich, a 24-year-old New York writer, became one of the moving pieces, living almost entirely as the Indians do."

I read it over and over: "A New York writer."

Well, I thought. *Well.*

It's easy to see now that much of what I had written was trite. It was almost all surface: descriptions of temples and landscape and quirky incidents. Yet there was something there, some spark, some freshness of feeling that made it possible at least to overlook its short-comings. The *Times* encouraged me to do more stories, and soon, without quite realizing it, I was beginning to make money from writing.

I had fallen in love with a young woman who lived two floors above me in my building in Washington Heights, a friend of friends of mine from City College. Like most of the women I was attracted to, Cornelia was the physical opposite of my mother: dark-haired and olive skinned, smart certainly, but unadventurous, and as self-doubt-ing as I was. She taught me to like *Casablanca* and *The Big Sleep*, and William Faulkner, and Aretha Franklin, and bourbon. Mostly we would meet in her apartment, in the afternoon; with the shades drawn so that it always seemed dim and penumbral, even in the brightness of midday. We would talk, drink bourbon, listen to soul music on the phonograph, and sometimes make love.

I was full of a terrific nervous energy that I could scarcely keep under control. When I drank, there was never enough; and when I started to smoke, I was up to three packs a day within weeks. Some-times I would borrow a car and drive the whole night through, down the West Side Highway and up the East Side or to Brooklyn and out the Belt Parkway, charged up like a battery with ideas about stories I wanted to write and places faraway that I still wanted to see, and surging fantasies of the life I might have with Cornelia. I imagined that she would settle down with me, that I would forget all the past and never go away again, and finish my degree, and become a pro-fessor, and teach history, and raise kids with her, or no kids at all if that's what she wanted. When I fell in love, I wanted nothing short of total surrender. It was the only way I knew how to love, the way I loved my mother, without limits or uncertainty, permanent and all-embracing. I was mystified when Cornelia, sensibly, dashed my hopes. "You're besieging me," she told me. "You're swarming over me, you're trying to colonize me like some Third World country."

Sometimes Cornelia would tell me that I was looking for my mother in her. Her words had a kind of logic, if you knew enough about me. But she was wrong. My mother was inimitable. I couldn't even imagine loving anyone who could come close.

AFTER I WENT ABROAD AGAIN the following year, I turned out a fairly steady stream of travel stories for the *Times* from Greece and Turkey, Afghanistan, Iran, and elsewhere in the Middle East. I usually wrote about exotic places, and sometimes with humor. When I look at these stories now, I see that there is often a hidden subtext of loss and bereavement transposed to the plane of history and geography, a preoccupation with the irrecoverable past. I began another novel based on a story I'd heard in Greece about the daring escape of a political prisoner who had been held captive on a small island by the Rightist junta that was then in power. The true story was heroic, but I twisted it into a grim tale about two men at odds with themselves: a prisoner who had secretly betrayed his convictions and was determined to refuse salvation, and a rescuer who in the end would prove incapable of saving himself.

I continued to move restlessly from one country to the next: a month in Egypt, another month in Cyprus, two or three months in Greece, shifting restlessly from island to island, town to town, hotel to hotel, never at ease, never quite able to rest. When I look at the journals that I kept in those days, they frighten me. I do not like the person I see in them. I felt increasingly empty of everything except the need to keep moving, a feeling that came up out of me like a sweat. "Places grow tight and I shed them," I wrote in my journal in Rawalpindi, Pakistan. I gravitated toward empty places and toward ruins. When I looked later at the photographs I took, I realized that they were devoid of human presence, as if I didn't see people at all, or had censored them out, or had no idea where they fit in things.

Collapsed walls, shattered columns, tumbled battlements soothed me. They brought a strange exhilaration, as if I had come home.

Early in 1973 I was in northern Pakistan, recuperating from a misdiagnosed case of hepatitis. I retreated to Lahore, the great city of the Punjab made famous by Kipling, who lived there when he was young, and a place justly proud of its intellectual tradition and its gentility and manners. I settled on it in part for that, and partly, secretly, because among the splendid Mughal tombs and palaces that graced its outlying districts was the garden of Shalimar. The garden's attraction for me had nothing to do with history; it was the name of the perfume that my mother favored, and just the sound of the word could often bring back her presence and with it, like a door flung open, a tumult of memories of us together on my birthday walking up Fifth Avenue, and lunching at the Carlyle, and at the Metropolitan Opera seeing *Un Ballo in Maschera*, and the city glowing all around us the way it will for a child who notices none of its grit and stink and human failure. Shalimar perfume came in a handsome little bottle that resembled the picture of Aladdin's lamp in my book of the Arabian Nights. So that when I was very young I thought of it as a kind of magic lamp too, the source of dreams and stories and wonders of which the fragrance was only a foretaste. I would ask my mother to open the box for me and let me run my fingers over the bit of opulent purple velvet in which the bottle nested, and she would remove the glass stopper, and the rich and mysterious odor that was inseparable from my mother would fill my nostrils until I thought I would float.

Going there on the bus from Lahore was a pilgrimage of sorts. Perhaps I expected to find the humid air laden with the opulent aroma that I remembered. Or, against all reason, that I would find something of my mother there, as if even her ghost were infused with the scent and so linked forever to this place, and that setting foot there could somehow bring her back to life almost a dozen years after her death. The garden lay a few miles south of the city on a congested local route that meant that the bus stopped often to pick up or let off people at the factories along the road. Of course, in the end, it could not possibly have been anything but a disappointment. It was an unimpressive place, more a park than a garden really, and not very well kept up. There was no palace, no poignant Mughal ruin, no enchanted landscape: just a few trees, a rectangular pool and in the center of it, on a tiny island, an unimpressive pavilion built of red sandstone and white plaster. I sat for some time on the edge of the pool thinking what a fool I had been to come here, knowing that now when I thought of Shalimar no longer would it bring back a child's memory of a magical urn but instead a forlorn scrap of landscape and the honking trucks and squalid factories. But I had learned not to tamper with the past, so fragile was it that it could disintegrate at my touch.

WHEN I HAD RECOVERED sufficiently from the hepatitis, I moved to Teheran, where I worked for a time as an editor and reporter for an Iranian-owned English-language newspaper that was read mainly by foreign residents of the capital. The popular discontent that a few years later would become the Islamic revolution was only a distant tremor then. There were rumors of restiveness among the clergy, and of political shootings near the bazaar, of a paramilitary corps that was said to be in training to take over many of the functions of the mullahs, but we were never allowed to investigate such things. A picture of the Shah had to appear on the front page of the paper every day, and in it the Shah, a very short man, had somehow to be shown standing taller than everyone else in the picture, a conundrum that prompted many feats of creative photography. One day, working with a Farsi-speaking photographer on a story celebrating slum clearance in south Teheran, I was arrested without warning by men in civilian clothes, who turned out to be members of the Shah's secret police; only later, after hours of interrogation, I was informed that it was "against Iranian law to interview poor people." When I could take no more of this sort of thing, I quit.

I traveled west, by way of Baghdad, through Syria and Lebanon to the Mediterranean. In the course of this journey I saw sides of myself that troubled me. The trip out from Teheran was a pleasant one, through sweeping thinly populated valleys that spread away beneath pale-gray mountains that, because of some quirk of the atmosphere, seemed to hover in the cerulean sky as if they had no weight at all. I crossed the border into Iraq without incident. An hour later, however, I was standing at a checkpoint with my baggage in the dust and my hands in the air, watching my bus disappear into the desert. A soldier was pointing a rifle at my chest and a policeman in plain clothes was shouting at me that my visa was out of order and that I was a spy, an agent of the Iranians or the Israelis or the CIA, or all three. The gun-pointing and the shouting went on intermittently for hours, until nightfall, when I was driven to the nearest town and into a police compound, where I was surrounded by more men with guns. What was going to happen to me I didn't know, but I supposed that it was going to be bad. Strangely, I felt as if a burden were about to be lifted from me. This was as apt a way as any for my life to end, far from home, the result of some consular clerk's stupid error, perhaps no more than a rubber stamp not having been pressed hard enough on my passport; I would just disappear, in my way, like the Spanish girl into the jungle, cut short the way my mother was cut short before her time, the last thing that we would have in common. Anticlimactically, the police chief, into whose office I was finally led, recognized that some kind of mistake had been made and after a few more questions sent me on my way to Baghdad, leaving me to ponder as I rode across the darkened desert why I was so ready to yield up a life that had had so little effect.

Two or three weeks later I traveled to the small Syrian town of Salkhad to see a Byzantine fort I had read about that was the empire's last outpost on the edge of the vast desert of Arabia that spreads away south to Mecca and beyond. There, in a kind of through-the-looking-glass reversal of what had happened to me in Iraq, I was captured by a flood of gaily chattering schoolchildren who, thrilled to discover an American in their remote town, seized hold of me and led me everywhere, finally depositing me in the home of their teacher, where a meal was instantly prepared for me and I was peppered with friendly questions and begged to stay and to help teach English to the

kids. A quarter of a century later I wish I could say that I readily surrendered to the torrential hospitality, that I remained in Salkhad, and
that I was remembered ever afterward as the friendly American who
came to dinner and stayed. But it didn't happen that way. Instead of
pleasure I felt panic at the swarming friendliness, as if it were a kind
of aggression, and I fled on the next bus as soon as I could get away,
mumbling dishonest excuses about how I had to get along.

I look at these two scenes now, turn them over in my mind, hold
them up to the light as if they could be made transparent and I could
see within them the true character of the person I was then, this
younger self, who today seems such a stranger to me. I see him in
Salkhad surrounded by friendly faces, and then in the police station
in Iraq expecting to be savagely beaten and possibly killed, so ready
to see it all ended. What had I become that I was more at ease with
a gun pointed at my chest then with laughing children begging me to
share a meal with them? And what would my mother have thought
of me? Perhaps she would have appreciated my adventurousness, my
curiosity about things, my affinity for the foreign, my determination
to write. But how could she, so vital, so full of self-confidence, always
so certain of what needed to be done, have had any respect for the
rootless and increasingly callous man I was becoming? I wanted desperately to be like her, but in the ways that mattered most I was not
like her at all. At forty-nine, when she died, she was a woman in her
prime; at twenty-six I felt like an old man. I had none of her exuberance and spirit, or her way with people. She was afraid of nothing
that I ever saw, while I was plagued by anxiety and dread. She lived
to make a difference in other people's lives; I was doing nothing for
anyone at all, so consumed was I with the need to keep moving, to
keep shifting ground, to keep one step ahead of my conscience. She
was filled with affection for the living, while I, had I the honesty to
admit it, and I did not, loved only one person, and she was dead.
There was little room left in me for anyone else.

·   ·   ·

LATER THAT YEAR I was living in Germany with a woman I had met in Greece. She was a sweet-tempered, lonely woman, a chemist, who as a child had escaped from East Prussia just ahead of the Soviet army and who grew up without a father and with little skill with men; she was part of the generation that rebuilt Germany and that for all its youth knew little besides work and shame. On the balmy night in the Plaka when we met, I was drinking and full of stories about India and Iran and the East, and I made her laugh. I talked about writing for the papers and about novels I'd written, or at least half-written.

We agreed to meet when I was in Germany. I was only in town a few hours when we decided that I would move into the tiny apartment with white walls and white furniture and white curtains where she lived in a gray town on the Rhine. Almost as soon as I moved in I felt trapped by my promise to stay.

Every day I began drinking soon after Ursula left her work at the lab. First I would set a bottle of wine on the table in front of me. I would tell myself that I could have a sip when I'd written five hundred words, or three hundred, or even fifty. But instead of writing, I would stare at the bottle and think about how much better I'd feel if I drank something now instead of just thinking about it and worrying about whether I'd written enough to deserve having the drink. So I would take the drink. Then maybe I would write for a few minutes. Or maybe not. Maybe I would just take a second drink because I already felt better having taken the first. Then I would think that since I'd already drunk that much, I might as well go ahead and have some more, might as well finish the bottle, since there's more where it came from, and what difference did it make anyway, since I could write anytime I wanted. Why spoil a good drink with worrying?

Sometimes I passed out on the bed, sometimes on the floor. Sometimes I lay there feeling that my life was draining away like dirty water and that I was powerless to stop it. Sometimes I would see my mother in front of me on the road in Vermont, calling my name, and I would try to catch up to her and fail. And then I would see it all over again. But I would be too drunk by now to feel anything about it at all.

I would wake up an hour later, or two hours or three hours later, exhausted and muzzy, and aching if I was still on the floor. I would take a shower and drink mugs of strong coffee so that I would be able to talk to Ursula when she got home from work.

I imagined that Ursula knew none of this. She may not have known about the passing out and the work that was not getting done, because I lied shamelessly about that. But she couldn't have missed all the bottles that were disappearing and how, when we went for walks in the vineyards in the steep hills along the Rhine and stopped at the nearest *Weinstube* to sample the local vintage, I never wanted to leave. Sometimes I would burst into tears for no reason, or fly into a rage and blame her for whatever popped into my mind: failing to make the coffee strong enough for breakfast, or because there were so many drab gray buildings in the town where we lived, or because the trains stopped running too early at night. Sometimes I would be blacked out when this happened, and when I came out of it she would be crying and I would put my arm around her and say, What's wrong?

Having lost a home, and lost a father, and lost years of her life when she was younger when Germany was broken and poor, she was, like me, used to losing things. But unlike me, she was grateful to have survived. She expected so little from me: a little loyalty, a little companionship, no more than a little of anything, but still far more than I had left to give.

I watched her slender, precise chemist's fingers splayed over her lap as I told her that I was leaving her, and they were so stiff that I thought they would crack.

IN THE EARLY MONTHS of 1974 I found myself living in the medieval fortress town of Monemvasia, a small island attached by a causeway to the southeast coast of the Greek Peloponnesus. Wealthy Athenians had begun to rehabilitate some of its ruins as summer homes, but in the winter only twenty or thirty people lived there, mostly widows along with a few fishermen and laborers who worked on the mainland. It was an eerie place, whose shattered domes and vaults and dark tunneled alleys were redolent of the tragedy that characterized its bloody history of sieges and sackings. Over the town rose a thousand-foot-high cliff that was so out of proportion to the ruins at its foot that it seemed disorienting, as if the earth had somehow been upended and were about to fall. When the wind was high, waves hit the old city walls like cannon shot, exploding off the rocks. The atmosphere of violence suited my state of mind. I lived in a room that looked out over the old walls toward the uneasy sea, trying to write. At night I hiked to the modern town two miles away to dine in a tavern that resembled a pothouse in some old Dutch painting, low-ceilinged and smoky and filled with men pounding their glasses on wooden tables and shouting about old grudges, and where I drank myself into numbness every night. In April I calculated that there had not been a night that I had gone to bed sober since early January. More and more often in my journals I find comments like "Too much wine again last night," or "Drunk again," or handwriting slurring off the page. "I have reached the end of something," I wrote.

I dreamed every night about cliffs. Sometimes I was standing on the cliff above the town fighting a wild wind that threatened to blow me over the edge. Sometimes the wind carried me over and I clutched wildly at stones that came away in my hands. Other times I dreamed that I was driving a car around a sheer cliff on a road that narrowed to a vanishing point and finally disappeared into the stone. When the front wheels spun out into the air I woke up gasping for breath, frightened that I was already dead.

5

IN THE SUMMER of my twenty-sixth year I came home. Newspapers were filled with stories about lay-offs and rising prices, dire predictions of even worse unemployment, and speculations about a war with the Arabs to take over the oil fields. It all seemed to be taking place in another world, one in which I no longer belonged. I stayed for a while with one friend after another, first in Manhattan, then in Brooklyn, then back in Manhattan again. In subway stations I found myself staring at the tracks as trains pulled into the station and imagined my body in front of them. I thought that the worst thing would be that I might not be damaged enough to die. In November I phoned Sam and Essie Liebowitz, the last people I still had nerve enough to call, an elderly couple who lived across the street from where I had grown up and who had always liked me as a child. I told them that I was writing a book and was down on my luck and needed a quiet place to stay for a few weeks while I finished it.

They had fixed up a corner of the basement with a bed and a metal desk. There were a couple of shelves of old children's books. On the other side of a sheetrock wall was the furnace. The washing machines were through the door in the garage. There was a narrow window over the desk. Standing on the desk, I could see the place where my house had been. As with so much else, my father had let the house slip through his hands. He had rented it out for several years, finally to a woman with bleached hair and several boyfriends who, when she skipped out on six months' rent, took off with what was left of my mother's jewelry. After that my father let the house run to seed. Vandals broke through the cellar door and ransacked what was left. Pipes froze and flooded the basement. Eventually my father sold the house to a man who resold it for a quick profit to the city, which tore it down to make way for an arterial road that was never built. There was now a mound of overgrown earth and gravel where it had been.

I tried to write, but I had nothing at all left to say, not even to myself. I sat for hours staring at blank sheets of paper in my typewriter, trying to will something onto the page. I was no longer capable of imagining lives worse than my own. The darkness of my fiction had flooded back into real life. My imagination had in the end proven too weak to stem the steady seepage of reality. My journal entries become increasingly infrequent and disturbing: "Waves of sadness roll through me . . . The silence is unbearable."

I would lie on the bed and almost instantly find myself on that August morning in Vermont. By now remembering had become a kind of illness, an infection of the imagination. I saw the boy padding to his mother's bedside, the childish pleading, the horses gathering speed, the body falling away into the Vermont air. Sometimes I seemed to be the rider hitting the ground, sometimes the one struggling to catch up, sometimes both.

My mind rewrote the events of that morning over and over. In one version I trot into my parents' bedroom. I poke my mother awake. I see the anxiety and exhaustion in her eyes. *She needs rest*, I think.

I tell her softly, "We can go riding tomorrow."

I kiss her cheek; she smiles, rolls over, and goes back to sleep. I tiptoe out of the room, silently pulling the door shut behind me.

In another version we are in the Buick, driving toward Wally's farm. Rain drips onto the windshield. I can hear the hiss of wetness beneath the tires. We see Wally on his tractor. I notice the irritation on his normally friendly face.

"I don't think Wally wants to ride today," my mother says.

I say with a smile, "It doesn't matter. Let's go home."

My mother wheels the Buick around, and we drive back to the lake. Looking into the mirror, I can see Wally waving to us from the tractor.

In the next version my mother and I are trotting up Fiske Road. My mother nudges Pepper into a canter and then a gallop. I do my best to keep up with her. The only sounds are the creak of leather and the gathering beat of hooves I feel the breeze quicken on my cheeks. We spur the horses into a gallop. The speed frightens me. I fear that I'll be unable to control my horse. As Pepper pulls away from me I shout, "I'm scared!"

My mother looks back with annoyance. I can see that she is disappointed with me.

"Mom," I shout, knowing that she won't refuse me. "Please don't go so fast!"

She slows down, waits for me to catch up, finally suppresses her annoyance and smiles. Soon the others join us. We trot back to the farm.

My mother lives another forty years.

With concentration I slow the speed of the images. The horses' hooves are poised impossibly in the air, floating like swallows. My mother glides effortlessly through the bright air. I can bring the scene to a crawl, but I can never quite halt it completely, never quite stop time in its tracks. Against my will the horses press inexorably up the hard-packed road. Finally the effort to hold them back is simply too much, and I let them go, and the horses leap suddenly forward toward the inevitable conclusion.

For a brief while I would believe in these revisions. Occasionally I even felt a gush of relief, even joy, which was quickly dashed when the truth once settled in and the familiar cycle of remembering began again.

Sometimes I thought of gassing myself in the garage in Sam's car, or slipping off the Odell Avenue bridge onto the tracks of the New York Central. The thought of it was the only thing that gave relief.

Once in a while my father picked me up and we drove to bars he liked in Elmsford or White Plains. As bad as things were for me, they had gotten easier between us. His marriage had fallen apart a few years before. There had been some conflict with his wife's family, some kind of ultimatum given, and she had chosen them and not him. He seemed to like to drink with me more than anything we had ever done together, and I thought that perhaps all my life he had dreamed of sitting like this at a bar with his son, like pals, drinking buddies, swapping stories, getting loaded together. We would talk about the collapse of South Vietnam, and about Watergate, and the Nixon pardon, and Gerald Ford's failure of nerve. On one of these visits, when we were both insulated by drink, my father told me that my mother had disappeared the night before she died. It was characteristic of my father to reveal something that truly mattered and that ought to have been talked about and made sense of only when it was too late to make a difference, when all the damage that could possibly be done by the not talking had been done. He didn't know where she had gone, or why. She had abruptly disappeared in the white Buick, gone off without saying anything at all, or at least without saying anything that even years later my father cared to repeat. She was gone all night and had only come back after dawn. When I woke her, she had been asleep for only an hour or two. Why was he telling me this now? He said he had never thought to tell me before.

My mother should never have gotten on a horse that day. She must have been mortally exhausted. No wonder she had panicked, had judged things so badly. I felt as if a sinkhole had opened up inside me and was sucking me in. Why hadn't she told me? Why had she gotten up, dressed, gotten into the car? Why hadn't I seen that something was wrong? It was clearer than ever that I had pushed her beyond what she could bear.

MORE AND MORE, memories of countless things that seemed of no importance at all took over my conscious mind. I remembered a girl named Barbara who had lived long ago in a blue-trimmed house across the street and who had once been my friend, and I remembered a fat tan-and-white dog named Gizmo that belonged to the Hemples, who lived around the corner on Odell Avenue. I remembered my father holding me on his shoulders to see President Truman when he came to Yonkers to campaign for Adlai Stevenson in 1952. I remembered the way corn stood on a hillside in Nebraska in 1958, a Buddha painted on a rock in a valley in northern India.

But I could no longer remember the touch of my mother's hand or the timbre of her voice.

The only thing that interested me was the empty space across the street where my house had been. It became a private theater. For what at least seemed like hours on end I stood on the desk and went back into the house of my childhood. I was aware even as I did this that it was absurd and pathetic and that I was surrendering to something dangerous in myself. Nevertheless, day after day, I stared across the street into the emptiness in an effort to bring my mother back from the dead. I relaid the slate path to the house, reerected the white-shingled walls with their green shutters, walked through the front door. There was the living room to the left, to the right the dining room, and opening out from it, through a swinging door, the kitchen. Upstairs lay my grandmother's bedroom, and my parents', with a section of it walled off for me. I searched everywhere in this house of my imagination for my mother. Sometimes I heard her throaty laugh, or heels tapping on the floor, leaving a room just as I entered, or caught a whiff of Shalimar, or glimpsed an evanescent smile fading on the air. After a while I began to be able to see her. Sometimes I saw her curled on the living-room sofa, beneath the cliffs of books, head bent over the Sunday *New York Times* crossword, then over pages and pages of yellow legal pads, writing without letup. I tried with all my will to compel her to look up, to see me. Sometimes I saw her in the dining room, torrents of ideas spilling out of her over the dinner table. I strained to hear her, but it was as if she were speaking a language that I had never learned. In the garden I found her on her knees with a trowel planting roses, her small, vigorous hands covered with peat moss and loam. I knew that if she could hear me, she would come to me, but I was mute.

I felt a growing sense of foreboding that something terrible was about to happen and that it could not be forestalled. "The day promises nothing but tension and fear," I wrote in my journal. "I have no hope at all." I avoided Sam and Essie as much as I could. I told them that I was having trouble with the novel and needed to be by myself. When they passed through the basement on the way to the laundry room or the garage, I jumped to the typewriter and smiled and pretended to write. I stared at the telephone, afraid to pick it up, afraid to hear another human voice on the other end. I no longer knew how to keep up a conversation, and indeed no longer wanted to. People called me less and less frequently. Sometimes now the phone never rang for days at a time. Even the sound of my own voice scared me. Increasingly it sounded like something left over from long ago and that was no longer mine, an artifact whose use no longer made sense. I rarely went out during the day. I was afraid to run into neighbors on the block, frightened that someone would ask who I was and what I was doing there, and that I would not know how to answer. I felt as though I had become as transparent as glass, that people could see through me, as if my webs of veins and arteries and nerves were exposed to everyone's view. Sometimes on the street I seemed to hear strangers behind me whispering my name, whispering my secret in voices too low for me to quite hear the words.

The past crowded in on me like a physical presence. In Asia, when I had hepatitis, I was once mistakenly shot full of atropine—a powerful chemical that is used to revive patients suffering from heart attacks—by an incompetent doctor. For more than a day I lay in my bed, nearly paralyzed, hallucinating that the cracked ceiling was pressing down on my chest, squeezing the life out of me until I could no longer breathe. I fought from moment to moment to retain consciousness, fearing that if I lost it, it would never return. I felt something similar now, as if I were suffocating from memory. I knew instinctively that my life was coming to an end. Increasingly, all this seemed like something that had happened long ago to someone else, whom I hardly knew. For a while this frightened me. Then it no longer seemed to matter.

When I drank, the pressure eased a little. But I drank now without pleasure or release. No matter how much I consumed, I could no longer lift myself out of depression. Usually I came upstairs to sit with Sam and Essie during the eleven o'clock news. After they went to bed I began drinking. Although they almost never drank, they kept a few bottles for guests in a cabinet and more, still in their holiday gift wrappings, in a closet down the hall. Hour after hour I sat in front of the TV pouring tumblers of rye or Canadian and watching anything that turned up on the screen until the drumming of memory stopped and for an hour or two and I could imagine a future for myself. When I had drunk enough, I thought, I will learn Russian someday, I will go to China, I will write books. I knew these were lies, but for a few hours in the dead of night it didn't matter. Before dawn I took the empty bottles out the front door in my stocking feet and placed them as silently as I could in the garbage can by the curb, spending long minutes removing the can's zinc top and then gently replacing it to muffle the sound.

I feared my bed because I feared my dreams. Every night I told myself, without much hope, that perhaps I would simply fall asleep. I repeatedly dreamed the dream that had begun in Monemvasia—that I was driving on a narrowing road that clung to the side of a cliff high above the sea. There was no way to turn the car or to go back, and then I could see where the road simply disappeared into the stone and that any second I would topple away into oblivion.

I clung to books as if they were a life raft, trying not to fall asleep. I read paragraphs over and over, but I could no longer concentrate and it was as if I had never read them at all. I stared at the pages anyway, terrified at what was becoming of me. The past, memory—everything was gone now. The only thing that remained was to remove myself. I could smell death on me like sweat. So long in pursuit of a ghost, I had become a ghost too.

Sometimes late at night when I couldn't bear to face the basement, I slipped out of the house and walked over the stone bridge that spanned the New York Central tracks and the Saw Mill River Parkway and out onto the parkway and hitchhiked into New York City. Once a car of stoned Puerto Ricans dropped me on One Hundred and Twenty-fifth Street in Harlem. Another time a truck driver going to work left me in Hunt's Point in the Bronx. There were other rides that I was too drunk to remember and from which I came to at dawn on a street in Manhattan or on a subway, sometimes with money in my pocket and sometimes without, and having to borrow or beg it from one of the two or three people I still talked to in the city, and with nowhere to go but back to the basement in Yonkers.

Often I stopped at the top of the bridge and looked down over the stone parapet at the tracks. Sometimes I stood there a long time in the suburban silence, listening to the traffic light at Nepperhan Avenue click from green to yellow to red to green again, grasping the rusty iron railing in my hands and thinking, *Just climb up*. I loathed my fear of what I wanted to do. When I was a boy, more daring friends had climbed onto the parapet and challenged the rest of us to lean out over the tracks. I disliked risk then and never would. Now, along with the fear, I felt a wild exhilaration, the kind of vital tension that I used to feel when I wrote or when I crossed a border into a new country. I wondered each time I walked over the bridge whether, this time, I would have the courage to go over the parapet. What, after all, would be lost—the memory of an afternoon on the shore of the Arctic Ocean, or of a ring of Indians on the Dakota prairie in 1958, the sound of horses' hooves, a woman's cry on a crisp morning in Vermont? Somewhere in the distance a train would already be coming toward me. My train.

IN THE LATE HOURS of a night in December I came out of a blackout in Manhattan, in Cornelia's apartment. My memory of that terrible night is confused, like the effect of random flashes in a dark room—the image of a table here, a face there, a picture that may or may not be a window—that leaves the afterimages of familiar objects seeming unstable and suspended in blackness. There had been a car ride into the city, then an angry scene in the apartment of another couple I knew, then a long walk up an empty avenue searching for somewhere to go. Coming out of the blackout, I see Cornelia sitting at her kitchen table. I am leaning over it from the other side shouting into her face and realizing that I have no idea what I am saying but only that I can only make myself heard if I shout. What I do understand—I recognize it instantly and feel sick at it and can do nothing at all to bring myself under control—is the contempt in her eyes, her palpable fear of someone she once trusted who has now changed beyond recognition. I feel a terrific rage well up. At what exactly? I don't even know. At my own helplessness? At her, simply because she is there and will live and I will not? I stand over her and rave until I physically choke. I go on until my rage seems to seep out through my pores like sweat.

Leaving my friend at the table weeping with fear, I went out to the street and into the subway at One Hundred and Tenth Street, drawn northward by nothing more than habit, toward the province of childhood, certain only that I had come to the end, had become voided of everything, at last even of memory. I left the train at its terminus at Two Hundred and Forty-second Street in the Bronx and walked east to the Major Deegan Expressway and went out onto the highway and into the traffic. Headlights swarmed toward me, swerving. Cars raced past with their horns blaring. I told myself, *Just step into the next lane, just one more step. Just pick a pair of headlights and step into them.*

I do not know who picked me up, or how, or even where—whether someone stopped right there on the highway, or if I wondered off onto the shoulder, or for that matter hiked halfway to Yonkers.

I have a faint image of myself in a car, but this may well be something that my mind created after the fact in an attempt to fill in the blank spaces. The driver must have let me out in Yonkers, because I next see myself clearly walking along Tuckahoe Road just west of the New York State Thruway, empty of all feeling. There is nowhere to go but the basement and that is where I am going. I am walking through the landscape of my childhood past Barbalette's store, where we always bought the Sunday papers, and my father's favorite gin mill, the Lighthouse, and the railway overpass where once a truck had crashed, strewing its cargo of candy all over the road, and past Eddie's house, and Alan's, and the field where we hit flies, and, once when I was very small, tried to dig a hole clear through to China, and then the empty space where my own home once had been. It must have been close to dawn when I finally reached Sam and Essie's.

I slept for most of the next twenty-four hours. I cannot say that when I woke I felt any new determination to live. I was aware only of a profound exhaustion. I felt, if anything, even emptier than before, empty of the mindless rage that had consumed me, empty of the will either to live or die. And yet something had happened.

The look of contempt on Cornelia's naturally gentle face, its reflection of what I had become, had penetrated in a way that nothing else had. It told me that I had lost all claim to understanding or to pity and that I had been cut off from virtually the last person to

whom I could turn. There was something else too, subterranean—
like one of those implausible fish that glow faintly near the floor of
the deepest seas—an awareness of the complete failure of the course
that my life had taken for the last thirteen years. I knew now, with
hard certainty, that if I continued in this way I was going to die, if not
this day then the next, or the one after that.

6

TWO OR THREE WEEKS after that awful night I told Sam and Essie that
I was "giving up on the novel." I borrowed money from them and
rented an apartment on West One Hundred and Fourteenth Street, a
gloomy place, dark and thick-walled and silent, with windows that
opened only onto an interior air shaft, like living in an envelope. For
months I lived a troglodyte existence, driving a taxi at night and
sometimes not returning until dawn, coming out again only at the
end of the afternoon to drive again all night. I wrote nothing, saw almost no one. I would go three or four days without a drink, then
think that I might as well have a beer, and have it, and then not be
able to stop. It went on like that through the spring.

For a while I saw a counselor in the alcoholism unit at Roosevelt
Hospital. Eddie had once been a punk in the Bronx, and even though
he had gotten sober and gone to school, he still had the street tough's
blunt way of talking. "You think you're smart," he would say, con-
temptuously waving big, flat, square hands at me. "You don't know
anything! You don't know it's the first drink that gets you drunk, do
you? So what do you know?"

Sitting tight-lipped, afraid to walk away because I didn't know
where I would go, I would think furiously, *I know about the Plantagenet kings, and what the madeleine means in* Swann's Way, *and
what it's like to face down the Ku Klux Klan, and what dawn looks
like on the Acropolis . . .*

"Once a pickle never a cucumber again," Eddie would say.
"You're a pickle, my friend. You can't drink anymore. You keep on

drinking, you're going to wind up in a mental hospital, on the street, or dead."

One night after turning in my cab I stopped at a bar I knew on the West Side. It must have been two o'clock in the morning. I was drinking stout and ale mixed together, drinking without really knowing why anymore. Alcohol no longer provided any kind of release but only left me feeling muddled and depressed and not knowing what to do. Looking at my face in the mirror, I felt a violent physical repulsion that had nothing at all to do with what I had eaten or drunk that day. Then, looking around at the man in the beer-stained business suit weeping soundlessly next to me, the gap-toothed drunk beyond him at the bar, the blowzy young woman across the room, I saw only reflections of my own helplessness. The bartender was offering me a refill on the house. I said no thanks and got up and left, not knowing then, in April of 1975, that it was the last drink that I would take, not even intending then never to pick up another one, but only wanting to get away from the sour reek and pathos of the place and knowing only that I was sick in a way that I never had been before, of being lost to myself, and sick of everything that smelled and smacked of alcohol and of the life that I had led for the past thirteen years.

Eddie kept telling me to go to Alcoholics Anonymous. He said if I didn't there was no way I was going to get sober. To quiet him, I went to the address that he gave me, in a church rectory near where I lived. I looked through the window into a lighted room, where I saw people sitting with their backs to me in high wooden chairs. I walked around the building once and then a second time, but I couldn't make myself go in. I felt that the last shred of my dignity depended on my being able to turn my back and walk away. So I did, feeling angry and depressed and thinking that if I couldn't stop drinking by myself, then I didn't want to stop, and to hell with Eddie and the counseling and the people in the room, whom I never even saw except for the backs of their heads. For the next week I managed to keep away from alcohol, but it was harder every day. At night after I dropped off the cab, I did anything just to keep myself inside for fear that if I went out again I'd drink. I couldn't concentrate enough to read, and I couldn't afford a TV. I painted walls that didn't need painting. I washed dishes and glasses and silverware over and over. I spent hours every night on my hands and knees stripping the floor of my apartment with a toothbrush, inch by inch, until I was exhausted enough to sleep.

Finally, having lost what hope I had that I could survive on my own, I went back to the AA meeting. For weeks I came late, left early, and hardly talked to anyone. But I didn't drink, and slowly things people said began to penetrate. People talked about how they'd lost marriages, children, jobs, homes, fortunes. The stories were different, but I understood the gaping sense of loss; how everything that was important to you and that seemed permanent could fall apart around you while you stood by, realizing—half-realizing, anyway—that you were the cause of it and could do nothing to stop it, and now seeing, too, that if you were going to survive at all, you would have to understand that things could never again be as they were. I would like to say that I toughed it out, that I stopped drinking just like that, never worried about it again. The truth is that for more than a year I never stopped thinking about alcohol. Every time I lit a cigarette, or ate a meal, or got ready for bed, or tried to write, and most times in between, I wanted a drink, often so badly that I gasped with the effort of not taking it. Sometimes at night I dreamed that I had begun drinking again and couldn't stop, and I would wake up weeping with shame.

For a long time days and weeks of deep depression blurred into ones of inexplicable exuberance and then back again into depression. Daily life slowly became more manageable. I began to take an interest again in things that I had long forgotten; I started going to the theater, the opera, museums, became aware of weather, architecture, smells in the air. Although there still remained in my heart that private place hidden from everyone else's sight into which I could suddenly be drawn, that place where the horses were always galloping and where my mother's cries were always alive in the bright air, the compulsive remembering, the seductive nostalgia gradually abated. Increasingly I felt that I had an existence apart from memory and loss.

Gradually I made friends with other people who were getting sober. We went to meetings together, had coffee afterward, talked each other out of drinking that day and, sometimes, out of despair. They told me simple things that seemed at first immensely hard to understand and then made a lot of sense once I got them: that if I didn't pick up that first drink I'd never get drunk, and that I didn't have to decide to stop drinking for the rest of my life but just a day at a time. I had persistent trouble with just one thing: they said it wasn't a religious program, and strictly speaking it wasn't, but whenever I said I was confused and frightened somebody urged me to pray, to put my trust in God, to accept His will for me. I kept thinking, how could anyone believe that there was a benign and intelligent higher power in a universe where six million Jews had been industrially slaughtered, and where *right now* Cambodian civilians were being herded into the countryside to be butchered by the Khmer Rouge, and where my mother, whom I loved more than anything on earth, had died senselessly at my feet? But I kept such thoughts to myself. I continued going to AA meetings and to rely on them as a bulwark against discouragement and depression and the recurrent impulse to drink. But when I didn't think I could go on, it was not the notion of God but my mother's image that came to me, Winston in hand, blue eyes glistening and alert, surrounded by Indians, telling me that if I gave up hope I would be killing what she had loved most of all.

When a Jewish friend of mine died after a long illness, I sat in the living room after the funeral while her mother and brother and the family she had made read aloud from a book of prayers: "You give meaning to our days, to our struggles and strivings. In the stillness of the night and in the press of the crowd, Yours is the voice that brings joy and peace . . . Let our darkness be dispelled by Your love, that we may rise above fear and failure, our steps sustained by faith. You give meaning to our days: You are our support and our trust." Listening, I thought not of God, of whom I had never thought in any serious way, but of my mother. It was only by thinking of her that I could even begin to grasp the import of these words, for like a protean force she had given life to everything that mattered to me. "Thus even when they are gone, the departed are with us, moving us to live, as in their higher moments they themselves wished to live." I didn't need God: I had my mother. She was irrefutable. She was unfailing. She was a ghost of boundless love.

ONE DAY my father called me from where he lived upstate. After his marriage ended he had put my mother's library in storage with most of the rest of his belongings in a barn. Now he was cutting his losses, clearing out what he didn't need, simplifying. "Take them, or I'm going to get rid of them," he told me. I took a bus up from the city, and he met me at the station and we drove to the barn. "Take whatever you can fit into the trunk," he said. I had always expected to inherit the library, imagining, without really thinking much about it that it would always remain intact; there was nothing else from our home in Yonkers that was left. Looking at the books now, piled around the barn, the ghostly rooms of my childhood seemed to rise up around them like something alive, and through them, through the heaps of books, I seemed to see my mother's roses and the willows and the Japanese cherry tree that she loved, and across Saw Mill River Road to the railway tracks, where a steam engine was pulling into Grey Oaks station and preparing to release her from another day in the city. The sense of her immanence was so intense that I felt it as almost a physical pressure in my chest. As the afternoon waned, I picked over the books as quickly as I could, working feverishly, setting aside the ones I would take, carrying them in teetering stacks out to the Rambler. I took Suetonius and Herodotus, and Gibbon, and the enormous Dante that my mother had read to me as a child, and the Ovid that I wasn't old enough yet to understand, and Chaucer. I took the copy of *Moby Dick* with Rockwell Kent's eerie woodcuts. I took Carlyle's *History of the French Revolution*, and the books of Durrell's *Alexandria Quartet* that I remembered her reading the last summer of her life. I started to collect the volumes of of my mother's beloved Temple Shakespeare—the pocket-sized set with gold lettering and paper that felt like cloth to the touch—but they fell apart in my hands, so I left them. I took the Nebraska novels by my mother's friend Marie Sandoz and everything I saw by Oliver LaFarge. There were hundreds of books about Indians. I grabbed them randomly—a biography of Black Hawk, a study of the Seminoles, a book on Hopi ethics, a chronicle of the Sioux, but not knowing what meant the most to her I would wound up leaving most of them behind, depressed at the sight of them and thinking of all the Indian places where I would never again go with her. Dusk was coming, and it was getting cold. I worked faster. I took everything by Henry James and Theodore Dreiser and Richard Wright, but I left Saul Bellow and Katherine Anne Porter, and most of the rest of the modern novels. I left the Romantic poets. I left the 1929 Encyclopedia Brittanica that I had grown up with. I left the complete set of O. Henry's works. When I had filled up the Rambler we drove back to the city, riding in silence, just myself and my father's silhouette. I thought of all the piles of books left behind, standing like the chimneys of houses that had been razed in a city that had been laid waste. I felt as if I had committed a crime.

FOUR MONTHS after I stopped drinking I went back to City College. I had just two semesters left to complete my degree, and I was desperate to do something with myself besides drive a cab and polish glasses and dishes and scrape the floors and paint walls that didn't need painting. I had tried to go back to the novel that I had left off when my drinking got out of hand, but when I wrote fiction everything I put down led back to death and catastrophe, to inner revulsion and, when I slept, to the nightmare of the road disappearing into the cliff. I went back to school tight with fear: frightened that I might not be able to make sense of anything anymore, frightened at being in classes with people ten years younger than I was and to whom I could say nothing about what had happened to me, frightened of being asked to explain what I thought because I was afraid that I couldn't put two sentences together without garbling them. But no one asked me what I was doing there. No one told me that I made no sense or to shut up. I did well, and a professor who took an interest in me urged me to go on to graduate school. I spent the next year at Columbia University, where I earned a master's degree, having written a thesis on urban renewal on the West Side of Manhattan, a choice of subjects that, I can see now, was hardly accidental. After graduation I was invited to stay on, part-time, as coordinator of admissions at the Graduate School of Journalism, an arrangement that appealed because it would allow me time to write.

Around this time my neighbor Howard died. When I met Howard he was in his late sixties, a man of the mildest temperament, a retired university librarian and, like me, trying to figure out how to stay sober. We would sit in his apartment off Riverside Drive talking about how many times that day we had wanted a drink but hadn't picked it up: small victories but real ones, and for me the first evidence I had that I might survive after all. As he came to trust me, Howard gradually revealed that he had had only one important intimate experience in his life, a brief romance that had taken place decades earlier, not for a long time making clear whether its object had been a man or woman (it turned out to have been a man) or had even been consummated, revealing all this as one might a treasured piece of chinaware or silk, unfolding it from its wrapping by slow and clearly delicious degrees, and telling me in his feathery voice how it was the only thing that had ever really mattered to him in his life and how the only thing that he lived for anymore was the remembering of it. For a long time Howard had been the only person I felt comfortable with. Then he began drinking again and became reclusive, and I was busy with school and driving the cab, and then graduate school, and for a long time I didn't see him. One day another neighbor who had a key to Howard's apartment and had missed him for several days found him dead on the floor, crusted with hemorrhaged blood and covered with cockroaches, with his two starving dogs dying and whimpering at his side. Howard's death frightened me because it left me with no doubt that if I drank again I could die as ugly and pathetic a death as he had. But I also recognized something central about myself in Howard: I could see how his life had withered around its core of fantasy, how memory had sapped him, had stolen his entire life, and how if I allowed it to, it would steal mine.

Increasingly I craved reality, the concrete, something indisputable to hold onto. I felt an urgency to get at the world as it was. I began reporting small stories for New York newspapers and magazines about city planning and the rehabilitation of slums. Beneath the superstructure of arcane housing codes, federal regs, sweat equity, and the like, I can see the intimate personal subtext of regeneration and rebuilding, of the clearing away of ruin and debris. (What a slum I had made of my own life . . .) Facts were a bulwark against nostalgia and memory and remorse, proof that I existed in the present and not the past alone. Writing the factual truth of things, I wrote myself back into reality. None of these stories holds much interest more than twenty years later, but they were truthful and increasingly self-confident. I assumed nothing anymore. I looked at things clinically, distrusting sentiment and often my own instincts, which had so often (it seemed) cheated and betrayed me, trusting instead now only what I could see and had checked out and gotten confirmed and checked over again. I wrote with single-mindedness, driven by a panicky sense of years wasted and by a deep and abiding wish to, finally, be the kind of man my mother had wanted me to be.

We were alike in many ways, my mother and I; in our bookishness, and our impatience, and our love of silence, and our perpetual moral unease. But I knew that I lacked her charm, her way with people, her ability to subsume herself in others' causes, to take on their needs and vulnerabilities as her own, her ability to inspire hope and to invent solutions where there had been none before. Where she had readily committed her heart, it seemed to me, I hung back; where she had led, I could only observe. But like her, and thanks to her, surely, I was drawn, as she had been to Indians, to the foreign, to the elusive Other, the stranger as a puzzle and also as the gateway into another world that one could, with patience and humor, enter. Also like her, I craved risk like food, not for its own sake, I think, but rather as a kind of moral litmus paper, a way to test the sincerity of what I claimed to believe.

I began to go abroad again, first tentatively, writing a modest travel piece about the aftermath of race riots in Bermuda. I was nervous at first, not having much confidence that I could travel without drinking; then, realizing with relief that I could, I returned to the countries that I had traveled in years before, writing mostly for magazines now, no longer searching for the reflection of my own mood but writing mainly about politics and economics, the mechanics of the larger world. When my self-confidence or my energy flagged, I often thought of my mother. I could see her anytime—it was like turning on a switch—the Winston jammed between her lips, puffing to keep herself alert on endless Dakota roads, always in motion, hurtling from one dust-blown reservation town to the next, hunting up men and women who when they first met her were incapable of trusting strangers and whites, and then sunk deep in someone's buckled sofa, listening to stories so awful that I wanted to run away from them, away from the sour stink of poverty and the naked snotty kids and the dust seeping through holes in the chinked walls. But sooner or later, in the midst of the awfulness, they would all be laughing and having a great time, my mother plainly so happy to be there that anyone could see it and that it was not put on for effect, more at ease than at home in our living room on Mayfair Road. She would tell me, "Never mind the dirt and the smell, just keep listening, just pay attention." And I would think, *That is the kind of person I want to be.*

In 1980 I crossed illegally into Afghanistan from Pakistan with a group of anti-Soviet guerrillas, dressed in a turban and baggy *shalwarkamis* to disguise my light hair and pale skin. We walked through denuded mountains beneath skies the color of lapis lazuli, and through narrow valleys where desperate farmers were trying to bring in their harvests before the Soviets returned. The Afghans reminded me of the Sioux Indians: long-limbed and laconic and taking pride in their warrior tradition and their connection to the raw and difficult

land where they lived. We communicated in broken English and fragments of Farsi that I remembered from my days in Iran, and squatting in mud-walled villages that smelled of dust and urine, trying to
unravel the snarl of religious passion and patriotism and tribal loyalty and xenophobia that made them fight, trying to understand their
blunt willingness to die, I felt ashamed of my own frailties and vulnerability, and of my years of self-absorption. Wherever I went, the
Afghans begged for Stingers—heat-seeking missiles shot from a hand-
held tube, like rockets—insisting that they were ready to die in whatever numbers were needed because dying was nothing, but they
needed the Stingers to knock down the Soviet MiGs that streaked
overhead devastating their villages and dropping payloads of butter-
fly mines—small, deadly things the color of soil that would blow a
man's foot off if he stepped on one. The guerrillas I was with would
scour the trails for them and collect them and set them off by smash-
ing them against rocks.

I had turned down a lucrative story about celebrities on a rent
strike in Manhattan to come to Afghanistan. I had no certainty of
publishing what I wrote, and I was traveling on a shoestring, but having known Afghanistan before the war and thinking that something
I wrote might benefit the Afghans somehow, and caught up in the
sheer thrill of adventure, I had come anyway. Some of these, at least,
were good enough reasons to be camped in the Hindu Kush wondering whether I would be caught there in a Soviet attack and ever get
out again. But why, I wondered, not for the last time, did I feel so at
home where my life was in danger? Perhaps there was no single answer, but part of one came to me one day several years later in another war in another country. I was interviewing a guerrilla leader
whose command consisted almost entirely of young boys, many of
them not yet even in their teens. The man was a brave fighter and famous among his people; he was also a religious fanatic who stroked
a Bible as we talked and in whose eyes I could see the radiant glow
of a man thrilled with the idea of martyrdom. As we talked, I thought
how he was getting ready to die and how he would think that he was
leading his army of frightened children to everlasting glory when he

sent them to their deaths. And then I thought that in my own way I was still not so very different from him, that I was still testing the courage of, and perhaps still punishing, a fourteen-year-old boy who had been too scared, too confused, too foolish to know how to save his mother.

BETWEEN ASSIGNMENTS I worked on contract at the United Nations for its Department of Public Information, covering meetings of the General Assembly and special committees and preparing press releases for the correspondents who reported on the UN for newspapers abroad. Because of this work at the UN, in 1982 I was invited by the Chinese national news agency, Xinhua, to spend a year in Beijing training the agency's English-language news department in what it called "modern" journalistic techniques. Officially I was to help speed the department's evolution into a plausible news operation whose product would be respected by foreign publications. I was asked to help to edit outgoing copy and to lecture on subjects like interviewing and fact-checking and research, things that were routine in the United States but, I quickly learned, were fraught with danger for Chinese journalists under a system in which, for decades, people had been jailed or worse for daring to question authority. My role then was a quixotic one when it was not farcical. China had barely begun the reform of its socialist economy, and politically it remained a tightly controlled police state. Since its inception the news agency had served as a conduit for official propaganda rather than a vehicle for the dissemination of news, and the writers on my staff who dared to employ the very practices that I had been engaged to teach were often reprimanded rather than praised.

The better I came to understand China, the more depressed I was by the magnitude of human destruction that had been wrought by the decades of communist rule. One day I met a man who had been jailed for more than twenty years as an alleged American agent simply because he had attended college in Oregon. I met another who during the Cultural Revolution, because he had what the Communists called a "bad class background," was compelled to stand at the gate to his factory each morning while every worker spat in his face as he entered. Only a handful of my colleagues dared to visit me in the compound where I lived; one of them, who came just to interpret for another whose English was poor, was denounced to the authorities by her own husband for the serious crime of "consorting with foreigners" and forced to make a confession in front of the office's party committee. Discouraged by the oppressive atmosphere of the capital, I traveled outside Beijing every chance I could, to Inner Mongolia, Shandong, the Yellow River basin, the south, learning enough Chinese to make my way around on trains and buses. I was drawn by the chimera of a lost China that must once have existed and that I thought I glimpsed sometimes through cracks in the totalitarian crust, a quest that would eventually lead, a few years later, to my first book.

At the end of the year I left China on the Trans-Siberian railroad to Moscow, and on through the gloomy capitals of Eastern Europe, which were still years away from the end of Communist rule. I came to rest in Athens, where I lived for the next year and a half, writing again mostly about the eastern Mediterranean and retrospectively about China, and commuting back to New York every few months to meet with editors. Opportunities steadily opened up; my stories began to appear in national publications.

When I went home for a few weeks at the end of 1984, an acquaintance in Athens asked me to say hello for her to a friend in New York. The friend's name was Jean Parvin, she said, and she spoke Greek like me and used to live in Greece, too; would I just call and give her the Athens news? When I got to New York, I made the call, and we agreed to meet at a Japanese restaurant near where I had an apartment in SoHo. Just as I was leaving for the restaurant, the phone rang; she said that she was lost somewhere near the docks and in some kind of empty building where there was nothing but a phone, and would I please come and find her. I said all she had to do was start walking east and that I'd meet her at the corner of Sixth Avenue in a minute. "Would you please just come and get me," she asked. As soon as I saw her I forgot about being annoyed. I liked the look of her thick, dark hair and large brown eyes that suggested a Mediter-ranean origin of some kind, Spanish or Greek, or maybe Jewish. And I liked the look of her trim business suit, and the brimmed hat tipped rakishly over her brow, and I was touched by her embarrassment at not being able to hide being lost and frightened.

We walked away from the gloom of the warehouses and across Sixth Avenue into SoHo, where among the boutiques and still-open galleries and stylish crowds Jean felt, if not at home, then at least se-cure. She told me that she was an executive with a company that was drilling oil in Greece and that before that she'd been the press secre-tary for a United States senator defeated in the Reagan landslide, and before that a journalist in Florida where she grew up. "Not Miami," she made a point of saying. "In Clearwater, a regular kind of place, not what you New Yorkers think of when you think of Florida." I liked her disdain for artifice and flash, and the incongruous political bent, and the foreign travel, and the ancient Greek that she had ma-jored in at college, and the modern Greek that was so much better than my picked-up lingo. Despite the dark complexion and the illu-sory hint of the foreign, she was descended on her mother's side from North Carolina Quakers and on her father's from people who had come over on the next ship after the Mayflower and had been raised the strictest of Methodists, in a home where few films besides Walt Disney's were permitted, and where a red skirt was treated as an il-licit provocation.

I had been planning to return to Greece in another week. I didn't go. We saw each other again a few days later, and then again a few days after that. What drew us together so quickly? Physical attrac-tion, certainly, and shared interests; but also, I think, an unexpected ease in each other's company, the absence of straining for effect or the need to impress. I was thirty-six years old. There had been other women, in New York and abroad, affairs that were sometimes pas-sionate but always circumscribed by travel or doubt or my native re-serve. I felt no doubt now, no needling suspicion, no need for an alternative strategy if things fell apart. Besides the Greek that I so ad-mired, and the political bent, and the American wholesomeness that, for me, raised around New York and having lived so much abroad, bordered on the exotic, there were subtler things, things of character, that I couldn't fully articulate even to myself, but that in time came clear. While I was truly comfortable only when I was in motion, Jean was an anchor, steady where I was volatile, tolerant where I was quick to judge, chronically optimistic about things in a fresh, American way where I was still often inhibited by the drag of the past. She was trusting of human beings and their motives in a way that I had not been for years. "Getting into you was like breaking rocks," she told me once, a long time afterward. Later Jean remembered me proposing to her; I remembered us deciding together, hardly even putting it in so many words, guided by an instinct that, at least as I thought of it, the fit was exactly right, like a well-made joint. I can see now that in marrying Jean, I was beginning, though only beginning, to relinquish a vision of myself that was still rooted in that morning on the road in Vermont, the image of a man who trusted in little besides his instinct for survival, the power of language, and the ghostly presence of the still-powerful dead.

Jean, who came from a large and close-knit family, thought of me as someone with no family at all except, of course, for my father. We would visit him from time to time in Lancaster, Pennsylvania, where after his last marriage fell apart he retired to be near his sister and my cousin Ellen. His last home was an apartment in a red-brick row house on East Lemon Street, where he immersed himself in books and in his last years enjoyed a certain local notoriety as a prolific writer of letters to the local newspapers, mostly tweaking the pieties of Lancaster's conservative establishment, typically attacking military spending, antiabortion crusaders, and "Creationists" and defending public schools, taxes, and the legacy of the New Deal. We would have lunch at a bar that he liked and talk about politics and where I had been traveling; in old age he had become proud of me, of what I had become professionally, writing stories that he could clip and show around the bar, and proud that I had made my own way and happy, too, that I was settling down with a woman he liked. Once, thinking that with Jean there he might be more forthcoming about my mother,

I asked him what she had been like before I was born, what it was that had attracted him to her. "She was a woman," he said, shrugging. That was all. Did he mean to imply something erotic that I was supposed to understand, or was this some kind of defiance, a way of telling me that I had no business asking, or was it just being old and uncertain and no longer knowing how to answer? It was impossible to tell.

Only in time did Jean discover the tight, small enduring place in me where my mother's ghost lived, and she began to resent it as a place where she could not go and into which I would still sometimes disappear, and to recognize that disappearance as a kind of betrayal. "I feel that I'm fighting a chimera," she said to me once. "If LaVerne were alive I'd have a living, breathing person with real strengths and weaknesses to deal with. It's hard to be compared to an icon when the icon is dead and you are alive with all your real-life weaknesses exposed. It's like fighting a shadow. It's like you're there with her and not with me. Sometimes I feel that I fall short on every count because I'm not her and I'm not dead."

INEXORABLY I had begun to revise my mother's life. More and more I seemed to remember a lonely, driven, even self-destructive woman, for whom Indian country may have been less an arena of success than a bolt-hole from the complacency of life in Yonkers, from middle-class mediocrity, and from our family. There was nothing analytic about this. It was more like an anxiety that seeped into my consciousness by imperceptible degrees, revealing something that I hadn't seen before or wouldn't have believed, like a palimpsest that had lain long hidden beneath other layers of texts that had now faded. Sometimes I thought that the key to everything lay in her mysterious disappearance the night before her death. Why had she fled? Where had she gone? *Weren't we enough for you?* I would think. *Did we fail you so terribly without even knowing it?* Or was all this something I made up later and only convinced myself that I remembered because, wishing to be like her, I also wished her to be like me, and thus to have shared the hopelessness of my years after her death, as if it were something that we had in common. The ease with which I could rewrite what I thought of as memory was unnerving, for it implied that any past, any history, was equally equivocal—not a gallery of fixed images like statues bolted to the floor of a museum, but a kind of boiling stew of truth and fiction in which it was no longer possible to tell the two apart. What was clear was this: that my mother was steadily losing reality, becoming mythic, slipping away from me. Sometimes all that remained vivid and immediate, and unyielding, was the sound of the hooves, and my mother's cry.

I WROTE MOST of my first book, *Cathay: A Journey in Search of Old China*, at a desk that looked out the rear window of our bedroom across the tarred roofs of Brooklyn, where we then lived. I was at the desk on a Saturday night in December 1989, revising a chapter on the descendants of Confucius, the oldest surviving family in the world, when Jean yelled at me to get the car. Within minutes China and Confucius and the enigma of the past were forgotten, and we were rushing into Manhattan and up the FDR Drive to New York University Hospital, where in the early hours of the next morning our daughter Chloe was born. The middle name we gave her, inescapably, was LaVerne.

There was nothing easy about fatherhood for me; nothing came naturally. I hardly knew the first thing about children, and I learned only slowly and painfully. I changed diapers, tried to make sense of gurgles and whimpers, clapped when she pulled books from the shelves with her tiny hands and opened them and stared at the pages as if she were reading (I wondered, *Was this something my mother had done?*), pushed her in her carriage along the Promenade in Brooklyn Heights where I would point out, meaninglessly, for she had no context for such things, but just so that she would hear my voice and never forget that I was there, the docked freighters and the glistening bay and the towers of lower Manhattan. She was without precedent, disruptive and radical, stealing my attention from the past and from myself and from Jean, taking it all into her greedily, leaving me no time or energy for longing for what I no longer had.

A YEAR AFTER the Gulf War I was asked by a national magazine to travel to the guerrilla-held sector of northern Iraq to assess how the Kurds were surviving. I was led in by a former British intelligence officer who had served there during the war. With bodyguards lent to me by the Kurds we drove across the corrugated, winter-raw landscape of Kurdistan, through villages that had been leveled to the last stone by the Iraqis, fording rivers where the road had disappeared, at one point wrestling our Land Cruiser by main force up the side of a mountain where the road had frozen up. I interviewed guerrilla commanders, soldiers dug in a few miles from the Iraqi lines, refugees living under plastic tarps, women in a village all of whose men had been taken away one night and never seen again and were rumored to have been buried alive in the desert. In the city of Sulaymaniyah I was guided through the cells of the former police headquarters by a turbaned Kurd who had been imprisoned there and liberated when it was captured by the guerrillas. He showed me patches of his dried blood still on the floor of his cell, and the wall where he had been chained when he was tortured with cattle prods and through which he could hear a woman's screams coming from the next cell where they told him they were raping his sister. In the ruins of the city of Halabja I listened to a young man tell me how government planes had dropped gas bombs on his city, how he had survived and had gone home and looked in the basement of his home to see the bodies of everyone in his family, thirty-one of them, dead in a heap, and how he'd had to move their bodies himself, since all his neighbors were dead, and how he had decided to live his own life in the same house— the one where we now sat—because it was as near as he would ever be again to everyone he had loved.

In a land that had been systematically ravaged and ransacked and tortured beyond belief, Halabja was the last circle of hell; it was the end of the road, final proof, if any were needed, that there was no ultimate moral order in the world and that savagery was as much the normal state of man as was innocence, and deliberate cruelty as much our fate as love. And I thought how, as terrible and meaningless as my mother's death was, I had managed to keep her alive, at a price. I had given her death some kind of meaning, and was doing it even now, here in the mountains of Kurdistan, just by listening to the young man's story, being able to feel something, however incomplete, of what this had meant to him, and being able to come away and write about it in the hope that by bearing witness other people in other places might, perhaps, have the courage or foresight or whatever it took to stop it from happening again. I had no confidence that this was so, but it was the best that I could do.

7

ON FEBRUARY 29, 1992, two weeks before my father's eighty-fifth birthday, my cousin Ellen Turnbull telephoned me from her home in Pennsylvania to tell me that he had been found on the floor of his apartment, having suffered a stroke in the middle of the night. A neighbor coming home at five o'clock in the morning, had heard him feebly tapping on the wall with his cane and had called the police. He had been in the hospital for a week before the doctors notified Ellen. Probably Harold had ordered them not to bother anyone, thinking that he would be out of the hospital in a few days. He had survived two heart failures, arterial surgery and the insertion of a pacemaker at the age of eighty. He must have imagined that he would ride out this event too. In spite of the alcohol and cigarettes, he seemed indestructable. Then he had the second stroke.

I drove down to Pennsylvania in an icy rain across a landscape that resembled an underexposed photograph. I found my father with an oxygen tube taped to his nose and hooked around his ear, and an IV taped to his forearm. I had lived in dread of this moment for decades, in dread of reliving the catastrophic despair that had followed my mother's death; not because we were close, because we weren't, but because I feared with the intensity of a phobia that his death would, like my mother's, infect everything I thought and felt for years afterward. But now I felt unexpectedly at peace. For the best part of the next three days I sat by his bedside, sometimes talking into his silence but mostly quiet and waiting, writing notes to myself hour after hour, clinically, as perhaps Harold himself would have done had he been able to observe his own death. I was determined to miss nothing. I wanted no space in my memory for mistakes or guesswork.

2/29 His head is thrown back in the pillow—his mouth open like a pit, soft, stained red with blood. An unpleasant burbling in his throat—Breathing is heavy, labored—inhale ... then a gurgling, wheezy exhalation.

When the nurse turned him I realized that I had not seen him naked since my childhood. I was embarrassed but I forced myself not to look away. His shanks were thin and white and flaccid, his legs white and helpless-looking. His forearms were almost hairless. His chest had no hair either. Has it all fallen out?

Once his eyes open, first slits, then wider, but grayish & filmy, unseeing. Then slowly they slide shut again. No glimmer of recognition.

Does he dream? Of what? Of his childhood in Brooklyn? Of finely made boilers? Or has the infarction stopped even his dreams?

3/1 A businesslike young doctor talked to me. He said my father's brain was already irreparably damaged. The infarction would continue to spread. He would "at best" be a vegetable for a few more weeks or at most months.

The doctor told me that I would have to decide what to do, whether to pull the tubes, and if they were going to be pulled, then when to do it.

I asked him if there was any chance whatever of a functional recovery. "None," he said.

I could almost hear my father snorting in disgust at the prospect of lingering on in this condition. He had planned his departure from the world as if he were plotting the most efficient route for an air duct or feeder pipe, leaving detailed instructions for the disposition of everything he owned, down to his collection of old whodunits. He had prepaid his cremation and arranged for the body to be collected and transported to the crematorium in Harrisburg. He was a tidy man, always a minimalist. I knew that he meant to save me trouble, but I had the feeling that he had excluded me even in death, as if it had nothing to do with me, as if it were not part of my life and were his alone. His will stated that no extraordinary measures were to be taken to prolong his life. I sat alone for several hours with the knowledge of what I was going to do, thinking that after trying so hard to keep my dead mother alive, I now held my father's life in my hands and that I was going to let him die. I looked for some clue in his face, the barest hint that he would return. But there was nothing.

I told the doctor to remove the tubes.

3/2 Night. His wet, phlegmy breathing now takes over the room . . . harsh, rhythmic, monotonous. I touch his head. It's damp beneath the palm of my hand. His hands are purple.

His knees are drawn up a little under the white sheet. His body is straining to stay alive. Doesn't it know that it is supposed to die? That there is nothing more? That it will never walk again? Doesn't it know that in a couple of days it will be a handful of dust? Why does it go on like this?

Two nurses come in and turn him over. Suddenly his eyes open. It is the first time I've seen them in two days. They seem, strangely, to have no color. Weren't they always brown? I look into them and say, "It's great to see you." But there is nothing there. They're blank. They are already dead. It was just a reflex.

Is this still my father? Or has he become something else, no longer a man, no longer mine? Has whatever he was gone now, slipped away somewhere between last night and this one?

Outside, in the night, I can see an ocean of yellow metallic streetlamps, the shadows of brick row houses, the facade of the railroad station sepulchral in the eerie light. There, for the last sixteen years,

I usually met him, where he waited for me in his wretched old Plymouth. We would drive to the Stockyards, where he would drink and ogle the waitresses, and then we would go back for a few hours to his little apartment that stank of stale nicotine.

I began cleaning out the apartment today. The stink was awful. There were seven sacks of garbage that had been sitting there for days. Meat in the refrigerator was turning green. There was the picked-up furniture that he had collected from somewhere or other, a jumble of mismatched chairs and end tables and bookshelves. It was always a fight to get him to accept anything from me: a paint job for the apartment, carpeting, a new bed, new drapes to replace the ones that had turned brown with nicotine. Now they all seemed paltry and inadequate. On the wall there was an old railroad map of northern New Jersey, framed pictures of New York harbor, a couple of M. C. Escher prints, a poster advertising a Fourth of July festivity near Lancaster sometime in the early 1970s, with our tickets still stapled to it. I remembered it as a frustrating evening of strained conversation, small-time rides and mediocre fireworks. But something about it had moved him enough to commemorate it for more than fifteen years. So much of our life together was like that.

I went from room to room, picking up books, stuffing old clothing into plastic bags, as I erased step by step the final event of my father's life. There were audio cassettes of Haydn, Telemann, and Tartini, alps of old railroad magazines, crumbling Norwegian picture books from the 1910s, a history of the Brooklyn Bridge, an illustrated history of train wrecks, thick manila folders filled with copies of the hundreds of letters that my father had written to the local papers. From his desk—a vast homemade affair with an abundance of ledges, hooks, clasps, overhead lamps and enough table space to spread out blueprints and maps—I swept up bottles of the medicine that had kept him alive so long against the odds. In the kitchen I found two bottles of vodka, and two more half-gallons of it in the back seat of the Plymouth, all of them open.

As I picked through my father's things, I realized that, as always,

I was looking through him in hope of discovering some trace of my mother. A thrill ran through me when I stumbled across her baptismal certificate and then the certificate of her first communion, her 1934 Phi Beta Kappa, and a certificate of service to the Oglala Sioux Tribe, and then the cards and letters and prayer books that were sent at the time of her death. Even at the cusp of his own death it was still my mother that mattered. Although in the last decades of his life I had worked hard to conceal it, he had always interested me less, had always faded in her shadow. He must have seen that, must have known that he could not compete.

3/3 Night. It is foggy outside. The railroad station seems to hover in the grainy, yellowish air. The whole scene seems tentative, as if the old station, the automobiles, the brick row houses might turn to vapor and disappear any minute, like a landscape in a Chinese scroll.

His hands don't move anymore. He lies with the sheet pulled neatly and cleanly up to his chest, like a child. A day or two ago I needed to look into his face, to touch him, to connect. Strangely, the impulse to do so is gone now.

The gaping hollow that was his mouth seems to have grown deeper. His cheekbones seem broader, sharper than I have ever seen them, and his shut eyes slitlike. It has become alien, no longer my father's face, as if some primeval Asiatic imprint buried in his genes were only now revealing itself on the eve of death.

A man in the next room is eating Chinese take-out food. Its aroma radiates through the hall. From somewhere else the chatter of television commercials fills the room: ". . . more chances to win . . . great recipes start with Campbell's. . . ." I wonder if these are the last sounds that will seep into my father's dying brain.

3/4 He's gone. I finally went back to the hotel at 2:00 A.M. to get some sleep. The hospital called me at 8:00 A.M. to tell me that he was dead. Somehow they'd gotten the idea that they were not supposed to disturb me at night. He died at 2:30 A.M., only a half-hour after I left.

I got in the car and drove down to the hospital to see Harold's body where it was being held in the freezer. His mouth was frozen open in its last gasp. I ran my hand over his forehead. The chill was unnerving and lingered on my hand. I wanted to shake it off but couldn't. Before I left I kissed him, the only time I had ever done it. I said, "I love you, Harold." Even now I wasn't sure if I meant it.

The crematorium was in the basement of a two-story brick building in a suburban strip just off I-83. My father lay in a cardboard casket on top of a stainless-steel gurney, covered to the neck with a plastic sheet. The stout, thirtyish man in charge—his name was Craig—enjoyed explaining his equipment to me. "This is considered a pretty sophisticated piece of crematorium here." He explained that the body would be burned in a brick-lined retort whose chamber would be heated to 2,750 degrees Fahrenheit. "I mean, it's hot in there! See that hole up there?" He pointed to an opening in the ceiling of the retort. "That's where the flame comes out. And this is the preheat." He showed me one of the controls. "You got to warm that up first. Then your master flame kicks in. It's all automatic. Then it goes into this pulverizer. It's got a wheel in there that rolls it until it consists of ash. It makes the consistency almost of flour."

Craig cranked the gurney up so that its top was level with the floor of the retort. He leaned against the casket and shoved it hard into the retort. "I'm not being disrespectful or anything, but I got to get it in there," he said apologetically. He pushed a metal lever. "Now I'll just kick it on." A green light flashed. There was a sound like an air conditioner being turned on.

I went out to read the *New York Times*. When I came back, Craig handed the ashes to me in a Ziploc bag inside a small cardboard box. I stared at it. What did I expect, after all? My father's instructions were explicit: "The ashes are to be neither buried nor kept." What did he expect me to do with them—toss them into the garbage? That probably was just what he did expect. He was devoid of sentimentality about such things. Too much feeling was like a misthreaded screw, a loose connection. I said good-bye to Craig and took the box with me. I put it on the seat next to me and drove home with it in the

Toyota, searching my memory for moments in which I could see my father and me together untainted by inhibition and disappointment. I couldn't think of any.

A FEW MONTHS LATER I stood on the bank of a river in Burma asking myself whether I was really about to walk into water that was laced with submerged mines. I was reporting a story about rebel Karens who had been at war for decades with the Burmese government and were on the brink of what would soon prove to be final, bloody defeat. The Karens, like Indians, were tribal people, quiet by nature, fierce when aroused; having been abused, starved, and enslaved by their Burmese rulers, they had a just claim on the conscience of a distant world, and a story worth telling. On the other side of the river I could see the Karen redoubts. To reach them I would have to wade across the river. There was a path marked out by sticks, but it looked vague and treacherous. A few months earlier Burmese regulars had attacked the Karens, circling through Thailand and coming at them from the east through the river where I now stood, sending waves of teenage conscripts against the rebel fortifications in a frontal assault. Many of them were blown up in the water. Another attack was expected any time.

I knew that the mere fact that I was even here on the bank of a mine-filled river would horrify my wife. I knew that I would lie to her later, tell her that there had been no danger, tell her about the jungle and the elephants that I had seen and the kindnesses of simple people, but not about the mines and the jumpy children with Kalashnikovs. I told myself, knowing that it was only a small fraction of the truth, that I didn't want her to worry.

I stood hesitating for a long time on the riverbank, riven by guilt and by a quiet struggle between betrayal of the person my mother had made (or at least my notion of what he was supposed to be) and of my duty as husband and father: between past and future. I thought of Jean, and then of my daughter and how I loved her primitively and without ambivalence or restraint, the way I had never loved anyone

but my mother, and how in her few years she had encroached on ter-
ritory that had always been my mother's alone, had colonized it,
made it hers, and begun after all these years to bring it alive again.
The thought of never seeing her again made me feel sick in the pit of
my stomach. How many risks like this could I continue to take before my daughter lost her father as I had my mother, and as my
mother had lost her own father, and my grandmother her mother before her? *Doesn't someone in this frail line deserve to grow up with
two parents to her name?* I stared at the water as if I could see the
deadly metal discs that lay in the mud below. I knew what my mother
would do. *You wouldn't hesitate. You would say, Those people deserve to be heard. Go listen to them.*

I thought, *I never want to do this again*, knowing that I probably
would. Then, finally, I took off my shoes and rolled up my trousers
and stepped into the water.

Part Two

❧

The Woman
in the Box

Already a fictitious past occupies in our memories the place of
another, a past of which we know nothing with certainty—not
even that it is false.

—JORGE LUIS BORGES
Tlön, Uqbar, Orbis Tertius

I HAD AVOIDED Lake Willoughby for more than thirty years. Then, in the summer of 1993, I had an impulse to show my daughter where I had spent my summers as a child. It seemed like a simple thing at the time, an offhand notion on a steamy weekend in New York. I told her about the steep forested hills that rolled and pitched into craggy knobs and always made me think of the bodies of a race of giants submerged in an ancient green sea, and rowing far out into the lake that to a small child seemed as vast as the ocean, and swimming from the dock below the Lyndon, and August nights so cold that you split wood and built a fire and scrunched down for warmth into old chairs that were as deep as trenches. The lake had for so long had the force of a primal imprint—so vividly remembered that it was as if it had veiled my retina like a membrane through which every other image had to pass—that when I actually returned that year, I had the sensation of simply seeing what I had always seen before my eyes. I recognized many of the names still on the mailboxes. Almost nothing seemed to have changed in thirty years.

Although I hid it from my wife and daughter, and as best I could even from myself, I had been afraid of what I might find, afraid of what monster of pain might still lie dormant like some horrid, scaly thing beneath the lake's waters, waiting implacably for me to return. However, virtually from the moment we arrived, I felt an unexpected and irrepressible joy. Perhaps it was the water's long-forgotten but instantly familiar numbing chill that reawakened long-buried sensations, or something in the crisp air. I remembered—strange that I had forgotten this—that I had been tremendously happy here. Memories swarmed back: hurtling off a dock with our two family dogs, Dinty and Susie, learning to ride with my mother in the woods off the Barton road, playing Parcheesi and cards on the veranda, the early-morning aroma of pinewood and bacon, languorous days that seemed to stretch to infinity. At the same time when I thought of my mother, I felt less the expected presence of death than I did a thrilling closeness to her, as if she had remained there, preserved intact along with the strange time-frozen ambience of the lake. As I taught my daughter to swim from the small beach, again and again I seemed to see my mother nearby, diminutive, blond, and intense, slicing through the water with the same determined stroke and obliviousness to physical discomfort with which she had approached everything in her life. This was of course déjà vu, a trick of the senses, a memory suddenly released from decades of hibernation. All the same, it was as if I had come home, as if a door had opened into the past and I had but to walk through in order to possess my mother again as I had known her in life.

One day, while Jean remained on the beach, Chloe and I drove down the east side of the lake to see if the Lyndon was still there. Just as I remembered, at the top of the hill just past the general store there were a couple of small cottages, then a sweeping lawn and beyond it, overlooking the lake through a gap in the trees, the Lyndon, rambling and rustically Victorian, with its pitched roof and double verandas, and in front of it the ferny boulders that I used to scramble over for hours on end with stubborn fascination. A sign indicated that the Perkinses, Earl and Jeanne, still owned the property. Another advertised the maple syrup that Earl tapped from his own trees on a ridge above the lake. I hadn't intended to stop, but then I saw that someone was in the sugar house alongside the driveway. Even after thirty-one years Earl's long-jawed face and merry blue eyes were instantly recognizable. I told him that I had stayed at the Lyndon years before, and he stared at me for a while and then said that they still rented it, and then with amiable bluntness, "I can't say I remember you." Then he bent down and asked Chloe if she wanted to see a trick. He gave her a quarter and told her to drop it through a slot in the roof of a miniature privy that he had made from scraps of wood. When the quarter hit a spring inside, the walls exploded. "You wouldn't want to be sitting in there when that happened," Earl said innocently.

Chloe laughed uproariously and begged to do it again and again. As we left Earl said to me, "But your name sounds familiar."

We spent only a few days at the lake that summer, but I was drawn back irresistibly. A few months later I telephoned Jeanne Perkins and said that I wanted to rent the Lyndon, and when I told her my name she gasped. "Oh, my God," she said. "That was the worst day of my life."

The next summer we rented the Lyndon for two weeks. I knew that it was a risky thing to do. Jean had misgivings; she worried that staying there would hurt me, that it would force on me emotions that would be hard to contain, but she understood that with my family gone, and the house in Yonkers gone too, Vermont was one of the few windows Chloe would ever have into my childhood. But as soon as we walked through the door of the Lyndon, I felt embraced by its old wood and sagging sofas, by its creaking stairs and the deep shadows that lay, like well-kept secrets, within its broad verandas. Hardly anything was different. The painted plank walls that I remembered—one a watery blue, another yellow, a third pink—had been covered by paneling, and the ceilings by tiles made of some synthetic stuff. There were new cabinets in the kitchen, and the huge old dreadnought of a wood-burning stove had been replaced by a modern gas range. From the cottage a path ran down a steep slope to a boathouse and a patch of sand between some large boulders, where a pair of aluminum rowboats were pulled up onto the sand and a small dock, just as I remembered it, extended out into the lake.

It was a while before I could bring myself to ask Jeanne Perkins about the day my mother died. Like Earl, still vigorous well into her seventies, she was pushing an old hand-propelled mower across the vast lawn, which she tended as meticulously as a potted garden. She leaned on the mower and we talked. "I was in the kitchen when the phone rang. It was Gertrude Hunt. She was crying. She told me to go over to the Lyndon and tell your father that your mother fell off a horse. I can still see him there sitting on the railing. I told him, 'LaVerne's hurt. They need you at Wally's.' He put his arms around me. I was doing the crying. He said, 'She'll be okay.' He just looked as if—I can't explain it . . . Then he just got in his car and took off. When he came back, he cried. Boy, did he cry that day." Jeanne pushed the mower a little while I walked alongside her. Then she said, "I can remember her so well. She had beautiful eyes, beautiful hair. When she came up that year, she was exhausted. I went in and perked a fresh pot of coffee for her. We sat there and had coffee and doughnuts, and she told me, 'I need these two weeks more than I ever needed two weeks in my life.' "

It was disconcerting sometimes to see Chloe here, as if I were witnessing my own childhood restated. We swam from the tiny beach at the foot of the Perkinses' property and built miniature villages with twigs in the sand, as my mother had taught me to do. We passed the time playing Candyland and Monopoly and doing jigsaw puzzles that revealed fluffy kittens and New England villages. We went to see a maple-sugar factory in St. Johnsbury, and to Montreal, which in the 1950s had entailed an expedition of grandiose proportions, requiring a predawn departure and the car to be stuffed with blankets and pillows and box lunches to be eaten along the way, but was now a mere two-hour jaunt on the interstate highway. From the veranda I watched her worry the same boulders that had obsessed me as a child, running at them full tilt trying to reach the top, slipping back down, and trying again and again with fierce determination until finally she managed to grab hold of the narrow top and crowed with delight. And I realized that it was she, more than anything else, that had made it possible for me to return to the lake. Her childhood had finally, as nothing else had—not literature or professional success—overwhelmed my own, cracking apart dark memory with her enthusiasms and her irrepressible faith in the ever-unfolding future.

Now, looking back, I am not so sure that coming back to Lake Willoughby was as casual a decision as it seemed at the time. What was it that I really meant to show my daughter? Or, unwittingly, was I using her as a shield, a kind of amulet that would enable me to enter my own subterranean darkness again, to descend into its depths and to confront what lay at the bottom of it? Was I not, without realizing it at the time, becoming again the frightened child that I had been more than thirty years before and transforming my small, unknowing daughter into the parent, the protector, and asking her to lead me by the hand back into my own past?

Each summer after that, we returned again to the Lyndon. For Jean, coming to Vermont became part of a tacit familial quid pro quo, a kind of insurance that I would make time to spend with her relatives. She didn't love the place as I did and had nothing like my emotional stake in it. A sociable person by nature, and now a journalist again with many demands on her time, she found the whole area, while beautiful, lonely and remote. "I feel like I'm in a time warp here," she said. "I feel like I'm in the 1950s." She was right, of course, at least in the obvious sense. Not much "happened" around the lake except an occasional church supper or bake sale. The closest phone was outdoors and half a mile from the Lyndon, and the nearest movie theater a half-hour's drive distant in Newport. Having grown up in Florida, she found the water too cold for swimming, and the Lyndon gloomy and dark. One night she told me, "I'm afraid it's going to burn down. I'm afraid of the electrical system. I have nightmares of waking up with it on fire and not being able to get Chloe out. I'm afraid to have a fire in the fireplace or have the heater on." But for the most part she accommodated herself with her usual grace and tolerance. She passed the time reading, making curtains for our home, baking gingerbread, hiking to the phone. "I feel that when we come here, we're doing something with your family," she told me. "You don't have a house, any living relatives, a place. You have nothing except memories. Now they're ours too."

In the Lyndon I could see into the past itself. Often as I looked across the living room at my wife sewing or reading, or at Chloe wrestling with one of her puzzles, I could see the rest of us too—my mother curled over the *Times* crossword puzzle, the red-haired boy immersed in his books, my father weeping at the table by the door—coexistent and simultaneous, there and not there at all, as real and as evanescent as the uncertain shapes of the junipers stirring in the evening breeze, or a shadowy figure moving over the grass, or the creak of wood on the stairs that seems proof of a human step that no longer exists. *I know this is not so: the bright room, Jean, Chloe, the fire, this pen, this notebook are the only reality. But I can see you. You are still here.*

One day I stopped by to talk to Dalton, Wally Hunt's son. Dalton was only a few years older than me, but square-built and raw-boned and always togged in overalls and rubber boots caked with mud and dung, so much part of the texture of the countryside that I couldn't imagine him anywhere except on the farm. But he quit farming after Wally died in 1981 and now ran the video-rental store in Barton. Farming had collapsed generally. He ticked off a long list of the farms that had failed since the early 1960s. He said, "Why should you work eighty or ninety hours a week and get nothing when you can work forty hours a week and get something?" He guessed that seventy-five percent of the population of Barton was either retired or on welfare. "You can't even get a job around here at four dollars an hour. There just aren't any. Zero." After that, when I looked more closely at things, I saw that open fields that I remembered from my childhood had gone back to forest or scrub and that farms that used to raise cows had become weekend or summer homes, and that away from the lake, where things were well kept up, there was an edge of seediness and neglect that I had not quite noticed through the gauze of remembering. Dalton reminded me that he had saddled our horses the day my mother died (I had forgotten this, but as soon as he said it I saw him at my mother's side, cinching the saddle, helping her up). "Then I went down to the field to do some haying and chase cattle. I was gone all day. It was evening before I heard what happened. My father was shooken up. I remember that. Dad used to say, 'I've got to watch out for her. She always wants to go fast.' He said that was her character."

"THE PAST," Harold Pinter wrote, "is what you remember, imagine you remember, convince yourself you remember, or pretend to remember." Recent research bears this out, having shown that it is difficult, if not impossible, for most of us to separate what we have actually experienced from a later memory of the experience, or from what others say we saw or did or experienced, or from what we have reconstructed in our own minds. Thus "remembering" is really a process of weaving recollections, guesses, and second-hand reports into narratives that we revise over and over to fit the "remembered" past. Although the machinery of memory records traumatic experiences more accurately than others, even these recollections are constructions rather than literal recordings. A false recollection may well be as potent and durable as a true one.

For many years I confused memory with knowledge, believing that remembering my mother was the same as loving her and that by remembering her without restraint, I also knew her completely. Now I began to wonder if I had really known my mother at all, or whether the person I remembered as my mother was just a function of guilt and remorse, a fiction that I had created to fill the empty spaces in my own life. Memory, which had always appeared to be my only link with my mother, had in fact been a wall: through it I could see nothing of the woman whose real life lay on the other side. What had really mattered to me was not the past as it actually was but the stories that I had created about my mother's past. I had turned her into a private myth. I distrusted idols and shibboleths of all kinds, yet I had created one that towered above all others and that I tacitly forbade myself to doubt or challenge. When I tried now to look at her with the same kind of objectivity that I would apply to any subject I was preparing to investigate—the plight of the Kurds, say, or German reunification, or the conflict in Northern Ireland—I was appalled at how much was mere sentiment disguised as fact. Apart from her work with the Indians, which I had witnessed from a child's vantage point, I knew that she had grown up in Mount Vernon, a few miles from our home in Yonkers, that she had studied Classics at New York University, that she had worked to get Japanese-Americans out of American internment camps during the Second World War. I knew vaguely that she had written poetry and that she had flirted with radical politics. How little I really knew about her!

Alone one day in the Lyndon, Jean and Chloe having gone to the supermarket in Barton, sitting at the dining table, perhaps in the very chair where my father had sat and wept that morning in 1962, struggling to read and failing, I asked myself over and over, *Who was this LaVerne Madigan?* What kind of woman had she been before she became my mother? She was thirty-five years old when I was born, a woman with more than two-thirds of her life already behind her. During the fourteen years that remained, I had been capable of observing her, of knowing her with anything approaching reliability, for less than half that time, and even then my judgment was still skewed by self-centeredness and immaturity and need. Who, really, was this woman who had died in the dirt at my feet a few miles from where we now sat in the Lyndon? Was she really the same LaVerne Madigan whom I remembered? What freight of life that I never knew was she carrying to its final destination that morning?

I was acutely aware of how much I still feared the events of more than thirty years earlier. Precisely what frightened me was less clear, however. Fear of revitalizing the horror of what had happened there in 1962? Fear, perhaps, of adulterating cherished memories with fresh experience? Fear—by confronting her death—of losing the last hold I had on my mother herself? Fear of finally coming to terms with my part in what happened? She was like a talisman whose power would be destroyed if her memory were examined too closely. I feared not only that I would lose her, but that she would lose me, that by probing into her past I would discover a person for whom I did not exist. Could I still love the LaVerne Madigan who had never even known me? Could I bear discovering a life in which I was not at the center? What kind of claim could I have on the stranger that I found?

Thus began a journey into the foreign country of my mother's past. I set out to peel away the layers of misinformation, skewed memory and deliberate self-deception. It was a process, in part, of salvage, an attempt to match memory against actuality in hope of finally getting at the truth. It was also a kind of assassination. For even as I began to recover my mother from the shadowy realm in which her memory had lived, I knew that I would eventually bring about the death of the ghost that I had loved for more than thirty years.

2

THE INVENTION of the lightweight and inexpensive box camera at the beginning of the twentieth century transformed photography from a specialized science that was difficult to perform outside a studio into a form of mass entertainment that was within reach of all but the poorest families. Like the rest of the American middle class, my mother's parents, George and Georgiana Madigan, loved photographing themselves. Scores of the pictures they took have survived, and in the late 1940s my mother collected them in a set of huge bound volumes and carefully identified them, often with wry humor. The pictures from her childhood record—a little deceptively, for they were all taken before simple flash attachments made indoor photography easy—a world of endlessly sunny days, blooming gardens and trellises fecund with their cargo of wisteria and grapes, a world where girls gaze into the camera with coy innocence, as if into a mirror, and men stand foursquare like soldiers with their legs planted wide apart, jaws jutting and hands clasped firmly behind their backs. I see her, here with her favorite doll Kewpie-Nut, and there, dressed in a tiny doughboy's uniform with a popgun on her shoulder, alongside a yellowed document certifying that she had collected five dollars for the United War Work Campaign in 1918, and there, in the backyard of the house on Washington Street, mugging beneath a Japanese parasol, pouring tea for a party of dolls, and frolicking with a seemingly unending series of terriers with names like Dix, Pal, Fritz, and Brownie. At first when I look at these pictures, still afraid of the bite of loss that I know I will feel, my eye shies away from my mother, darting to the frisking dogs, to the grim-faced Houlihan sisters, to Maddy's stunning gowns, to anything but my mother's face. When I finally force myself to look at her, at the curve of her prominent forehead, the subtle smile, the merry Irish eyes, her childish expression is so familiar that I have a disorienting feeling of dèjá vu, a bizarre certainty that I was there on those forever bright afternoons, standing just off to the side somewhere, smiling back at little LaVerne, waiting for the picture to be done so that we could return to our play.

LaVerne was fortunate in her parents, who doted on her, their only child. Why were there no others, I couldn't help but wonder. But I shall never know the answer. George and Georgiana Madigan (after her husband's death she took to calling herself "Madigan," which over time became "Maddy," the nickname by which I and everyone in the neighborhood knew her in the 1950s) were a couple clearly on their way up the social ladder, middle class but nevertheless well-connected and well-liked members of the local elite in a city that was regarded in the nineteen tens and twenties as one of the most desirable communities in the New York suburbs. When I look at them now, the two of them seem profoundly mysterious in their wonderful youth and beauty. Even after three-quarters of a century an aura of warmth and charm still radiates from George's beaming, square-jawed smile and from the self-confident gaze of a man who knows in his heart that life is going to deliver for him. Maddy's expression is harder to read, more equivocal, beneath an unending series of vast hats that look as if they had alighted upon her like exotic birds.

Although Maddy was born and raised in New York City, my father wrote years later that upon meeting her for the first time, she gave "the impression of Southern gentility fallen on hard times." When I was small I begged her over and over to tell me the story of her father, James Patrick Farrell, the Irish rebel. She would sit me down next to her on the living-room couch and pour herself a cup of tea and tell me how he had fled Ireland to escape arrest by the British, joined the Union army during the Civil War, and then somewhere on a southern battlefield miraculously met his own brother face to face, and that both of them wept as they flung down their guns and fell into each other's arms. After the war, she said, James Patrick walked the streets of New York and was turned away from job after job by signs that proclaimed, "No Irish Need Apply." By dint of hard work, however, he made his fortune in the Irish linen trade ("the finest linen," as she would pointedly put it), and rose to a leading position in the Friendly Sons of St. Patrick, a fraternal organization of considerable importance and political influence in a city that was then perhaps twenty-five percent Irish. He raised his large family in a pillared mansion on Shore Road in Brooklyn, a fashionable boulevard of posh country homes overlooking New York bay. Maddy, born in 1882, was the youngest of James Patrick's children. The only girl, she often told me how she was repeatedly saved from six of her seven brothers' cruel pranks by her one devoted brother, Jack, who eventually grew up to become the manager for Buffalo Bill's Wild West Show. "And then Jack came and made them stop," she would always conclude with a proud smile. "He told them, 'If you don't leave her alone I'll slap you down!' And they did."

While I cannot be quite sure about this, I like to think of Maddy as a protomodern young woman, searching for a career in one of the few professions that were open to women at that time, trying one thing and then another, and staving off marriage as long as she could. She attended Pratt Institute for two years, where she took courses in dress design and millinery. She later studied nursing and tended the author O. Henry, whose stories she loved, during his last weeks. His deathbed photograph was one of her treasures, and when I pleaded she would sometimes show it to me with a cluck of pity, one of her characteristic, most self-consciously Catholic modes: "The poor man." She had been an exquisitely beautiful young woman in her youth, with sparkling blue eyes and pale-blond hair, porcelain skin, and a face that was favored with both grace and sculptural dimension, by far the most attractive person that either side of my family has ever produced. She had no end of suitors (among them the son of Captain Paul Boynton, who built a once famous "bicycle railroad" to Coney Island), and she was surely destined to make a brilliant match.

The story that Maddy told about her father, James Patrick Farrell, was colorful and exciting, a quintessential American tale of determination, courage, and eventual success. Some of it was even true, but it is impossible to say how much. I have found no evidence that

James Patrick served in the Union Army, much less had a battlefield encounter with his "brother," of whom there is no mention in any family document. New York City business directories indicate that as early as 1870, when he was thirty years old, he owned a shop that sold woolen goods on White Street in lower Manhattan. While it is possible that he somehow went from rags to riches in just a few years, it seems more likely, if less romantic, that he came to New York as an investor, perhaps to develop an American branch of an existing Irish business. That he made a good deal of money there is no doubt. The Shore Road mansion still stands, a handsome Italianate landmark now dwarfed by modern apartment buildings. And the program for the Friendly Sons' annual St. Patrick's Day gala in 1882 shows James Patrick as one of those officiating over a banquet, whose guests included President Chester A. Arthur, ex-President Ulysses S. Grant, and other prominent figures. Curiously, however, old documents in Maddy's own hand make clear that James Patrick had not eight children but seven, and that five of them were daughters. While I have a tintype of Jack Farrell posing with Buffalo Bill, the Buffalo Bill Museum in Cody, Wyoming, has no record of his ever having been employed by the Wild West Show.

Apart from his apparently apocryphal Civil War exploits, James Patrick Farrell always remained a rather shadowy figure in my grandmother's stories. The explanation for this and for Maddy's fabulizing may lie in something that happened in 1909. It is a story that even my mother may not have been aware of, and which I stumbled on quite recently by chance. In 1900 James Patrick turned his dry goods and real estate business over to his older son James and accepted an appointment as superintendent of the Brooklyn Disciplinary Training School for Boys, a reformatory for delinquents located in present-day Bensonhurst. It is clear from what came out later that the job was a political sinecure procured for him by cronies in Tammany Hall. In late 1909 a scandal erupted over Farrell's management of the school. It was covered in detail by the *New York Times*. For the young boys aged seven to twenty who lived there, the school was a hellhole. They were fed often inedible food, deprived of facilities for learning useful trades, and endured a regime of almost hair-raising brutality, for which James Patrick Farrell was chiefly responsible. He typically beat boys accused of even minor infractions over the head with a heavy walking stick until they bled. Sometimes they were subjected to a punishment that Farrell called the "Star-Spangled Banner," in which the victim would be stripped and beaten with a club for the number of stars and stripes there were in the flag (fifty-nine in 1909). On one occasion he beat a small boy for forty-five minutes straight, driving him from room to room and floor to floor, ordering attendants to drag him from beneath beds and from behind furniture where he tried to hide. Another time Farrell brandished a pistol and threatened to "blow out the brains" of a boy he saw throwing a stone in the yard. "Suspected thefts were punished with a six weeks' diet of bread and water and floggings, during which the helpless victims begged on their knees for mercy," the *Times* reported. Farrell was often seen to cane the boys while under the influence of alcohol, and was sometimes noticed returning drunk to the school at dawn with the institution's female housekeeper. The school appears to have been a money-laundering operation for Tammany politicians, who siphoned off nearly all the funds appropriated for it by the city. Children were often kept there for years beyond their intended term in order to justify higher expenditures in public funds. It is impossible to say how much of this money wound up in James Patrick's own pocket. However, it would seem that at least a portion of the expense of running the mansion on Shore Road, of the salaries of his Swedish maids and coachman, of the family vacations in the Catskills and Smokies, of the cost of my grandmother's upkeep and of her education at Pratt were wrung from the lives of the unfortunate children in the Brooklyn Disciplinary Training School for Boys. When Farrell was finally fired in November 1909, citizens who crowded the school's downtown office applauded.

I had seen enough cruelty in the course of my journalistic work not to be surprised that human beings were capable of such atrocities against the innocent and helpless, but I still couldn't help being sickened by what I read. This was the "hero" who was in my mind when I went south to register black voters, the man whose Civil War record

I had once supposed had been my mother's model for her own commitment to social justice. I felt less betrayed—after all, the scandal
had taken place nearly a century ago, and almost forty years before
my birth—than I did intensely sad for all those little boys of long ago
for whom my great-grandfather must have seemed like some demonic
force capable of visiting terror upon them any time and without
warning. It also reminded me once again how much of what we think
of as our past is just a best guess, an untested hypothesis, that no matter how deep its fraudulence can still have an extraordinary power to
inspire.

While the "heroic" James Patrick was gone now without a trace,
the real one—drunk, sadist, Tammany bagman—shed some light on
how my grandmother had been shaped. One year after his ouster
James Patrick Farrell died "from apoplexy," according to his obituary in the *Times*. The scandal must have been a social disaster for my
grandmother, by then the only child who was still unmarried, and the
only one left at home to bear the brunt of the opprobrium that must
have fallen upon the family. She was already twenty-seven, well past
the age when she should have been wed. Whatever social cachet she
once possessed had now been wiped out. There was no chance of
marrying into the Bay Ridge elite. Just months after her father's fall
she suddenly married George Madigan, a parvenu three years her
junior and an outsider from the upstate Hudson River town of
Catskill who had recently graduated from the University of Pennsylvania's medical school with a degree in dentistry.

What brought George's father, John Madigan, my mother's pa-
ternal grandfather, from County Kerry to New York is unclear. The
only picture I have of him, taken shortly before his death in 1915,
shows a wizened old man whose small, rather inexpressive face seems
dwarfed by an enormous white walrus mustache. The facts of his
early life in America so closely resemble those that Maddy attributed
to James Patrick Farrell that I suspect she simply appropriated them.
According to notes my mother left, the Madigans were patriotic Irish
nationalists, and soon after his arrival in America, John Madigan enlisted in the Union army determined to help save his new country. Re-

cently, I found Civil War documents which indicate that he enlisted as a private in 1861, in a regiment that became part of the famous Irish Brigade, and served until 1865, when he was demobilized with the rank of major—an impressive record, by any measure. While not much was ever said about him in my house, I grew up with the distinct impression that he was a professional man, probably a doctor, and that he had raised his family in one of the large Victorian homes on the heights near St. Patrick's, the plain but substantial red-brick church that served Catskill's large Irish Catholic community.

I found John Madigan's name quite readily in several of the old directories that listed nearly all the residents of the town in the later decades of the nineteenth century: "Saloonkeeper, 24 Bridge Street." The address lay on the west side, the "wrong" side, of Catskill Creek, which separates the commercial district and the Victorian mansions from the frame tenements that housed the town's industrial class and poor. Indeed, John Madigan himself may well have come up the Hudson, like so many Irish did after the Civil War, initially to seek work in Catskill's brickyards, mills, and cement plants. The barroom where he sold whiskey and lager is still there, a narrow two-story frame structure, now occupied by a florist. The directories indicate that the Madigans lived on the premises, which could only have been upstairs, over the bar, from where, while he listened to the raucous shouts of workmen below, my grandfather, the immigrant's son, would have looked out across the creek toward the grand homes of the wealthy and successful, ascending like risen souls up the heights to the east. While my mother remembered her father as a man of charm, wit and generosity, he must also have had great determination. That he made it off Bridge Street and went to college at all was remarkable enough, much less that he earned two degrees, the first from Albany City College and the other from one of the preeminent dental schools in the country. Still, both he and Maddy had something to hide. There was a symmetry to their match, the declassed beauty and the saloonkeeper's dashing son, the scandal in Brooklyn weighed against the room over the bar. By marrying, they reinvented themselves, became new people, left the embarrassing past behind.

They lived first in Clifton, New Jersey, where my mother was born on September 13, 1912. The following year they moved to Mount Vernon, from which it was an easy commute for George via the old Boston and Westchester Railway and the Third Avenue el to his office at 66 Wall Street, just down the street from the New York Stock Exchange. Mount Vernon liked to think of itself as a progressive city, a term that occurs repeatedly in the promotional materials of the era. "Mount Vernon is a wide awake community," proclaims a brochure published in 1913. Another, clearly aimed at the middle class, promises "the ideal Children's Paradise, free from the crowded conditions of the Great City and its many and varied temptations." Mount Vernon's tax rate was the lowest in Westchester County, and its death rate was the lowest in the state. There was a brand-new Carnegie library. The fire department sported a magnificent new "automobile apparatus," and the mostly mounted police force even included a motorcycle squad.

George Madigan soon became a well-known figure in the local Republican Party, which was, as one publication put it, "the dominant political persuasion." The credo of the Republican Club stated, "It contemplates the upbuilding of a political Utopia wherein the beneficent influences of a stalwart Republicanism will make life one grand sweet song." There was also a Women's Republican Club that was "theoretical rather than practical, inasmuch as women without the franchise are not likely to become conspicuous political factors, and even with the ballot, it is believed that not very many of them—certainly not the cultivated class—would care to invade the domain of practical politics." Although Mount Vernon was more receptive to immigrants, Jews, and blacks than many other Westchester communities, theaters and restaurants were segregated by custom if not by law. Catholics declined to swim with Protestants at the YMCA. And when a priest at the Madigans' church, Sacred Heart, began inviting black families to mass, he was quickly hustled away to a parish in Harlem. Although Mount Vernon had a large and prominent Jewish population, no Jew was hired to teach in the city's schools until 1930, the year my mother graduated from high school.

For a time when I was small my mother put me to sleep by read-ing me entries from her childhood autograph book. I would pick a page and she would tell me a story about the boy or girl who had written the limerick on it. I still have this book. It is full of jokey lim-ericks and girlish sentiments about the "golden chain of friendship" and the like. Then one night I picked one that made her hesitate. It went like this:

> *Remember the present*
> *remember the past*
> *remember the fun*
> *in the 7-B class*
> *and don't forget*
> *the children too.*
> *-P.S.-Please don't marry*
> *A dirty jew*

"One day," my mother told me, "I was standing at my window when I saw a small boy running for his life down Washington Street. He was running as fast as he could, and there was terror in his eyes. Close behind him was a gang of bigger boys. They were shrieking as they ran, 'Onion Ernie is a Jew! Onion Ernie is a Jew!' I was fright-ened for the little boy. I wanted to help him, but I didn't know how, and then they were gone." My mother kept staring as the boys ran out of sight, hating, even thirty years later, that she had been small and a girl and had not known what to do. "What happened to Ernie?" I asked her. "I never knew," she replied. For days afterward I fell asleep with tears in my eyes, feeling as helpless as my mother, terrified of what they had done to Ernie when they caught him.

THE MOUNT VERNON that my mother knew disappeared long ago. African-Americans now make up somewhat more than half of the city's population. Many are middle-class refugees from disintegrating sections of the Bronx, which lies just to the south. North of the railroad tracks that bisect Mount Vernon from east to west, tree-lined streets and single-family homes still predominate, as they did in my mother's youth. The south side has suffered badly, however. Crime, often attributed to interlopers from the Bronx, is a severe and pervasive worry. Vacant lots abound where once-attractive buildings have been gutted and burned. Menacing young men with too little to do jockey for space with bottle gangs on the corners. Much of Fourth Avenue, where the Madigans shopped, has become a dilapidated mélange of empty storefronts and discount emporiums.

Washington Street has held its own better than might have been expected. Sometimes I would drive by the house where my mother grew up. It is a plain home with porches front and back and a pitched and gabled roof, nothing like the mansion that Maddy grew up in but still roomy and well-proportioned. The new plastic siding that now sheathes the Madigans' old clapboard, the well-kept yard, and even the wrought-iron bars at the windows suggest a precarious but determined stability. As I drove past, the house seemed to me like a tropical islet magically transported to the New York surburbs, brightened by the sunny smiles of my mother and her friends and their frolicking pups. One day I noticed someone opening the front door. On impulse I pulled over to the curb and ran up the path to the door.

The man was elderly, perhaps in his seventies, and had the bent, slightly deflated look of someone who had spent a lifetime at some kind of hard physical labor. I explained that my mother had once lived there and asked in what I hoped was a mild and ingratiating tone if I might look inside.

"We've remodeled," he said, not unfriendly. "It don't look the same."

I told him that that didn't matter, that I would be grateful for just a few minutes, just to see where she had lived. He said that he would ask his wife.

From where I stood in the doorway I had a momentary glimpse of the interior. I could see stairs to a cellar, a swath of cheap wood paneling, a room to the left, perhaps the kitchen, and to the right another room—the living room?

"It's a strange thing to ask." A woman's suspicious voice now came from what I took to be the kitchen. "Things happen in places," she added cryptically.

I could understand their uneasiness. It was clear that they had no idea what I really wanted. I was something irregular, a disturbance, and therefore suspect, perhaps even dangerous in some unclear way.

I wanted to shout, How can you say no to me?

"My mother went to Sacred Heart," I said, hoping they might be Catholic.

"Oh!" the woman's voice exclaimed brightly. "In Mount Vernon or Eastchester?"

"Mount Vernon."

I could feel the faint flicker of her interest seep away.

"Oh, our granddaughter goes to Eastchester." The voice grew cold again.

"You don't think it would be possible for me to come in few just a few minutes?" I asked again gently.

In front of me the door began to close.

"I'm sorry," I said, as much to the ghosts that inhabited the rooms that I now would never see as to the invisible woman behind the door.

GEORGE MADIGAN died prematurely on July 16, 1926. My mother almost never talked about his death. For a woman as expressive as she was, it seems to me that in this instance, at least, her silence was eloquent, the only event in her life that I can think of for which she had almost no words. The only thing she told me was that it had destroyed her faith in God. "I thought, how could God have let my father die?" she told me.

I looked up the *Daily Argus* for July, 16, 1926, on microfilm at the Mount Vernon Public Library, which lies just a short walk from the house on Washington Street. My grandfather's death was the lead story that day. "Dr. George F. Madigan, a well known and highly esteemed resident of Mount Vernon, who was prominently identified with the Republican organization in this city, a past exalted ruler of the Elks and an active member of several local organizations, died at 6:30 o'clock this morning at his residence." He had first become ill in March with pneumonia and was several times reported in critical condition. The obituary reported that "poisoning" had developed and was listed as the cause of his death. "Due to the fact that the patient rallied several times and seemed to be on the road to recovery, the news of his death came as a shock to his many friends." His part in civic affairs had won for him "great respect and admiration," the obituary declared. It went on at length to describe his membership in the Knights of Columbus, the University Club of Mount Vernon, the New York Athletic Club, and the prestigious Winged Foot Golf Club. He had served as a volunteer fireman and on the city Board of Health and on other unspecified committees. "When called upon to serve in various municipal positions, important in questions concerning the city, he readily volunteered."

I had never realized before how much his life, on its smaller scale, had foreshadowed my mother's: the public service, the personal commitment, the impression of boundless energy and warmth. The house on Washington Street must have been filled constantly with local politicos and power brokers. Even the mayor had attended George's funeral. There must have been a glow about him and about the Madigan home, an aura of importance and the promise of a comfortable and significant future. What a shock his death must have been to the tiny household. Devout Catholics, my mother and Maddy must have prayed fiercely for his recovery. The priests would have reminded them that his fate lay in God's hands, that it was their duty to trust in His loving care, that it was well known that faith could move mountains. After all those years at Sacred Heart School the possibility that God could fail to save her father, this always-beaming man, so beloved in his home, so admired in the community, may never even have entered her head. Each time he rallied, the priests must have assured them that God was answering their prayers. Over and over again she must have told herself that life would soon return to normal. Then suddenly the golden glow faded and the future disappeared.

Did you fly into hysterics? Did you deny it all, as I did your death? Did you flee into your room and into books? Or did you stand silently and watch, drawing it all into yourself, boxing the horror into a cell somewhere deep in your being, filing everything away, knowing that you would need to understand everything if you were to go on in your life?

George Madigan died at the age of forty-one, when my mother was thirteen; she died at the age of forty-nine, when I was fourteen. The symmetry was unnerving. Staring at the grainy microfilm, I felt suddenly there with my mother, a teenager like myself, knowing what she felt more intimately than I could ever know anything else about her as she stared at her father's stretched-out corpse, grasping for the first time the terrible knowledge that life would never be the same again, that it was damaged utterly and beyond repair. Had she lived for her dead father as I had for her, I wondered, carrying his unlived life in her heart as I had carried hers? This, I thought, was something that we would share until the end of my own life. But there was a difference, too. She was spared guilt. She had watched death gaining inexorably on her father for six months, had seen him weakening physically from a microbial infection over which she knew that she had no power. She knew that if anyone was responsible for his death, it was not she but God, Who, the priests kept reassuring her, had the power to save him, but then hadn't. She at least had someone else to blame.

On another day I asked the librarian if there was a copy of the 1930 high-school yearbook anywhere. She went to a tall cabinet in a corner of the room, poked around in it for a while, and eventually came back with a large leatherbound copy of *Maroon and White*. I skimmed through the pictures inside. Frozen here on the threshold of life, they stared out at the camera with a steady, sober gaze that made them look much older than today's laid-back eighteen-year olds. Among the boys jaws were squared and hair slicked and parted with knife-edge precision. Girls struck a pose of modesty and reserve. The mottoes that these children of the Roaring Twenties placed under their pictures were noble and optimistic to a degree that seems almost unbelievable seventy years later: "The mould of a man's fortune is in his own hands," "Sail in the boat of ambition and anchor in the harbor of success," "He who conquers conquers himself," "A worthy motive is better than a long life." On the threshold of the Great Depression and the advent of fascism, only one student even hinted at an interest in politics: Joseph "Joe Library" Blatt's motto was "Down with Mussolini." There were only three black students in the class. Among them, Walter C. Prevost's face fairly smouldered on the page above the motto, "Life is a struggle hard and cold." I felt overwhelmed with sadness looking at them. They would be dead now, almost every one of them.

And there was my mother.

She peered out at me from the page with her ineffable smile, never imagining on that day in 1930 that I would discover her here on a bitter winter afternoon in the basement of the Mount Vernon library, searching for a window into her heart. Her entry was one of the longest in the yearbook: "Editor-in-Chief of Maroon and White, '30; Maroon and White Staff, '27, '28, '29, '30; Oracle Board, '27; M.V. Hi-News, '28, '29, '30; Contributor to M.V.H.S. Anthology of Verse, '29; Representative at Columbia Scholastic Press Conference, '29, '30; Junior Debating Society, '28; Senior Debating Society, '28, '29, '30; Secretary of Senior Debating Society, '29; Alpha Tau Delta, '29, '30; Prize Winner in Senior Girls' Extemporaneous Speaking Contest, '30; Chorus, '29, '30; School Publication Committee, '29, '30; Concert, '28." She was one of the handful of graduates who did not provide a nickname amid the jolly crowd of Pinkies, Bunnys, Midges, Dots, and Dollys. Her motto was original but puzzling: "Justice is having and doing what is one's own." Turning the pages, I saw her everywhere, in the group pictures for the yearbook and newspaper, the service clubs and the debating team. She stood out immediately, smaller than anyone else by a head and always tilting forward and a little to the side, a little off-center, as if she were the only one in these orderly rows of graduating seniors to step out of line.

She had edited the yearbook I now held in my hands. The classical theme would of course have been hers as well: the fluted columns that flanked each page of photos, the toga-clad figures who introduced each section of the yearbook, the ubiquitous classical allusions.

She must have been written the book's thematic editorial, too:

> For a moment we pause to pierce the mists of time. Two thousand years have died and with them the temporal might of imperial Rome. Yet her ancient civilization and the poet Virgil in whom it was consummate have not passed. His songs have come unsullied through the ages and in them is the culture of a race which is no more. And it is in homage to him and that eternal civilization of which he was a part, that we vest this book with its Roman theme. The wisdom which is ours—the verse of our nation—our swiftly progressing science—all have sprung from the seed sown in the age of ancient Rome. Let us marvel at this culture which is ours, and trace its path to future heights. But in our wonder, let us not forget that it is but the heritage of Virgil and his race.

In the yearbook I could see the proof of her intelligence and her amazing energy. Yet her face gave off something mysterious and new to me, an impression of someone who, though well-liked and even admired, in some indefinable way did not quite fit in.

The librarian told me that if I wanted to find out more about Mount Vernon in the 1920s I might try calling Dr. Larry Spruill, the city historian, who worked for the Board of Education. Spruill, an expert in black history, suggested that I try to find a woman named Ginny Moskowitz, who had collected most of the materials in the library's local history room. All he could tell me was that she was retired and now lived somewhere in Connecticut. There was only one phone listing for a Virginia Moskowitz in Connecticut. As I dialed I felt, as I would often in the years that followed, a strange and uneasy mingling of emotions: the thrill of the hunt and a cold professional hunger for hidden facts and satisfaction at getting at them, and along with all that a rush of relief that I was close to my mother in a way that I hadn't been since her death, a feeling that was indistinguishable from love. When I explained what I was looking for, and mentioned the name LaVerne Madigan, the elderly voice on the other end of the line exclaimed, "Was she a small blonde girl?"

Moskowitz told me that she had attended the high school at the same time as my mother, a year or two behind her.

"How well did you know her?" I asked.

"Oh, just from a distance," Moskowitz gasped, sounding suddenly like the shy teenager that she was nearly seventy years ago. "I was just a lowly person. She was the elite."

The Mount Vernon that Moskowitz described, the city of my mother's youth, still had a certain nineteenth-century quality. "It was a wonderful place to live," she said. Serious crime was virtually unknown. A theft of three or four dollars warranted front-page coverage in the *Daily Argus*. In an era before the advent of electronic entertainment crowds gathered to watch Clydesdale horses pull wagons up the steep Oak Street hill, and Italian funeral bands that would parade through the streets with trumpets and trombones, and gypsies in bangles and colorful clothes who picked dandelions on people's lawns in order to make wine. For a night on the town there were vaudeville shows at Proctor's theater, where you could sometimes see Eddie Cantor or dancing Siamese twins. On the Fourth of July everyone young and old piled into streetcars and went to St. Paul's Church, where the Declaration of Independence was read aloud, bands played, and the church bell was rung thirteen times, for each of the first states.

Moskowitz had a copy of the 1930 high-school yearbook. She went through it for me and mentioned people she thought were LaVerne's friends. "Ernest Halton. He's dead. Eddie Lee. He's dead. Beulah Hoffberg. I don't know what happened to her. Augie Petrillo became mayor. He's dead too. Howard Duffy worked for the *Argus*. He's gone." As so it went. I asked, did she know anyone at all left from the Class of 1930? She mentioned a man named Phillip Robbins. "He did well as a pharmaceutical salesman." In 1930 he had been snapshot editor of the yearbook. And there he was in the photo of the yearbook staff, in the row behind my mother and a little to the left. I found a phone number for Robbins in the town Moskowitz had mentioned and left a message on his answering machine.

When Robbins called back the next day, tension hardened in me like a rock. In spite of my curiosity I knew that I was afraid of what Robbins might tell me, afraid that I might learn of a person who would disappoint me, afraid to hear of a life that I had never shared and never could share. His voice was startlingly vigorous for a man in his mid-eighties. "She was well-liked, very lovable, very smart," he remembered. "Everybody loved LaVerne. Most of the popular girls were untouchable, so to speak, you couldn't get near them. But LaVerne never snubbed anybody. Her attitude was that she accepted people for who they were. She was into everything. No matter what you were doing you'd run into LaVerne there. She was extraordinary. Everyone knew that she'd amount to something." Robbins gave me a telephone number and urged me to call Dr. Herman Weissberg, another member of the Class of 1930, who had only recently retired from a long career as a general practitioner in Mount Vernon. "I think LaVerne was the brightest woman I ever knew," Dr. Weissberg told me. "She was one of the stars of the school. She could do anything she set her mind to. She wasn't snooty. She had a right to be, but she wasn't. Everybody was her friend."

Weissberg said that most of the survivors of my mother's generation had long ago retired to Florida. So many of them now lived there that hundreds gathered annually for a Mount Vernon Day festival every February. By coincidence, this event was to take place the following week. The organizer of it was a retired judge, who gave me the name and Florida phone number of a retired postman named Stanley Wolar who had taken over the organization of Mount Vernon Day. The day after the event he called me back and apologized because no one had responded. "They're probably all gone," he said.

Then he said, "Hey, wait a minute." He went away from the phone to look at a list, and when he came back, he said that there had been one attendee from the Class of 1929, a John McCaffrey. "He used to be a policeman," Wolar said. He gave me a phone number in Mount Vernon and wished me luck.

"Sure I knew LaVerne," McCaffrey boomed when I reached him. "Her family got a paper called the *Catholic Visitor*. I used to deliver it." McCaffrey had grown up on First Street, a couple of blocks from the Madigans, and had gone to grammar school with LaVerne at Sacred Heart. "Everybody liked LaVerne," he said. "But she was different from everyone else. She did everything different. She read every book she could get her hands on. She read and read and read. She always seemed to be a step ahead of the rest of us."

A few days later I drove down to Mount Vernon and met McCaffrey in the apartment where he had continued to live since his wife's death a few years earlier. He was big man with the gruff and gregarious style of an old-time street-corner cop. He had joined the Mount Vernon Police Department during the Depression and had eventually risen to become chief of detectives. After his retirement he had done well selling security systems as the city's crime rate rose in the 1960s and 1970s. We sat, in the living room that his wife had elegantly furnished with a mauve carpet and curtains and floral slipcovers, looking at old photos and talking as the Catholic Channel, McCaffrey's favorite, flickered lullingly on the TV across the room.

McCaffrey was in the photo that I had of LaVerne and her classmates on the steps in front of Sacred Heart School in 1921. There, grinning out from the sepia rectangle, was McCaffrey's round moon of a boy's face, the face of a life still empty of experience, and next to me the same face, the face of a man with no future at all left before him. I was overwhelmed with an intensity of feeling, as if, with McCaffrey, I could step back into the picture, take the little girl by the hand and lead her away to safety, to warn her: *Never climb on a horse.* . . . Then the moment passed and I had the unnerving sense of an entire life having raced away before my eyes, of eighty years having fled in a twinkling.

McCaffrey was talking about Sacred Heart, about Sister Monica who was so strict, and Sister Laurentia, everyone's favorite, who if you made a mistake in class, turned red out of embarrassment for you. "Religion was very important in those days," he said. "No one even thought of challenging a nun or a priest, or doctrine. If someone fell away from the church, we'd really resent it. We couldn't understand it. It was incomprehensible." Then he told me that he used to go to parties at the Madigans' house on Washington Street. "There were always parties at LaVerne's. There were games, three-legged races. Her mother loved those parties as much as LaVerne did. I think the mother was the instigator. She was always involved in them." This was unexpected. It was still difficult even now to see through the detritus of Maddy's ruined personality, through the madness and the bitterness of her later years to a woman capable of joining in children's hilarity, and to the cold maternal pragmatism that McCaffrey now described. "When we were older, she wanted LaVerne to marry a doctor," he continued. "She was willing to pay some Catholic boy's tuition all the way through medical school if he would marry LaVerne. One day I was delivering the paper, and she sat me down at the kitchen table and after a while I realized she was interviewing me to see if I would become a doctor. I think she did that with everybody, although you didn't always realize you were being interviewed at the time." It was as hard to picture this still-youthful Maddy as it was to see back through the tough and independent woman I knew as my mother to this young girl tangled in the web of the future that her mother was weaving around her.

George Madigan had left a small fortune at his death, sufficient for Maddy to believe that she could buy LaVerne a secure and conventional life. I wondered what she saw in her daughter as she prepared to graduate from high school. Ultimately a ticket to the restoration of the patrician life of her own youth, a redemption of the family name from dishonor and misfortune? Perhaps. She would marry an Elk, play golf at Winged Foot, live out the life that had been cruelly stolen from Maddy by her husband's premature death. Of course Maddy could not foresee the catastrophe that was about to occur and that would wreak havoc with her dreams. The old photos of sunny days on Washington Street are images not only of one fam-

ily but of all of middle-class America, of an entire optimistic generation that thought itself safe from the vagaries of politics and economics, and whose security hung by gossamer threads that were
about to snap.

THE SIGNIFICANCE of the stock market crash of October 1929 was
largely lost on Mount Vernon High School's Class of 1930. There
was no mention of it in the yearbook. On Black Tuesday, October 29,
when the greatest break in the history of the New York Stock Exchange slashed away billions of dollars in value in a single day, the
lead story in the *Daily Argus* concerned a local man who had been
killed in an air crash in Arizona. On Wednesday the Argus optimisti-
cally reported, "The market came back smashingly today," as the excited buying of bargains left from the previous day's crash heartened
Americans who had become accustomed to an era of unshakable confidence in business. It was clear that no one realized what was in
store.

In spite of the crash my mother managed to go to college in the
autumn of 1930, as a freshman at New York University's School of
Commerce. Although she earned top grades, in the fall of 1931 she
transferred to the liberal arts program at NYU's Washington Square
College, enrolling in courses in ancient languages, English Literature,
European history, and—this last a hint of how the country was
changing—labor problems. Thereafter nearly all her credits were in
the departments of English, Italian, and her beloved Classics, where
she became expert in the decipherment of ancient manuscripts and
ostraka, the potsherds on which the ancient Greeks used to keep their
household and business accounts. Although an English major, in her
junior and senior years she was registered for no regular English
courses at all, but rather for Reading for Honors, the equivalent of
today's independent study, a highly unusual arrangement at that time,
the university registrar told me. She would graduate in 1934 with
high honors and a Phi Beta Kappa key.

Tuition at NYU was only about three hundred and fifty dollars per year in the early 1930s. Even so, so few qualified students could afford it that admissions standards were jettisoned and virtually anyone with the money to pay was allowed to matriculate. Almost everyone commuted by subway, mainly from lower-middle-class neighborhoods like the central Bronx, Crown Heights, Flatbush, and upper Harlem, which was then still predominantly white. Although there was a leavening of students from Irish, Italian, and other backgrounds, the vast majority were Jewish. Men wore suits and ties to class, and women wore hats. Students ate at the Lychee Garden on Tenth Street, where a full Chinese buffet cost a quarter, or at the Waverly Cafe on Broadway, where soup and a sandwich were just twenty cents. For the truly impoverished, lunch might be a "ketchup sandwich" at the Horn and Hardart Automat for a nickel. Although prohibition was still in effect, needled beer could be had at a popular Italian speakeasy on Charles Street or at Chumley's on Barrow Street.

My mother's four student years at NYU coincided with the darkest period of the Depression. In the spring of 1930 five million Americans were unemployed; there were ten million in 1931 and fifteen million at the end of 1932, roughly one-third of the nation's workforce. All but one-fifth of the steel mills had shut down; farm income had fallen by two-thirds, with cotton selling for six cents a pound, one-fifth of its value in 1929. More than a thousand banks failed during the last three months of 1931 alone. In some regions of the country currency virtually disappeared. By early 1933 deposits were shrinking at a daily rate of thirty-seven million dollars in gold coins and a hundred and twenty-two million dollars in banknotes. In New York City blocks-long lines of men and women waiting for bowls of soup were a common sight. There were panhandlers in front of Judson Church on the south side of Washington Square, and there was a Hooverville of shanties, where homeless families lived in an excavation for a new building at Abingdon Square, to the west of NYU. The film critic Stanley Kauffmann, who studied drama at NYU from 1931 to 1935, sometimes saw dead bodies on the sidewalk as he walked to school in the morning from the subway at Astor Place, probably the same route taken by my mother.

Many Americans feared that the machinery of representative government and the capitalist system had broken down beyond repair. Al Smith, the 1928 Democratic candidate for President, declared in 1933 that the Depression was a greater crisis than war. "And what does a democracy do in war?" he asked. "It becomes a tyrant, a despot, a real monarch." Malcolm Cowley, then an editor of the *New Republic*, wrote that same year, "I do not doubt that the United States will have its revolution," though like many of leftwing sympathies, he feared that it was destined to follow the German path rather than the Russian one. He added, "The only thing that can turn us aside from that steep path into the sea is the influence on the middle classes of the Russian experiment, the success of 'socialism in one country.' " A straw poll taken among NYU students before the 1932 elections gave Norman Thomas of the Socialist Party eight hundred votes, Franklin Roosevelt seven hundred and sixty-eight, Herbert Hoover six hundred and sixty-eight, and Communist William Z. Foster a hundred and thirty-eight. And when Communist Party chairman Earl Browder gave a speech in Washington Square Park, students from NYU flocked to hear him. "It was the first time I ever heard a Communist with a country accent," Kauffmann, who was born and raised in Manhattan, told me. "We thought there was a lot of hooey going on politically—we thought, maybe Roosevelt means well, but now we'll get the goods. All my experience with Communists up to then was of New York types. When we heard Browder, our feeling was, now we're getting the truth."

In Mount Vernon unemployment reached forty-three percent. On the first day of 1932 two hundred unemployed men stormed the mayor's office in a frantic appeal for jobs. By 1933 Mount Vernon was desperately trying to negotiate loans from New York City bankers to pay thousands of city salaries that had been in arrears for months, and the mayor was begging large taxpayers to make payments in advance. City officials were even talking seriously about issuing scrip to be redeemed when the city's financial situation improved. A few miles away in Larchmont the president of the Larchmont Bank and Trust Company shot and killed himself in his basement when it became clear that his bank would never reopen. Respectable people began un-obtrusively renting out rooms in their homes to make ends meet. The Madigans would soon be among them.

Nearly all the Maddy's assets had been placed in the Mount Vernon Trust Company, the city's largest bank. On March 4, 1933, the Trust Company's three branches were ordered closed along with thousands of other insolvent banks around the country in accordance with the federal bank holiday that was proclaimed as Franklin Roosevelt's first act as President. When the Trust Company reopened, only ten percent of balances were released to depositors. Thousands of depositors, including my grandmother, were ruined. It was widely rumored that the bank's officials and their local Republican political cronies had milked its assets before the crash. There were several feeble attempts to reorganize the bank. Depositors were at one point issued common stock and assured that they would "participate in all profits of the bank." Maddy received several handsome certificates printed colorfully in orange, green, and brown ink and engraved with the state seal of New York. They had a value of one-half cent on the dollar. "Hold on to your certificates," the Trust Company's president O. H. Cheney declared a few months before the bank closed for good in 1934. Maddy was still holding on to them at her death in 1965.

With the failure of the Mount Vernon Trust Company, the Madigans sank abruptly from comparative affluence to the very brink of poverty. Everything "the doctor" had placed his confidence in—the bankers, the Republican Party, the golf-playing country-club gentry—failed them now. My mother left nothing that tells me what she felt as the society that she was raised to trust disintegrated around her except a single sonnet that she published in a literary magazine at NYU:

> *Moistly into my palm I gripped the dime*
> *I had to spend and was particular*
> *To want no more than I would want a star.*
> *The gowns where solemn dragons, white as milk,*
> *Crawled over transparencies of silk.*
> *My coin—sweet coin—would buy a butter jar.*

3

MY MOTHER'S TRANSCRIPT told me little about what she had actually done at NYU. However, I found in the garage among Maddy's few surviving papers, along with the worthless stock certificates and a few notes on the long-ago deaths of her brothers and sisters, a yellowed clipping from the *Daily Argus* that she had taped to a piece of manila board. The article, a long interview, dated from August of 1936. It gave me a glimpse of how accomplished my mother had been as an undergraduate.

Greek, Latin Hold No Terrors For Young Mount Vernon Woman

LaVerne Madigan, Attractive, Blond, Unlike Usual Conception of Learned Scholar; Delves into Past; Her Poetry also Claim to Fame

The Greeks had a word for it! And it's Miss La Verne Madigan's delight and diversion to decipher that word.

For this erudite young woman, the daughter of Mrs. George F. Madigan, of 126 Washington Street, and the late Dr. Madigan, is a profound student of paleography both medieval and ancient.

Paleography involves the handling of the actual ancient manuscripts; not merely the translation of the meaning into English, but the deciphering of the strange and faded old hand writings in which they were written.

Miss Madigan explained that the task is complicated by the fact that people, even scribes, wrote as illegibly and spelled as badly then as now.

"The medieval manuscripts are worse in this respect." she said: "the writers had an extremely imperfect knowledge of the Latin language which had become pretty mutilated since the fall of Rome. Moreover, they had a trick of abbreviating words: for example, 'bet' might be their abbreviation for 'benedicta.' A row of such ligatures, one after the other, is enough to turn the hair white.

"I have worked over some medieval documents which are called palimpsests; in this case, because writing material was scarce, a monk has taken one of the old Greek or Latin manuscripts stored in his monastery, scraped off the ancient writing, and then written upon the clean surface himself. It is possible, with much labor, to translate both the old and comparatively new inscriptions on the palimpsest.

"My most important piece of medieval paleography was a translation of the previously untouched Bodleian Manuscript, 649; it was a sermon of the early Middle Ages, significant in relation to conditions in England at that time and as a contribution to the great body of mediaeval allegorical literature."

"Going back farther into antiquity," she continued, "I have done my most interesting work of this sort. That was the study of Greek civilizations by means of the tattered bits of papyrus unearthed by archaeologists. You seldom have a complete document to begin with; usually your working material is a box full of scraps and shreds. These you place together like any puzzle, although they are so old and fragile they must be kept under glass."

But paleography and archaeology are not the only interest of this remarkable girl who, in her youth and animation and attractiveness, is completely unlike the conventional conception of a scholar as a severe, bespectacled, person, weighed down with the burdens of knowledge.

No, indeed—those involved subjects occupy only part of her time, for she is also engaged in writing a modern novel based on the translation from the Greek of Homer's "Iliad"; she has just completed "Miracle in Dust," a collection of 100 sonnets, one of the most difficult mediums of poetic expressions, and is now working on another 50 or so to be entitled "Scattered Agamemnon."

I imagined sometimes as I hunted down my mother's classmates and scoured the columns of old newspapers that I was carrying out my own private archaeology, trying to make sense of a person whose basic shape was recognizable, like the foundation line of a building that had disappeared long ago but whose life before my own still remained a jumble of scraps and shards and faded memories. I tried to work as methodically and clinically as I could, though I felt a terrible urgency, sometimes almost a terror, that things would disappear before I got to them and that the last people who knew her would die before I talked to them: none of them could be younger than in their seventies now, and most would be in their eighties, if not older.

I knew that one of my mother's closest friends during the 1930s was Dr. Catherine Ruth Smith. Photographs of her show a homely, plainly dressed woman with a fleshy, peculiarly inexpressive face. Later, in the 1940s, as the editor of a small poetry magazine, she published two or three of my mother's sonnets; from the magazines I also knew that she was a professor at NYU. There were more than fifty telephone listings for the name "Catherine Smith" in the New York area. I called them one by one. One of the last on the list lived in Yonkers, just a couple of miles from my childhood home, in what I knew to be a largely black neighborhood. But in the end there was no one else left, so I finally called.

A youthful female voice answered the phone. "She's dead. She died in 1996."

The young woman, Frances Brunner, told me that she had grown up down the block from Catherine Smith's home, and that she and her mother had cared for her at the end of her life. Smith had left the home to them in her will. She hadn't gotten around to shutting off the phone yet. "Hardly anyone calls."

I asked if, by chance, Smith had left any papers.

"She left a whole house of them. I don't think she ever had a thought that she didn't write down, and she never threw anything away."

I had expected a small frame house of the type typical in Yonkers. Instead I found a towering wreck, dormered and gabled and painted dark green, built into a steep hillside that must once have given it, before later and less grand buildings blocked the line of sight, a panoramic view of the New Jersey Palisades. In spite of Brunner's herculean labors, the house seemed beleaguered by a deep exhaustion, an ingrained decay, that seemed beyond human power to remedy. Walking through it, I felt an unsettling sensation, a kind of temporal vertigo. Paint was scrolling crazily from the ceilings. In the hall an ancient grandfather clock had stopped at one twenty-two on some now forgotten afternoon. In the bookcases that were everywhere multitudes of ancient volumes in gilded leather gleamed dully beneath skins of dust. The dark old furniture, the dim aqueous light, the heavy drapes, the ornate lamps with japanned shades that crouched everywhere on dusty end tables seemed to hold past time in them like a soaked sponge. *You were here. I can feel it. How many times did you sit in this room, gazing out over the peaked roofs toward the Palisades and running your fingers over the old upright Schomaker Angelopian piano? How you must have pored over the cabinets of books, exclaiming at new discoveries, trolling for gems to take home. Perhaps you even cradled me here as an infant, showed me off to your friend.*

Brunner, an ebullient woman in her early thirties who was studying to become a pastoral social worker, said that she had never heard Smith mention my mother. But then the Brunners had only moved to the neighborhood in the late 1960s. She told me that Smith had lived in the house almost her entire life, first with her parents and then alone until her death at the age of eighty-nine. "She never married. I don't think she ever went out on a date with a man or a woman. Dr. Smith—no one ever referred to her as anything but 'Dr.'—had an incredible mind: witty, retentive, a great critical intellect. She never forgot anything. But she tended to reject what didn't fit into her world. The modern thing was not her cup of tea. She just didn't think there was anything in it. Her mind was anchored in the classics. She could write a satire about the garbage man in the language of Shakespeare. But she was not interested in thinking about anything new. She became more self-centered in her later years, and she gradually drove people away from her. She wanted to be a warm person, but she didn't know how. She was an intellectual snob. She didn't accept anything less than perfection. She couldn't have survived outside this house. It was always dusty because she'd rather write than clean. She had dogs and spoiled them mercilessly. She fed one paté on dog biscuits until it died of a stroke. Another was named Anubis, and it was so fat that it went upstairs backward."

Smith's parents, and after their deaths Smith herself, oversaw a small evangelical society that supported an ever-shrinking corps of missionaries in Eastern Europe and the Soviet Union whose ultimate ambition was the conversion of Jews to Christianity. Smith herself was something of a child prodigy. In the wreckage of her office I found a brief autobiography that she had written: "She learned to read at the age of three, read newspapers at five, read 'Ben Hur' through when she was six, began typing at seven. She studied by herself at home, and also wrote (on the typewriter) more than a dozen original novels." At fifteen she entered the Biblical Seminary in New York and at eighteen became its youngest graduate ever. She then studied at New York University, where she received a doctorate in classics and began teaching ancient Greek and Latin in 1929. That, of course, is how she would have met my mother, six years her junior, poetic, in love with the classics, a natural soulmate. As a junior member of the department Smith may well have taught my mother her first course in Greek, perhaps even have been the pivot upon which she swung away from the School of Commerce to liberal arts and the classics. "Like a lot of bright women," Brunner said, "I think she was taken advantage of by NYU. As brilliant as she was, they never gave her tenure. She was thrilled just to type the notes of Prof. So-and-So."

Brunner led me upstairs. We squatted for hours on the floor in thick dust, pulling open cardboard boxes, searching for anything that would connect Smith with my mother. There were snapshots of dogs long gone, old commencement programs from NYU, ads for Victory Loans, sixty-year-old coupons for condensed milk discounts, ration booklets from the Second World War. There were papers that Smith had written as an undergraduate in the 1920s: her own translation of Aristophanes's *The Clouds*, a twenty-page original play in Latin, erudite exegeses of ancient rhetoric. And there was her doctoral thesis, completed when she was only twenty-five, on the crossover of Egyptian deities into the Roman calendar. There were invitations to elaborate, bizarre parties. "You'd be there for hours," Brunner said. "She would invite the neighborhood grocer, the gas man, and the counterman from the Greek luncheonette to commemorate her dog's birthday or putting up a stone wall in the backyard." One hand-written program announced a two-and-a-half-hour-long, scheduled-to-the-minute party to celebrate the repair of her car. Brunner said, "There were always dog hairs in the cakes."

But there was nothing at all that mentioned my mother.

Finally I moved on to Smith's office. The floor was ankle-deep in papers. Boxes and file cabinets lay scattered amid them like crags in the sea of papers. She must have written incessantly, typing for hours every day in the smallest typescript that I had ever seen, sublimating whatever was missing from her life onto the file cards that surrounded me everywhere. There were thousands of them, tens of thousands. There were whole drawers packed with typed notes, many of them in ancient Greek. In still other drawers there were notes for plays that Smith planned to write. There were dense packs of news clippings under "Settings," "Costumes," "Music," and "Ideas." There were lists of hundreds of titles of performances that her characters might have heard, music they might have played, books they might have read. On card after card she had written things like, "read more Goethe: master hand, wonderful characterizations"; or, "Read about Pico della Mirandola and his uncle Giovanni." Gobs of dust dripped from the cards as I pulled them out. I felt uncomfortably that I had entered, as if into a tight crawl space in a vast unstable building, the very synapses of a woman whose brain would not shut off.

I knew that my mother was there somewhere. For a time I was so obsessed with the certainty of it that I dreamed nightly about the house and the alps of dusty paper. The dream was always similar. In it I struggled to read words without end on scraps of yellowing paper that crumbled in my hands. I would catch a glimpse of my mother's name, lose my place, and then start all over again from the beginning, choking on dust.

On my third trip to Smith's house I went back to a wooden file

box that I had looked through before in a cursory fashion. This time
I went systematically through every item in the drawer. Here and
there I noticed that there were envelopes folded double between the
cards. I took them out one by one, looking at the postmarks. Suddenly I saw what I had been looking for: "Mount Vernon, New
York," and the return address "126 Washington Street." Inside, on
sheets of yellow foolscap, was a long critique of a play that Smith had
written, entitled *The Dawn of Nothing*. The penciled handwriting on
the manuscript was unmistakably my mother's, bold and racing.
There were more sheets of foolscap, index cards, scraps of blue tissue
paper with scribbled notes. Apparently Smith would send synopses of
the plays or entire scenes to my mother, leaving a wide margin for her
comments. Most seemed to date from 1935 and 1936, although some
may have been earlier. "The comments on the accompanying sheet,"
Smith wrote, acknowledging my mother's critique of one play, "are
not those of a little girl who has just graduated from college, but of
a dramatic critic and a creative artist. I say this, not because of the
times when you approve of my work, but because of the points at
which you differ from it and criticize it. What makes you so good,
anyway?"

In another drawer I found a note in which my mother spoke of
coming here, to this house, to visit Smith. She wrote everything in
soft pencil, and I could see where she had turned its shaft in her small
hand every ten or twelve words to find a sharper point. Such a tiny
thing, such a thoughtless gesture, yet it made me feel so close to her
that I could scarcely bear it. I could almost touch her hand. Her voice
was unmistakable, coming to me across the years. I could have picked
it out from among a thousand chattering strangers on a crowded avenue. I could hear her cadences, her self-assurance, her cocky charm.
As I read on, I felt myself pulled into this conversation between two
ghosts, which had lain buried here, unread perhaps for six decades.

Especially in the earlier correspondence, my mother expressed an
awestruck gratefulness at having been admitted into the privileged
citadel of Smith's inner life. It was clear that she adored Smith's brilliance and aestheticism, her dazzling knowledge of the classics, her

ambition, her intellectual versatility, her apparent independence. "I'll bet you could carve statues and be a steeplejack if you wanted to," she wrote in one note to Smith. Smith in turn sanctioned my mother's determination to be a poet, her craving to make a career of what she loved most. The two would try to meet whenever my mother came into the city from Mount Vernon. They would exchange work, Smith giving my mother her latest play and my mother giving her poetry in return. "It's a sort of spontaneous combustion that we can't keep down," Smith wrote in a note to my mother. But for the most part they exchanged the kind of copious letters that enforced leisure and poverty encouraged among literate people during the Depression. On February 28, 1936, Smith wrote to my mother, "I've long since ceased to feel, in our work, the dividing line between *'meum'* and *'teum.'* Each of us automatically and instinctively does anything she can for the other. The thought of that is very precious to me."

But almost imperceptibly the two women's roles reversed. At the beginning Smith was clearly the mentor and my mother the student at her feet. Later on it was more often Smith who was asking for advice, guidance, criticism. My mother's tone is affectionate and encouraging. Her comments are acute, surgical, often arguing for emotional economy, for ambiguity, for an earthy realism to counterbalance Smith's spiritualizing loftiness. Smith's plays are mostly awful. Typically they revolve around mystical bonds between chaste lovers and dreamers who agonize over beauty, art, or service to science. In her notes to Smith, my mother argues for irony, ambiguity, flawed personalities, and a less conventional sense of morality. In one of these notes I discovered a comment that revealed something of my mother's attitude about love and sex, to which she had obviously given a great deal of thought. "I don't really have a complex about love affairs," she wrote. "But, to be as blunt as you were when you accused me of such an obsession, I'm not a minister's daughter. I don't blame you under those circumstances—although God knows I was reared as strictly as a Vestal. To put a market value on virginity and to 'hold out' for marriage is as disgusting and hypocritical as it is possible to be. Marriage makes love safe, I admit. *But it does not improve upon love.* An affair under the circumstances sounds as natural to me as drinking water when thirsty."

One of the drawers in Smith's office was packed from end to end with poems Smith had typed out line by line in her minuscule script. There were poems by Tennyson, Keats, Heine, Goethe, Kipling, Browning, Riley, Blake, Milton, Bulwer-Lytton, and dozens of others. I skimmed the master list, where each poem was systematically numbered, from one to one hundred and sixty-three and was identified by its first line. I was startled to see the name "Madigan." Under her name were scores of sonnets. I pulled them out one after another and stood for a long time in the dim aqueous light, for hours perhaps, amidst the blizzard of missionary tracts and half-century-old gas bills, and let my mother's words surge over me:

> *The icy stars whose fires did once exist*
> *And linger still in lower fathoms of air,*
> *Live in the life which drums against my wrist,*
> *And I were starlight were my self aware . . .*

I raced on to another poem, drinking in her words.

> *Were I a papyrus with a faded line*
> *Or tarnished coin, stamped with some Caesar's head,*
> *He soft would touch me, boasting, "This is mine!"*
> *But I, poor thing, am warm white flesh instead.*
> *O woe! His lean strong fingers play*
> *On time-cracked slabs alone, or shattered bowls.*
> *To win the man I must resolve to clay*
> *Interred, or hieroglyphs on crumbling scrolls.*
> *Will centuries be lifted as a shade?*
> *Then I shall house me in a dead queen's tomb*
> *And wait to be discovered by his spade,*
> *The shrouded issue of an ancient womb.*
> *For he were ravished if I came to meet*
> *My bride-bed in a dusty winding sheet.*

There were ninety-eight sonnets in all, many of which I had never seen before. Never could she have imagined as she typed them in her room at 126 Washington Street that I would someday read them here. I did not even exist in the imagination of this girl who was then less than half my present age. Yet here I stood, knowing her more intimately than anyone on earth, hearing her words as if they had been spoken to me only minutes before, filled with her memory, filled with love, filled with yearning for her voice and the touch of her hand.

Looking backward into Catherine Ruth Smith's life and seeing my mother looking forward toward a life full of promise, I felt an eerie sensation. It was as if we, my mother and I, were gazing into opposite sides of a two-way mirror. Looking into it, I could see her youthful face peering back from the other side, staring toward me into the invisible unknowable future. Between us, strange and transparent, was Catherine Ruth Smith, whose life, seen from LaVerne's angle, must have seemed so splendid in all its brilliance and promise, and which now seemed to me to be so shriveled and crabbed with failure.

Smith resigned completely from the larger world when her parents died in the late 1940s. After that she abandoned teaching, abandoned literature, abandoned any attempt to keep up with people outside the shrinking circle of her missionary activities, living on a minuscule stipend that may have been as little as two hundred dollars a month as the great house crumbled around her. She did finally write a book, a five-hundred-page history of her neighborhood Presbyterian church. Her last days were horrible. Brunner told me that the home attendant Smith hired to care for her gradually took over the house, renting out rooms to strangers and then subdividing rooms to fit in even more. Smith had a bed hauled into the dining room and lived there, behind a sliding door. Paint crumbled from the kitchen ceiling into the meals. Half-finished plates of food were everywhere. Smith became a prisoner in her home. Books and furniture were stolen. A social worker from the Yonkers welfare department found her in bed with cockroaches crawling over the bedclothes. The department evicted the attendant and her tenants and removed Smith to a nursing home. A year later Brunner and her mother brought her back to her own house and nursed her until her death from a cerebral hemorrhage. Her overcharged brain finally gave out.

I HAD SPENT MONTHS now ferreting out the broken shards of my mother's early life. Yet I had in my own possession—and had had for years—something of hers that I suspected would reveal more about her than I was likely to find out from strangers. It was an old file box made of thick, marbled cardboard that closed with a small brass hasp; apart from some of her books and the photo albums it was the only thing of hers that I owned. I knew only that it contained all that was left of what my father had preserved of her early writings. There must once have been more. I supposed that she must have thrown everything else away, although I could not put it past my father to have discarded anything whose utility was not apparent, the way that after her death he had packed up and shipped away every piece of her clothing, everything personal, until almost every trace of her physical presence had been erased from the house. It was quite possible that he had never even read what was inside the box.

By now I had made hundreds of phone calls searching for my mother's surviving friends and acquaintances, spent many hours reading microfilm, and many more hours foraging through archives at public libraries and at NYU. Although I had carefully preserved the box, had carried it from home to home for years, had stored it securely during the periods that I lived abroad, I had almost never opened it, had never done more than glance inside it and finger the old sheets of foolscap and onion skin and the small magazines where, I knew, she had published her poetry. In truth I was afraid of what I might find: afraid of being disappointed, afraid that I would discover her to have been shallow or conventional, and afraid, too—maybe even more so—that I would discover the opposite, that she was a better writer than I was and that after all my years of doing it, and of making a living at it, I fell short of what she had been capable of in her twenties. But there was really no alternative now; the cache that I had found in Catherine Smith's house had committed me, as if in this archaeological excavation of mine I had uncovered a buried crypt, and it now waited for me to open the lid. I had already brought the box in from the garage, and now it sat on a shelf in my office like a reproach, daring me to open it.

When I finally emptied it out, I found all sorts of things: the final report on my mother's resettlement of displaced Japanese-Americans for the War Relocation office during the Second World War; scholarly papers on James Joyce and George Moore, and on anti-Semitism in the writings of George Eliot. There were copies of an enigmatic exchange of notes with the silent film star Nils Asther, to whom she sent a Roman sesterce for good luck when he attempted a comeback on the New York stage. There were even children's stories that she had written for me when I was very small; in the one I liked best, a little Japanese boy and an American boy named Fergus set off with their fathers from opposite sides of the globe and met at the North Pole. But the great bulk of what was in the box dated from the 1930s. I found her translation of the Bodleian manuscript, a long and richly allegorical sermon in Latin and Middle English by an early fifteenth-century friar rebutting Lollard heretic attacks against the established church. There were copies of sonnets that had appeared in poetry magazines, a remarkable ninety-five-page novella set in Iberia on the eve of the Roman conquest of the second century B.C., and short stories that she published in college literary magazines; in one of them a meek shopgirl who suddenly comes into five hundred dollars hires a gigolo for a weekend on the town, and in another, possibly based on events surrounding her father's funeral, an orphaned child is exposed to the self-serving hypocrisy of callous adults.

There were also fragmentary notes, written on large index cards, apparently for a novel. Her thoughts were still unformed, and as far as I know the novel was never written, but they illuminated the furniture of her mind at some point in the mid-1930s like brief flashes of light in a darkened room:

Mechanization of everything in the end—sex, political relations, sympathy, all correct, all perfected, all mechanical.

Passions are replaced by obsessions—the emotions run in old streambeds—the Niagaras erode away and the water flows at dead level.

Frightened people do so much harm. And so many are frightened.

Women [are] like gardens—eternal, unfinished Spring—cultivated, fertilized, mulched, weeded in season and out—fur capes, gold cigarette cases, massaged bodies . . . violated, tender—trodden down, a footprint on the face, a bruised mouth and broken tooth.

As one aged and knew oneself too well, the happiest moments were those of meeting strangers and being seen as one was not.

She stopped resisting and let sorrow break over her in waves.

Dwarfing everything else I found in the box was my mother's poetry, hundreds of pages of it. There were a few poems dating from the 1940s and 1950s, including one, perhaps the last she wrote, on the death of Don Hollenbeck, a television newsman who was hounded to suicide in 1953 by McCarthyite Red-baiters.

I pictured my mother crafting her sonnets in her room on Washington Street beneath the eaves, from which she could look out over her beloved garden, a tiny figure curled catlike in the blue haze of cigarette smoke, legs tucked beneath her, head bent low over a yellow pad, her mind working with such intensity that I could almost hear it. We were at last, I thought, if only in my imagination, writers together. Our writing had little in common. My mother's was sometimes ornate in a way that was not always easy to read sixty years later but at other times hauntingly beautiful in ways that I envied and with which I could never compete. I had never written poetry at all, and what I did write was sparer and more earthbound. But I hoped that she would still have been proud of what I had written, that she would have seen that writing mattered to me as much as it did to her, that we had this in common, and that although she never saw a word I wrote, I still owed it ultimately to her: who had taught me to take words seriously, and to love them, and that there was a tribe of people in the world for whom they were a way of life.

By day my mother was, of course, working at NYU, and I could see her there, too, poring intently over lacunae, searching the empty space for connections, listening for the feathery rasp of ancient voices, trying to shut out at least for a few hours the sound of the imploding national economy, the grim uncertainty of politics, and her own passions. I knew that at some time after her graduation in 1934 my mother was appointed secretary of the Department of Classics, a significant job then as now, involving much of the department's day-to-day management. "LaVerne was tiny, buxom, with silver-blond hair, and smart, and witty, and gay," Lionel Casson's tartly cultivated voice on the telephone told me, and time seemed to dissolve. Casson had served as chairman of the Classics Department in the 1960s and 1970s and was a classicist of considerable eminence. Now in his mid-eighties, he lectured on classical subjects on cruise ships. I was lucky to catch him at home in New York City. In the 1930s he had been a lowly instructor grateful for a job. "The Madigans were very poor," he told me. LaVerne had started graduate work but had had to give it up for lack of money. "When she was elected to Phi Beta Kappa, there was some question whether she could even come up with the modest entrance fee. Kraemer thought the world of her, and I think that he may have come up with the money himself." Casper Kraemer, then the department's chairman, was a charismatic figure who brought the department a prestige far out of proportion to its small size. Under his leadership Classics was known throughout the university as a lively and convivial place, Casson said. The departmental office was then a single large unpartitioned room on the seventh floor of Washington Square College, overlooking the square. Each of the eight or nine members of the department had a desk there, along with my mother. As secretary, she was the intermediary between students and the department, took all phone calls, and typed the department's correspondence, final exams, and letters for the members of the faculty. Her fingers "were so small that she had difficulty reaching the keys," Casson remembered.

It was clear, Casson added, that my mother was underutilized as a secretary. I asked him whether she was planning on an academic career. Casson laughed dryly. "None of us had any idea what we would do later on. No one thought of jobs in the discipline. The department was cast in bronze. There were these professors, and no one ever got to replace them. There was nothing for anybody, so you could just enjoy what you were doing. It was marvelous. The school was young, the faculty was young, we were all young—young, able and devoted. The department was a tight group of people. LaVerne was the focal point of the room. I remember her smiling and laughing all the time, but one rarely caught a glimpse of what went on beneath her public exterior."

He remembered a poem that she had written about a visitation of the Virgin Mary. It had almost been published by *The New Yorker*. "She showed the rejection slip around the office. It was clear that just about everyone at the magazine had read it and been impressed with it, but the magazine had considered it too advanced, too erotic, for the readers. She was a heroine to us. Being published in *The New Yorker* was the pinnacle of success, and she came very close." I had a copy of this sonnet, and after talking to Casson, I reread it. My mother called it, with deliberate tongue-in-cheek irony, "A Prayer to Our Lady." Some sixty years after it was written it still had at least some power to shock:

> *Our lady, if you can remember now,*
> *Seated on pearls and diademmed with gold,*
> *A girl of Nazareth, instruct me how*
> *To live a certain story that is told*
> *Of her, and many another bonny bride,*
> *Who heard God knocking softly in the night*
> *And slipped in silence from a husband's side.*
> *And teach my body how to give delight*
> *But, Lady, after you have taught me this,*
> *Tell me how, when the long farewells were said,*

And heavy on your mouth clung love's last kiss,
You made your way back into Joseph's bed?
Did you console him with a gentle lie,
Or turn your face against the wall and cry?

I FINALLY CAME TO GRIPS with my mother's sonnets on a witheringly hot day in mid-July. It was nearly a hundred degrees Fahrenheit and the heat pressed in like a live thing, claustrophobic and insistent. What was I to make of this poetry? Her language was precise and often splendid. She had a wonderful feel for the pentameter line, and she handled rhythms well. Her imagery was often arresting. She speaks, in one sonnet, of "the drills of age that do their quiet work of havoc and corruption and decay"; in another she begs, "Take back the voided beauty of the sun." In another she speaks in the voice of a woman standing in her doorway addressing passing pilgrims, telling them of her own bitter journey back from love:

Then I shall tell them just how dear was bought
My brief hour's looking on the sovereign's face . . .
How first one paid a heart into his hand,
And, having seen, was starved out from his land.

There were echoes of Tennyson, Matthew Arnold, James Russell Lowell, and of course Shakespeare, but not even a hint of Pound, Eliot, or Stevens. In an era of creative reinvention of poetry she experimented not at all; she was creating Grecian urns. She could not have been unaware of the modern rebellion against the classics. It almost seemed as if my mother had deliberately entered a temple of erudite Victorianism like a sanctuary and closed the door behind her. But the voice at the center of the poems was hardly a Victorian: she was full of passion and sexuality, and a vibrant, irrepressible sense of herself. Why didn't she come out and say what she had to say in American English?

"Miracle in Dust" comprised by far the largest number of sonnets, all of them classically Shakespearean in form. The title referred to mortality, to the human "dust" that is so fleetingly and miraculously imbued with life:

> And yet of all that I have loved and ceased
> To love, I think I yearned and suffered most
> Not for the god who left me unappeased,
> Not for the moon on whom my tears were lost,
> But for such dust as must be had in haste
> Before a wind blows and it is effaced.

Generally the sonnet sequence charts the downward trajectory of a disintegrating love affair. But it is also a moral and spiritual journey of false hope, disillusionment, death and rebirth. She dedicated it to her father. I couldn't help but feel that the Exalted Ruler of the Elks Club and pillar of the Republican establishment would have been shocked by much of what he read. Apart from the eroticism, it was sometimes—and deliberately, it seemed to me—masculine in its repeated imagery of combat and confrontation and blood. At the same time the mother I was searching for in these past poems was, I could also see, a woman of great tenderness, who delighted in earthly pleasure but who also possessed an almost antique sense of personal honor and dignity, as well as frightening vengefulness. I was awed at times by her consciousness of her own strength and indominable spirit. Behind the medieval imagery and the sometimes archaic syntax there lay extraordinarily fierce emotion: love to the point of obsession and beyond, raw despair, rage and, to my mind, transcendance. In spite of what I had read in her notes to Catherine Smith, the erotic boldness of some of her sonnets at first made me cringe. Yet when I was a child she had always been remarkably open in her attitude toward sex, free in her speech about it and about the body, and contemptuous of puritan mores. I was not so much discovering a new mother in the sonnets as I was being reminded of one whom I had, in a sense, bowdlerized and sanctified, stripped of her sexuality.

The poet's lover is introduced in the first sonnet in the guise of a monk. He is already, and remains throughout the cycle, mostly beyond reach, entombed in a mirage of otherworldly concerns. In one sonnet, she writes:

> *Does he not know that fastings are but coins*
> *Which bribed the angels in a lost god's age?*
> *Shall all the power of his mighty loins*
> *Be wasted in an inland hermitage?*
> *Or shall I drag him back upon the shores*
> *To hunt the thunders that the deep sea roars?*

She glories in her own passion, celebrates it, drives it like a galloping steed:

> *Saddle me. Urge me with the spur and whip.*
> *Ride me in harness up and down the earth. . . .*

The affair seems to be a furtive one of public silences, sidelong glances, nervous assignations. She is increasingly ashamed of her "scared eyes" and "muffled feet," and of "how he makes my breast/a vessel fit for cowardice and deceit." Increasingly frustration turns into bitterness, and bitterness into despair. Eventually her obsession has become corrosive, a worm "who eats his tunnels in the healthy stem." She warns ferociously:

> *You would not laugh or smile again in life*
> *If you could know the peril in which you stood*
> *When I have longed to end you with a knife*
> *Or see a dog's tongue reddened in your blood.*

The cycle ends on a note of realism and self-acceptance, with a sense of human proportion that has finally outweighed all the buffeting emotions that have gone before: "Now and forever let the air belong/To gods and eagles . . ."

. . . And I no more
Am envious of the nomad bird who springs
To mock or challenge from a naked tor.
I walk the earth as if it were most sweet
To dwell these humble leagues below the sun
And go with those grown patient of their feet,
Whom flight eluded or whose flight is done.
Nor shall I leave this world of vanquished crowds
For any lonely conquest of the clouds.

Reading this last sonnet, I thought how, all the years I was growing up, my mother must have wondered and worried about me: *Has*
he an eagle's pinons? Will he soar? So often she had pushed and
tugged at my shyness and reserve as a child, trying to pry me out of
the solitude that seemed natural to me and into which I tended to slip
without noticing. Because of her, all my life I had wrestled with the
impulse to draw away from the world into myself. It was what I had
struggled with in the middle of the river in Burma, the desire to turn
away from danger and from what it hurt to see, and away from the
moral imperative to connect. I had done my best not to fall short, not
to fail her, and for the most part I had succeeded. But I was uncomfortably reminded that like the antiquarian in her sonnets, I, too, was
in love with a phantom in a tomb.

An obvious question nagged at me: who was her mysterious
lover? It was possible, of course, that he was a composite of one or
more people—an old boyfriend, an adored scholar, a bit of Christ
(the gaunt monastic image, the otherworldliness), and even her father, in some of the poems unattainable, sexless, dead cold. But I had
to believe that the cycle was rooted in some actual experience. His
physical appearance seemed fairly clear. He had a "lean" face with
"brooding" brows, "long brown eyes," and dark hair. He was tall, or
at least considerably taller than my mother: she had to look at him
with her face "upraised." From several fairly transparent allusions in
the sonnets I deduced that he was married. He was clearly someone

whom she saw with some regularity, a man of refined sensibility, and someone who she felt had elevated, even ennobled, her aspirations:

> *My dreams that were a tavern, driving trade*
> *With clowns who shadowed possibility,*
> *Are now a marble tower by the sea*
> *Among whose fluid columns flash and fade*
> *The streaming purple and the lordly face*
> *Of one who stooped not to that other place.*

Although Lionel Casson could not remember any man who fit the role, he must have been someone she knew at NYU, almost certainly a member of the Classics Department or an archaeologist, a man more attracted to "a papyrus with a faded line" and "time-cracked slabs" and "hieroglyphs on crumbled walls" than to "warm white flesh." I went to the NYU archives on the tenth floor of the Bobst Library on Washington Square and asked for all the yearbooks from the early and mid-1930s. I scanned the faces of the senior faculty of the Classics Department. There was only one woman, Catherine Ruth Smith. None of the men seemed to fit the image of the man in the sonnets.

There was, of course, Casper Kraemer, the chairman. In many respects he seemed the most likely candidate. A departmental photograph taken of him in 1930 showed a bespectacled man with sly, humorous eyes behind horn-rimmed glasses, a well-modeled symmetrical face, a wide forehead, and a slight, whimsical smile on narrow lips. Kraemer had personally supervised the translation of many of the papyri. My mother was his private secretary, and he had taken a special interest in her. Was that only for her acute intellect and her ability to type perfectly in Greek? Beyond that, however, Kraemer's warmth and extroversion and spiritedness simply didn't square with the inhibited, sterile man of the sonnets. On the other hand, I knew from a longtime friend and colleague of Kraemer's that he was unhappily married and that he was "something of a ladies' man." The friend, a retired professor now in his nineties told me, "If your mother was attractive, I think he would have made it clear to her that he would not reject an advance out of hand."

THE PAPYRI that my mother worked on are now part of the collection of the Pierpont Morgan Library on East Thirty-sixth Street in Manhattan. Sitting in its cloistered, oak-panneled quietude one afternoon, I felt an almost erotic sense of the riches in manuscripts and art that the financier had hoarded lying somewhere far beneath my feet in vaults cut deep into the city's bedrock. The Nessana Papyri, as they are known, were discovered by a wealthy amateur scholar named Harris D. Colt in the early 1930s in the ruins of a sixth-century A.D. Byzantine frontier post in the Negev. Most were written in various forms of late-classical Greek, in which my mother was expert, and a few in Arabic. Casper Kraemer had convinced Colt to lend them to the department for translation and eventual publication, which was not completed until the 1950s, a few years before Kraemer's death.

The papyri were delivered to me between panes of glass taped together at the edges, some of them perhaps even by my mother's own hand when she was Kraemer's assistant. Few of the fragments were more than a couple of inches square, and many no bigger than a postage stamp or fingernail. Lines faded into oblivion, words disintegrated, letters dissolved into enigmatic shapes that communicated nothing at all. In the ruined fabric I made out the shadow of a Greek phrase: "ΑΚΟΥC . . . ΚΑΙ . . ." and then "ΕΚΤωΝ . . . ΑΝΑΓ . . ." and then "ΓΙΟC.ΑΝΑCΤΑΓ . . ." It was something about a son. She would have sorted these fragments like a jigsaw puzzle most of whose pieces were missing, spending days studying a few strokes of an ancient stylus, looking for correspondences in penmanship, searching for the missing bit of an omega or an omicron, letters that she would painstakingly match and align according to the grain of the disintegrating papyrus. *How strange that we should meet here in this silent room, joined together by these pedestrian fragments of forgotten lives. Your eyes, like mine now, followed the scribe's slanting hand,*

leaping over these same lacunae, struggling to make sense of these is-
lands of shattered words. The scraps spoke mostly of unpaid taxes,
the sale of some fig trees, an inheritance, a levy of camels, wheat req-
uisitioned for the Byzantine army. Trying to make sense of them was
like trying to piece together my mother's life itself from its half-legi-
ble shreds, a story more lacuna than text that seemed as remote and
irrevocable as these enigmatic messages from a world that ended thirteen hundred years ago. Depressed at how much I could never know,
I stared at the blank spaces where the papyrus had broken away, and
I felt a sudden surge of sadness, realizing that she had left me with no
key to her text and that I had lost her, as surely as these forgotten
Palestinians were lost, to the infinite nothingness where she had gone.

4

By THE END of 1936 my mother was poised to embark on a literary
career. She had the ability, the command of language and the imagi-
native sensibility to become a serious poet. She had completed two
ambitious cycles of sonnets, apparently with the idea of publishing
them as books. In February one of her sonnets had been published in
the *New York Times* and several more were soon to be published in
Britain. The poet Stephen Vincent Benét had given her encouragement. She was planning a novel based on the Odyssey. She had a se-
cure job among congenial colleagues in the Classics Department. She
had time to write. It seemed an ideal situation. All her work since
high school had led up to this point. And then she suddenly stopped
writing. There were, it was true, some later poems, and they were always skillfully composed, but there was nothing like the complexity
of her sonnet cycles. Poetry was clearly no longer at the center of her
life. What happened?

"I haven't told you the most interesting thing yet," Lionel Casson
said to me over the phone. His controlled voice was redolent with the
barely suppressed excitement of a man about to divulge a secret that
he had kept for more than sixty years. "LaVerne was an active mem-

ber of the Communist Party. It was all covert, all hush-hush. She tried
to recruit me. She was passionate about doing good for people. She
always talked about communism in terms of helping the poor and op-
pressed. I remember her saying, 'This is the only party that is trying
to do that.' " Casson was unswayed. "I was a young cynic. I thought
it was promising far too much. But I know that she was appreciated
as a very active and devoted worker."

In the 1950s Americans did not chatter to their children about a
Communist past, and by the time of her tenure as director of the Association on American Indian Affairs she was an anti-Communist, in
the mold of a Hubert Humphrey or an Adlai Stevenson, and saw vigorous liberalism and commitment to civil rights and social reform as
the most effective weapons against communism's appeal. "The Communists' most effective opponents are not those who excuse [democ-
racy] for not working, but those who make it work," she wrote in
1960 in a letter to the board members of the Association on American Indian Affairs concerning Communist attempts to foment unrest
among the tribes. Nevertheless, what Casson told me was not a complete surprise. After my mother's death one day I came upon a stray
volume from Lenin's *Collected Works* in the attic of the house on
Mayfair Road. When I asked my father about it, he said, "Yeah, we
used to study dialectical materialism and all that." I recognized it
then as an experience that he had sealed up and discarded, and one
that, like so much else, he did not think deserved explanation. He
added a little more, but only a little, in a short memoir that he composed before his death in 1992. He described meeting my mother in
1937 and evenings spent talking politics on the porch of the Madigans' home. She had become interested in the Communist Party
through friends at NYU. "Eventually her interest spurred us to consider joining. We had meetings, we had talks. The leader would talk
for two hours about the glories of Communism and what we could
do to promote it here." Where had her radicalism come from? Whatever there may once have been among her papers that might have told
me was now gone. There was not the slightest hint in all her poetry
of someone on a trajectory toward the radical Left. If anything, the

sonnets were remarkable for their unapologetic classicism, their seeming rejection of anything smacking of the modern.

I began to read about the shifts and turns of Communist Party policy in the 1930s, searching for clues. In 1935 the Party made it much easier for intellectuals who were uneasy with doctrinaire Stalinism to become members. Up to then the Party had called stridently for the revolutionary overthrow of capitalism, the establishment of a Socialist Soviet Republic in the United States, and the complete abolition of classes; it attacked FDR as a "fascist" and federal jobs efforts as "enslavement programs," while denouncing even democratic socialists and reformist trade unions as "social fascists," with whom no compromise was possible. In that year, however, a crucial change in policy occurred when Moscow decided to seek new allies for the long-term effort to counter the threat of real fascism. The resulting policy, labeled the Popular Front, called for cooperation with socialists, non-Communist trade unions, and even liberals. Ernest Hemingway, W. H. Auden, Thomas Mann, and many other intellectuals of their stature lent their names to communist causes; as the novelist John O'Hara put it, "All the best people followed the party line." Shedding revolutionary rhetoric, at least in public, the Party embraced reforms like universal social security, health insurance, the construction of low-rent housing, more schools, hospitals, and parks, free higher education, debt relief for farmers, and—virtually alone among political parties at that time—total racial equality, as well as collective security against fascism. American Communists were directed to halt their attacks on Roosevelt and the New Deal, while party ideologues embraced "native radicals" like Tom Paine, Thomas Jefferson, and John Brown. Communist Party bands played "Yankee Doodle" on rostrums festooned with the Stars and Stripes. Party literature argued that the Declaration of Independence was a forerunner of the Communist Manifesto and likened Benedict Arnold to Stalin's nemesis Leon Trotsky. CPUSA Chairman Earl Browder asserted meaningfully that George Washington had favored a one-party state. The strategy worked. In May 1935 the Party had thirty-four thousand members; fifteen months later, with the Popular Front under way, it numbered forty-three thousand, and by 1939 it could claim a hundred thousand. One of them was my mother.

It appears from my father's memoir that he and my mother joined the Party sometime in 1937. It is less clear when they left it. He writes, "Many abandoned the Party on the news of the non-aggression pact with Hitler [in August of 1939]. Some rejoined when the invasion occurred [of the Soviet Union, in June 1941]. We did not. By this time, LaVerne was working for the Army." In fact, my mother was not hired by the War Relocation Authority, then part of the United States Army, until 1942. It seems to me likely that she and Harold began to separate from the Party after the infamous 1939 pact ("Pact Smashed Axis," the *Daily Worker* preposterously proclaimed at the time) but did in fact renew their membership after Hitler's attack on Russia, and then withdrew completely after my mother joined the WRA. "That was before the McCarthy era," my father writes, "but there was a McCarthyist feel in the air all around government offices, despite the fact that Russia was our ally. So that's when we left." In all, they may have been involved with the Party for as long as five years.

In 1937 the whole atmosphere at NYU was politically charged. A poll of undergraduates taken that year found that large majorities believed that the nation was headed toward public ownership, and that a fascist takeover of the United States was possible. (The same poll bafflingly voted the right-wing Charles Lindbergh the "greatest American personality of all time" and Wallis Simpson the "greatest living woman.") Almost every academic department had a definite political orientation. The Philosophy Department was Trotskyist, although its chairman, Sidney Hook, would eventually evolve into one of the country's most outspoken anti-Communist intellectuals during the McCarthy period. All the senior members of the Classics Department, including Casper Kraemer, were known to be Republican. History was also reckoned as conservative, the German Department as Red, and so on.

I supposed, mistakenly as it turned out, that it would be relatively easy to find people who had known my mother in the Communist

Party. But death and the party's secretiveness, and perhaps my mother's own housecleaning, had almost completely erased her tracks. People tried to be helpful. A retired labor leader provided me with the names of several men and women who were active in the Young Communist League at NYU in the late 1930s and early 1940s, but they explained that in accordance with the party's cellular structure, its youth wing was organized separately from the faculty and staff units, to one of which my mother probably belonged, and that there had been little or no contact between them. A friend led me to the daughter of a famous editor of the *Daily Worker*. She introduced me to her father's surviving friends, but none had worked with party units at NYU. Another friend gave me the phone number of an elderly English professor who, she thought, had taught at NYU. When I got no answer, I called back my friend, who checked and then told me with distress that the professor had just died. I managed to trace a writer named Ben Burns, who was a student at NYU in the early 1930s and later a sports writer for the *Daily Worker*, and who told me that even those who met my mother very likely never knew her name or who she really was. "You only knew about your close friends and people in your own unit. Nobody flaunted Party membership. If you had any kind of vulnerability, you had to keep your membership secret. You'd meet people socially but you'd never ask whether someone was in the Party. People were afraid of losing their jobs."

In order to join the Communist Party, it was necessary for my mother to have a sponsor who was already a Party member, "a Virgil to her Dante," to use one of her favorite analogies. He, or she, could not have belonged to the Classics Department. According to Casson, she was the only radical there. However, the English Department, in which she had taken her bachelor's degree, was considered a Communist stronghold: among others, Harvard-trained Edwin Berry Burgum, a nationally known Marxist literary critic and the cofounder, along with the eminent medievalist and linguist Margaret Schlauch, of the influential pro-Communist journal *Science and Society*; poetry professor Eda Lou Walton was an off-again, on-again member of the Party; Samuel Sillen, a former editor of a student literary magazine for which my mother wrote and now a professor, was also the book review editor for the the Communist Party monthly magazine *New Masses*.

There was not much material in NYU's archives on Communist activity at the school, with a single important exception. In 1949, NYU became the first private university in the United States to cooperate in the gathering national hunt for Communists in high places when the university's president invited the Senate Subcommittee on Internal Security to investigate the loyalty of members of its faculty. Edwin Berry Burgum was the committee's first and most prominent target. He was eventually cited for contempt of Congress for refusing to answer questions regarding his Communist affiliations, fired by the university, and jailed in 1953. He died in 1975. I looked him up in old university bulletins from the 1930s. He had taught courses on advanced composition, critical writing, nineteenth-century English thought, Victorian prose. None of these was a particular interest of my mother. However—my eye jumped to the words—in the early 1930s he had supervised the English honors program and must therefore have overseen, if not also personally advised, her two years of independent study.

Many of the yellowing clips and manifestos in Burgum's file also mentioned Margaret Schlauch. Rather than face investigation herself, Schlauch abruptly left for Poland in 1951, where she was named chairman of the English Department at the University of Warsaw and where she died in 1985. Checking the old bulletins, I saw that in the 1930s Schlauch had taught courses in the fiction of the Middle Ages—the great Norse sagas, the grail cycle, the Arthurian legends—as well as Chaucer, Anglo-Saxon, and Middle English literature. I knew, because my mother talked often about it, that she had studied most of these subjects. I still have the edition of Chaucer with Rockwell Kent's magnificent woodcuts that she bought in 1934 and that she would sometimes pull out and read to me with great vividness when I was young. I can still hear her voice lovingly caress the old words. Schlauch also taught linguistics, including a course on the

Indo-European languages. My mother once wryly told me how comparing the grammar of ancient Greek and Latin, Persian and Sanskrit, she thought that she had discovered an original Indo-European "mother tongue," only to be informed by her professor that such an ur-language had already been postulated in the last century by German scholars. That professor could only have been Margaret Schlauch. Her teaching probably influenced the Arthurian motifs and imagery of my mother's sonnets, and she may well have served as her mentor during the writing of them. No one but Schlauch, moreover, could have supervised my mother's translation of the Bodleian manuscript, the culminating effort of her honors work.

The English Department preserves a file of letters that Schlauch wrote to successive chairmen from the early 1920s up to and after her defection in 1951. They are small works of art in their own right, full of insight, wit, and colorful description. Several report on a summer in Iceland learning Old Norse, others on a trip to Mexico to compile the first dictionary of the Aztec language; in one she watches Hitler's abortive 1923 putsch from the window of her pension in Munich, and in another she describes life in Moscow collecting Russian folk tales during the terrible famine of 1932. "Although my hosts might have nothing more to offer by way of refreshments than tea, black bread and sliced cucumber, there was always lots of varied conversation and cross-examination. . . ." There was no mention of my mother in any of the letters. But I photocopied some of them and at home compared her distinctive, compact script to the hand-written comments that were in the margins of the original draft of the sonnets: it was the same.

Photographs of Schlauch show a slender woman with an affable, but conspicuously homely, doughy-featured face. She was recognized as one of the most inspiring teachers in the university, and in spite of a well-known hostility to the Catholic Church, she was often seen in the halls trailing a bevy of nuns enthralled by her elucidation of the medieval mind. May Katz, a close friend of Schlauch who visited her many times during her exile in Poland, and who knew her for decades as a fellow member of the CPUSA described her to me as "a real party stalwart." But there was clearly something more to Schlauch than Marxist cliché. Her scholarship was by all accounts impeccable. Even Katz described her with a kind of hard-bitten respect as "more or less independent and individualistic," a measure of remarkable character in the Stalinist Party of the 1930s and 1940s. She had even dared to write critically about Stalin's own crackbrained ideas on linguistics, a gesture of defiance for which, Katz said, she suffered the harshest attacks within closed Party circles.

I saw how my mother would have been drawn to a woman like this, as earlier she had been to Catherine Ruth Smith, by the older woman's intellectualism and originality, and her brilliant success in the male world of the university. Schlauch was, in fact, the first woman to be named a full professor at NYU. In contrast to Smith's religiosity, Schlauch—who was Irish on her mother's side—shared my mother's rejection of the Catholic Church. Where Smith buried herself in lofty, bloodless aestheticism, Schlauch was gregarious and self-confident, a world traveler, living proof that it was possible for a woman both to be scholarly and to take a hand in shaping the muddy uncertainties of modern life. Perhaps it was only coincidence, but by 1936 my mother's handwriting had lost its girlish loopiness and become compact and tense, like a spring: it had come to resemble Schlauch's own.

"JOINING THE PARTY was usually a very slow process," Morris Schappes told me. Schappes is probably the most prominent veteran of the Communist Party in the 1930s still living in New York City. Since the 1940s Schappes has edited a magazine called *Jewish Currents* from a nest of tiny offices in an old building overlooking Union Square, where Communists turned out by the hundreds of thousands for rallies in the 1930s. "May Day was a huge affair, not like the skimpy affair they have today," Schappes said. "They had them right down there." He tilted his head toward the Square. "It would be full of people." I tried to picture my mother there, a tiny figure wedged among the marching stevedores and machinists and garment workers. Now, on a warm spring day, the plinking of a West Indian steel band wafted up from the Square, gaily infusing the strange twilight of the office, where nothing—metal shelving, battered desks, oak cabinets, bare wood floors scraped by many decades of heavy wooden chairs—seemed to have been altered for decades. At ninety, Schappes wore heavy black-rimmed glasses, and tufts of white hair bushed from beneath the fedora that he wore even indoors.

Schappes, who once taught English at the City College of New York, was a founder of the Communist-controlled College Teacher's Union whose leaders at NYU were (no surprise, really) Edwin Berry Burgum and Margaret Schlauch. He was an intimate of the senior Party leaders of the day and taught ideology at the Party's school on East Thirteenth Street after he was fired by CCNY for Communist activity. Originally a Communist Party publication, *Jewish Currents* followed Schappes's own drift away from the Party and was now an independent socialist magazine reporting mainly on Israeli politics. Disappointingly, he knew nothing about my mother, but he did explain how as a professor he had influenced students in much the way that Burgum and Schlauch might have influenced my mother. "I felt a political obligation to radicalize people," he told me, pale fingers hovering and fluttering like small white birds in front of his mouth as he spoke. "I'd have to be impressed by the person's ability to influence other people in a radical direction, and I'd have to convey that to the Party leader of the unit that he was to join. I'd base this not only on conversations but also on joint action. Had he gone with me to demonstrations? Had he shouted the slogans that we shouted? Probably your mother shared the views of her teacher, and there was a kind of symbiosis. One day Schlauch might have said, "LaVerne, you might be interested in meeting some people I know. . . .""

According to my father's memoir, there were fourteen or fifteen members in their cell. There was a plasterer, a machinist, a young veteran of the Spanish Civil War, an Italian building superintendent. Meetings rotated among members' homes. Members were expected to buy copious amounts of books, pamphlets, magazines, and newspapers, which they were then required to resell. They were expected to be on call to distribute leaflets, to join picket lines, to collect money for Loyalist Spain, the Scottsboro Boys and any number of other causes, to take courses in ideology at the Workers' School at Party headquarters on East Thirteenth Street, to contact and influence potential recruits like Lionel Casson, and to report "intelligence" from their workplaces that might prove of use to the Party. Said Schappes, "The Party would want her to promote and spread the Party's ideas, whatever the current program was at the time."

The years of my parents' membership in the Communist Party saw some of the worst crimes perpetrated by Stalin against the Russian people. Famine induced by disasterous Soviet agricultural policies had driven millions to starvation. In some areas of the Ukraine peasants resorted to eating insects and earthworms and to cannibalism. Millions of the most productive farmers were herded into labor camps. Even as Earl Browder was proclaiming that "Communism is twentieth-century Americanism," Stalin was savagely purging the ranks of his own followers. Of the nineteen hundred and sixty-six delegates who had attended the 1934 Communist Party Congress eleven hundred and eight had been shot by the time of the next congress in 1939. Similar slaughters took place at every level of the Party apparatus. In June 1937, about the time my mother probably became a Communist, the purges reached the Soviet military: all those commanding military districts were shot, along with about half of the hundred thousand members of the officer corps. By the end of the decade an estimated fourteen million had died from famine and terror, and another eight million were incarcerated in slave-labor camps, and of those, millions were eventually to die from abuse, malnutrition, and exposure. So horrific was the death rate that the 1937 census was suppressed and members of the census board were arrested for "treasonably exerting themselves to diminish the population of the USSR."

Although the Popular Front Policy pushed Stalinist doctrine into the shadows, basic Party doctrine did not change. Members were still required to support the catechism that was laid out in the 1935 *Manual of Organization*. It stated:

> The State is an instrument in the hands of the ruling class for suppressing the resistance of its class enemies. *In this respect* the dictatorship of the proletariat in no way differs, in essence, from the dictatorship of any other class, for the proletarian State is an instrument for the suppression of the bourgeoisie . . . [T]he dictatorship of the proletariat cannot be "complete" democracy, a democracy for *all,* for rich and poor alike; a dictatorship of the proletariat must be a State that is democratic *in a new way (for* the proletariat and the poor in general) and dictatorial *in a new way (against* the bourgeoisie) . . . Only under the dictatorship of the proletariat is real "freedom" for the exploited and real participation in the administration of the country by the proletarians and peasants possible.

The manual spent several pages reiterating the importance of unqualified obedience to one's superiors in the Party.

> We cannot imagine a discussion, for example, questioning the correctness of the leading role of the proletariat in the revolution, or the necessity for the proletarian dictatorship. We do not question the theory of the necessity for the forceful overthrow of capitalism. We do not question the correctness of the revolutionary theory of the class struggle laid down by Marx, Engels, Lenin, and Stalin. We do not question the counter-revolutionary nature of Trotskyism. . . . We do not question the political correctness of the decisions, resolutions, etc., of the Executive Committee of the [Communist International], of the Convention of the Party, or of the Central Committee after they are ratified. Otherwise, every under-cover agent of the bourgoisie and every sympathizer of the renegades would have an opportunity of continually raising their counter-revolutionary theories in the Units, Sections, etc., and make the members spend time and energy in discussing such ques-

tions, thus not only disrupting the work of the Party, but also creating confusion among the less experienced and trained elements of
the Party. (As a matter of fact, this is what enemies of the Party are
always trying to do in the name of "democracy.")

How could my mother, with her irrepressible curiosity and restless intellect, have accepted this? I would like to think that she simply laughed off the agitprop, like many liberals for whom it was
enough to know that the Party was the ally of the enemies of fascism.
But the fact is, in order to become a member, she had to believe what
the Party required or something pretty much like it, had to swear to
it, had to think that the future that it proclaimed was necessary and
just, and that she would want to live in it. "Only those who agree
with the program of the Communist Party and the C.I. can become
members of the Party," the manual bluntly stated.

Like most Americans, she may well have been unaware of the full
extent of Stalin's repression. What news did leak out was denied as
propaganda by Western Communists and by sympathetic intellectuals who wished for the great Soviet experiment to succeed. George
Bernard Shaw claimed to have seen not a single undernourished
person after a chauffeur-driven tour of the Ukraine. "Were they
padded?" he asked with intended wit. "Were their hollow cheeks dis-
tended by pieces of india rubber inside?" Even mainstream news reports often portrayed the Soviet Union as a country that was scoring
impressive achievements in industry and agriculture, increasing the
standard of living while maintaining full employment, expanding ed-
ucational opportunity and health facilities even as it stood alone
against the onset of fascism. Walter Duranty, the prize-winning
Moscow correspondent for the *New York Times* wrote glowingly of
May Day marchers who paraded with enthusiasm "because they are
proud of the new Russia they are building, the new Russia, whose
motto is 'all for all instead of each for each.' They are proud of it and
they love it, and are eager and willing to give hours of their leisure
for its glory."

The international situation also provided ample reason for politically concerned Americans to look hopefully toward the Soviet Union. Hitler had just annexed Austria. Mussolini had invaded Ethiopia. Democratic Spain was falling to a military revolt armed by Hitler and Mussolini. The Hitlerite German-American Bund was filling Madison Square Garden with its rallies. Nazi films were showing in a theater on East Eighty-Sixth Street. Catholic followers of the anti-Semitic radio priest Father Coughlin were beating up Jews in Times Square. Stanley Kauffmann recalled, "Fascism was going from success to success. It was petrifying. We felt that nothing could stop this monster. I had things thrown at me on the street because I was Jewish. It seemed hopeless, or rather that there was only one hope, the Soviet Union. We didn't want to believe any of the bad things about the Soviet Union because it was our only hope. Where was the United States? It was naïve in a world full of wolves. There were only those two choices—Communism or fascism."

But there surely must have been something more, a more personal motive, or a web of them, that was seamlessly interwoven with the intellectual concerns that so many shared about war in Europe and the spread of fascism. In the letter that my mother addressed to her board of directors about Communist activity among Indian tribes she wrote, "If a political science exists, it is axiomatic that a Communist can win a following only among people who have failed to find fulfillment under democracy. The Communist does not win over people by expounding Marxist theory. He does it by shouting more loudly than the people themselves the just demand that, he believes inwardly, the democracy will never satisfy. Merely exposing the Communist as a Communist will not turn the people against him, for they do not follow him because he is a Communist. They listen to him only because the democracy he hates has left a deep need of theirs unmet and will reject him for what he is only when the democracy has met the need and his hatred is seen to be unchanged."

What was the "inward need" that by 1937 was so strong that it propelled her into the Communist Party? For much of the decade, of course, she had watched her middle-class world collapse around her. Her own family had descended perilously close to penury. Poverty and the sense of a safe future denied must have worked on her. In addition, for reasons that were not yet clear to me, my mother came to identify in a deeply personal way with the victimized, the underprivileged and abused. "Women like gardens . . . trodden down, a footprint on the face, a bruised mouth and broken tooth," she had written cryptically in the notes for the unwritten novel. I thought of the terrified boy racing for his life past the house on Washington Street—*"Onion Ernie is a Jew!"*—leaving my mother with a feeling of helplessness so deep that telling me about it in the 1950s, the memory of it still filled her with shame. Beneath the surface romanticism of the sonnets I could see a dark substructure of catastrophe and rage, a narrative in which faith has been destroyed, the hollowness of authority revealed, idols toppled, and order reduced to desolation. So perhaps they reflected the apocalyptic aspect of her era after all. But where was she to go from these ruins? By becoming a Communist, she finally left helplessness behind in the doorway on Washington Street, as it were, becoming one with the terrified boy, as the boy in turn became her entire world under attack and threatened with destruction.

Had Margaret Schlauch hinted to her that the romantic distress that she expressed in the sonnets was selfish and indulgent, a facet of the decay of her class? *The world is falling apart everywhere while you spend your days deciphering lacunae in Byzantine manuscripts. How long can you keep it up? How can you justify it to yourself? Do you have a moral right to do nothing about the wreckage of the nation that lies all around you—you who, alone, in your high school motto, proclaimed justice to be the important thing? Do you owe nothing to the world more than poetry?* What room was there anymore for the classical sonnet? In the age of crisis, political irrelevance must finally have seemed evasive and immoral, an aesthetic collaboration with the forces of reaction. No writer in the twentieth century could afford to see himself any longer as "some sort of ornament on the pillars of society," as Dorothy Thompson, the most eminent woman journalist of her generation declared in a memorable speech to the International Pen Congress of writers and publishers. "The days are Doric. There is no room for ornament." This is, I suspect, precisely the way my mother would have thought of it.

And perhaps poetry had taught her to understand why poetry wasn't enough. Lovely as the sonnets were—like ancient bronze, like Flemish tapestry—only infrequently did the voice of a real flesh-and-blood twentieth-century woman break through. Her poetry almost never ventured beyond the personal pain; it never grappled with the larger, political implications of the self. Having abandoned Catholicism, she had turned to poetry as if in search of God, a god of aesthetic perfection but also a god who made room for human passion and for the needs of the flesh. But she carried in her heart more dreams and ideals, and more pain perhaps, than the poetry allowed her to express. She couldn't break free from the old rhetoric. Here she was, after all, sitting in the Classics Department—it would be hard to find a more conservative and traditional milieu—writing provocative poetry but within a form that was as rigid as the Catholic catechism. She needed a larger stage.

I can only guess at what legacy my mother's years in the Party left her: deepened concern for social justice and for minorities, some grasp of community organization, and possibly a belief that was to drive her until the end of her life, that politics was as essential to human fulfillment—or at least to her own—as beauty and love. I can see now that in fundamental ways my mother was a rebel. Her intellectualism was, at least in part, a rebellion against the Elks Club conventionality of middle-class life in Mount Vernon, and the unembarrassed sexuality of her poetry (despite its classical cadences) a rebellion against Catholic puritanism and the proprieties of her time. Then in the Communist Party she rebelled against the political and economic system that had destroyed her family's security, although she did so within a new orthodoxy that was as rigid as the form of the sonnet. Just why she left the Party will probably remain as much a mystery as why, precisely, she joined it. I have no reason to think that there was a dramatic break rather than a process of political osmosis, a gradual seeping away from Party doctrine back into the political mainstream. Perhaps—I can only guess at this—she realized that she was not temperamentally fitted for the Party, that the routine, the stifling of initiative, the flattening out of intellectual life, the secrecy that forced her to live in two worlds had finally ground her down, even as she came to recognize the self-serving dishonesty that infused the Party's promise.

5

IN THAT INTERESTING YEAR of 1937 two things came to my mother: Communism and her future husband. My father would remain with her, in some fashion, for the next twenty-five years. It was an improbable relationship that is even more difficult to explain than her leftism. There is a set of photos that records one of their first dates. A note says that they were taken at Cranberry Lake, a large pond, really, in a patch of woods near White Plains. In two of the pictures my mother is perched on a large rock and dressed in loose white trousers and a polo shirt with her pale hair tumbling over her shoulders. In the third, the most interesting one, she wears a bathing suit and smiles directly into the camera with uncharacteristic coyness. She cannot possibly know that the face behind the camera belongs to the man whom she will marry three years later. I have searched these pictures again and again, as if some message lay hidden there just for me, in this record of an afternoon so many years ago, on a day when Franco's planes were dive-bombing the suburbs of Madrid and Japanese columns were on the march across North China, something that would open to me the heart and mind of this familiar yet not familiar woman with the tumbling pale hair and provocative smile. *Who are you now? What do you fear, what desire? What is it you see in the man on the other side of the camera?*

I strain to see them beyond the broad empty plain of their deaths, young people still rushing toward life. I still can't really understand what drew them together, the poet and the mechanic. Although it's possible that men, at least marrying men, were uncomfortable with her intellectualism and independence in an era when, apart from

Thompson and Eleanor Roosevelt and the ruthless Clare Booth Luce, autonomous women were an anomaly, still, she was beautiful, brilliant, witty, well-liked by everyone who remembers her, and she should have had her pick of suitors. Surely Maddy, who had set her heart on a doctor for her daughter, who had sacrificed so much to see that she got through college during the Depression's worst years, must have had in mind someone of loftier station and greater ambition than this likable telephone lineman who, though he had a taste for Shakespeare, lacked even a high-school education. Was marrying my father another rebellion, more defiance of what was expected?

I also wondered if it could have been Communism that had brought them together. My father's memoir made their introduction to the Party sound casual and superficial. To Lionel Casson, however, my mother already seemed deeply committed to the Party when she tried to recruit him "in 1937 or 1938." Was she already a secret member of the Party when she met my father? Was he a recruit, initially a political rather than a romantic conquest? This would not have seemed like cynicism to a loyal Party member but rather like the bestowal of political enlightenment. Harold was, after all, a worker, the genuine article, a man with calloused hands; she, the intellectual, would lead him into the charmed circle of historical grace. It's possible that it happened this way. Yet it seems unlike her, who so highly valued plain speaking and personal honesty.

It may also be that I have failed to give my father enough credit. Certainly he was not a glamorous man, hardly the sort who would inspire a woman to flights of poetry. Pictures of him from the late 1930s show a slim man, well-proportioned, with a mischievous smile hovering at the corners of his lips. He had a certain modest charm and a wry sense of humor. His mechanical talent may well have appealed to my mother: he knew about *things*. ("I found an engine in a sand heap in the Bronx," he relates in his memoir. "I broke it down to the last screw and bolt; replaced the piston rings, ground the valves and seats and removed the carbon. . . .") Although he had little formal education himself, he admired erudition, and he was driven neither by personal ambition nor social conventions that might have demanded that my mother sacrifice her own career. (In the late 1930s a majority of states still had laws prohibiting the employment of married women, and a 1938 poll that asked both men and women "Do you approve of a married woman earning money in business or industry if she has a husband capable of supporting her?" found that eighty-two percent replied in the negative.) Harold also had integrity: I never knew him to lie or to trim the truth in hope of gaining an advantage. He was steady, reliable, unsurprising, safe.

MY FATHER WAS BORN in 1907 in North Bergen, New Jersey, in a frame row house which, his memoir remarks with his characteristic irony, "still does not have a plaque on it." His mother died during his first year; his father, Charles, a walrus-mustached immigrant from Lofoten and a bookkeeper for a Manhattan textile firm, in accordance with Norwegian custom of the time, married the dead woman's sister, Anna. When my father was a year old, they moved to a cold-water railroad flat in Brooklyn, where my father would spend most of his youth. A sister, Dorothy, was born in 1910, and then a brother, Arnie, in 1917.

Although my father loved to read, he was an indifferent student. Inexplicably—or at least without any explanation in his memoir—he began to play hooky, gradually drifting away from school, exploring railway yards and riding the elevated lines to far parts of the city. "By this time Pop knew that I would probably not finish high school so he found a job for me," first as an office boy for a company that manufactured camphor and beeswax candles, and then as a file clerk for the Home Insurance Company near Wall Street. Then he falls in love with electronics and builds his first radio. "There was a great sense of accomplishment when I acquired a pair of earphones, tickled the detector crystal with the cat's whisker, turned the knob and heard the announcer on WJZ—my first reception." The rest of his working life would be tied to new, increasingly standardized technologies that mystified people of his parents' generation but that were soon to become indispensible parts of American life.

In 1927, the well-being of his family was rudely shattered when Charles Bordewich lost his job, and with it his self-confidence. Unable to keep up the mortgage payments, he lost the family home. When my grandfather worked after that, which wasn't often, he peddled electric blankets door to door, and sometimes rented setups for illicit drinkers at hotels during Prohibition. Although my father does not say so in his memoir, his father's failure hurt him deeply, leaving a sense of shame and embarrassment that lingered for years, and that perhaps accounted for his lifelong conviction that having a job, almost any job, and showing up for it on time was a defining measure of a man's virtue.

The family moved north to a rented house in White Plains, in Westchester, where a neighbor suggests that my father apply for a job with the New York Telephone Company. "Overnight, I ceased to be a commuter and a white collar worker. I had been afflicted with that dreadful disease which affected white-collardom. We were a cut or two above blue collar workers. Business managers cultivated this attitude for, like religion, it kept the natives from becoming restless." He soon became a field dispatcher with his own crew and was earning forty dollars per week, "a munificent sum." From this point on, my father's memoir becomes increasingly caught up in the discussion of technological change, of equipment and its function, as if in discovering the talent that would enable him to make a decent living while the rest of the country was falling out of work, he lost the capacity to see himself, or at least to describe himself. The more complex his life, the less he has to say.

There is a long courtship—six years—followed by a marriage of just six months to a young woman who works for the telephone company. "She was mousy, with no intellectual interests. She could play piano, her sole effort being 'To a Wild Rose.' " After the wedding they drive to the Adirondacks. "That honeymoon trip was surely an indicator that the marriage would not be forever." Peculiarly, or perhaps predictably, he says nothing about what happened between him and his bride on this trip. What he writes about instead is the Model A Ford he drove, and the engine he has picked out of a junkyard and

rebuilt. Then he talks about the two Chevys that he owned before the
Model A, and how between them he has replaced seven rear axles,
two differentials and a transmission. "There is no way of remembering how many spark plugs, vacuum tanks (predecessor of the fuel
pump), tires etc. were installed at one time or another." It is as if tires
and compressors and leaf springs took the place of emotions, and the
hardware of automobiles the place of the mechanics of human rela-
tionships, as if he found in the fine calibration of steel gaskets, the uncertain firing of spark plugs, the pulse of a compressor a clarity and
precision that he could not find, and perhaps could not even care
about, in the boundaries between human beings, and in the disturbing stresses of love and distrust, and the uncertainty of human
motives.

"I am convinced that I married B. more because of her family
than any other reason," he wrote. "I liked them, but that was not
enough to keep us together. One afternoon we had the customary argument. I packed everything that was mine, clothes, a couple of
books, and left her. This was strictly 'spur of the moment.' Since I
was then working out of an office in Mount Vernon, I decided that I
might as well locate there, drove down, picked up a paper and
checked the possibilities. I went past two 'for rent' locations without
stopping." The third turned out to be the Madigan house on Washington Street. "Maddy and I had quite a conversation during which I
was given the impression of Southern gentility fallen on hard times
because of crooked bankers. So, I rented a good room at $5.00 a
week with parking in the driveway."

In the evenings, there were many good conversations on the
Madigans' front porch, and sometimes on the more intimate back
porch. "We all liked a drink so it was natural for me to bring a bottle to the scene occasionally," my father recalled. Sometimes he took
a bucket to a nearby bar and had it filled with beer, and they drank
it as they read Shakespeare aloud with one or two of my mother's
friends from NYU. I like this scene. I like the image of my parents together among friends, with that bucket of beer, a quaint, antique
touch, happy in each other's company. The intricate Shakespearean

English coils and springs on their tongues. Marriage, the war, disappointment and death are still in the future, still out of sight. My mother is at the precise midpoint of her life, still filled with potential, without the slightest inkling of the future that lies in front of her.

MY MOTHER AND FATHER decided to marry as soon as his divorce from his first wife came through, which it finally did in December 1940. Neither of them—probably Communist Party members at the time—wanted to be married in a church. Therefore an elaborate "elopement" was arranged as a fiction to protect them from the disapproval, or at least the hurt feelings, of my mother's Catholic relatives. The nearest place they could wed without time-consuming formalities was Fredericksburg, Virginia. They traveled there by train, most of the way through a blizzard, managing to arrive at the Fredericksburg registrar's office only minutes before closing time. They planned to spend their wedding night in Fredericksburg, but discovered to their dismay that Virginia was a dry state. "We dashed across the street to see if we could get a train back to Washington. We could, we did, and wound up at the Harrington Hotel near Union Station. After a couple of drinks and a good dinner we were ready to turn in. The wedding night was not really satisfactory. Whether it was due to the day's frustrations or that we were not used to each other, I do not know. However, when we got home to Mount Vernon we did get properly sorted out."

MY PARENTS lived for the first year of their marriage in a corner apartment on South Fourth Street in Mount Vernon. Sometime that year Maddy sold the house on Washington Street. Did my mother miss the home that had enfolded her childhood, where her father had died, where she had written her sonnets, where she had met and been courted by her new husband? There is nothing that tells me how she felt, or if she felt anything at all, whether she grieved for the house, or whether she willingly relinquished its cargo of memory with relief, abandoning it as the symbol of the spent past as she embarked on married life. Perhaps she and Maddy were simply relieved to get a decent price for it in the improving housing market that came with the end of the Depression. In November 1941 my parents and Maddy left Mount Vernon for good to be close to my mother's job at NYU, moving into the city to an apartment at 235 Wooster Street, a block south of Washington Square Park.

It was a good time to be a New Yorker. Despite a decade of economic depression, in the early 1940s New York was approaching the apogee of its glamour as a city of the world, radiating prosperity while the great cities of Europe, one by one, were engulfed by war. The roof gardens at Rockefeller Center claimed to be four times the size of the hanging gardens of Babylon. New York's subway was the world's fastest, the George Washington Bridge was the earth's second-largest, and the Empire State Building—my mother worked there in the offices of the War Relocation Authority for much of the Second World War—was the tallest building. From all over occupied Europe displaced artists, writers, and thinkers were flocking into Manhattan and transforming New York's cultural life in ways that would resonate for decades to come. Visitors to New York found it a welcoming place. "Wherever the stranger goes in New York he will find people who really seem glad to meet him, and the appearance of rush is readily interrupted by the slightest excuse for showing hospitality," the British photographer Cecil Beaton wrote after an extended residence in the city in the late 1930s. He admired New Yorkers' sense of easy decorum. Girls in the middle-class homes were taught to curtsey to guests. Men removed their hats when women entered an elevator. Skirts were worn discreetly low on the calf, trousers were rarely seen on women, and blue jeans were something that only laborers wore. The streets were, for the most part, so safe that on merciless summer nights—in that age before air conditioning—New Yorkers by the tens of thousands slept outdoors on fire escapes and rooftops, and in the parks. In 1945, a representative year as far as crime is concerned, there would be only one hundred eighty-four reported murders, roughly one-tenth the number reported today in a city whose population has remained unchanged at about seven and a half million. A poll taken the same year would find that ninety percent of New Yorkers considered themselves happy.

Wooster Street was then considered part of Little Italy rather than Greenwich Village proper. The surrounding streets had something of the feel of an immigrant neighborhood, an ambience that pleased my mother, who enjoyed using her fluent Italian. She and my father liked to eat at the Grand Ticino and the Skaska, and the Brevoort Café, and the Sheridan Tavern, and at a place on the corner of West Eighth Street where, my father notes in his memoir, they once won a bottle of champagne and "we usually had as many free drinks as we paid for." Zero the dog went everywhere with them and drank whiskey from a dish. Sometimes in the Minetta Tavern my father bought shots for eccentric Joe Gould, who would sometimes recite a poem in what he said was the language of the seagulls. Occasionally they drank in the San Remo, a popular bar on MacDougal Street where they would have rubbed shoulders with the young Larry Rivers, John Cage, and Jackson Pollock and the still younger Allen Ginsberg and Jack Kerouac.

Their world begins to become recognizable to me now, almost my own. In my father's photos of the apartment on Wooster Street I see the furniture that will become the landscape of my own early life: the fat armchairs, the bookshelves supported by blocks of rippled glass, the strangely sensual portrait of a Renaissance Madonna next to the door, the copies of early Picassos—a clown in white and another in blue, not yet the clichés that they will later become—and in front of the couch the familiar round glass table with its fluted pedestal like a Grecian column and its perennial freight of cocktails and cigarettes. So deceptively familiar is this room that sometimes I think that I was really there, peering around the corner of a door, so close that I seem to hear even now the voices of people I never actually knew——Tom Roberts, Vaughn Kristeller, Catherine Ruth Smith in her amazing discus-shaped hat—but whose names would float disembodied on the air of my childhood.

I like to think of this period as one of homely domesticity that repels, at least for the time being, the increasingly tense mood of the country. I have to remind myself that my parents are still largely strangers to each other, that they are still discovering each other's hearts and bodies, that the "mother" and "father" that I see before me in the disintegrating fixative of my father's photographs know far less about each other than I do about them as I write this more than half a century later. My father is at last purging the failure of his first marriage, my mother yielding her fiercely prized independence, giving herself over to this mild man with the ready smile, who mixes a good cocktail, who admires what he calls her "poetic nature." A new flippancy is reflected in a poem that she wrote on December 30, 1940, a few days after her marriage. Perhaps she intended to read it aloud the next night at their New Year's Eve midnight dinner, a dining tradition that they carried on into the early 1950s: It is titled "Lines for the Threshold":

> My goodman will not hang us
> Because I bid you to eat,
> For he would rob a blindman
> Before you lacked for meat.
>
> And when the sad wind rocks us
> At the thick rope's knotted end
> It will not be because I
> Poured drink out for his friend.
>
> But, young man, you are gentle
> And my goodman's wife is fair,
> And oh! At dawn our shadows
> Shall dance upon the air.

There are no more eagles struggling toward the ether, no more gloomy monks; instead, gentle irony, a hopeful uncertainty. This is the way I want to imagine my parents-to-be on the eve of war. But I know that this is too pat. There are other poems that complicate things, poems that suggest something darker and unresolved. My mother's heart is still a rebel, a provocateur, defiantly defending an interior space of memory and longing in which my father does not exist.

6

ON SUNDAYS, my parents frequently had a late lunch at a luncheon-ette around the corner from the Wooster Street apartment. They were there on December 7, 1941, when a radio announcer broke the news of the Japanese attack on Pearl Harbor. I was six or seven years old, playing in our backyard in Yonkers, dropping rocks on plastic soldiers and ships, shouting "Bombs over Tokyo!" and pulling the ends of my eyes to make them slant, imitating Japanese in the way that children still did in those days, when my mother told me about the radio and the announcement, and then said, "The first thing your father said was, 'The yellow bastards.'" Even then I could see that it was painful for my mother to repeat this to me.

She told me another story about the war that day, sitting with me in the backyard in the sand box, amid the carnage of toppled soldiers and upended cruisers and battleships. Possibly she told this story to me many times, or else told it this one time with something in her voice that unsettled me, because I remembered it ever afterward with unusual clarity. In the story she has traveled to a camp in Arkansas where Japanese-Americans have been interned. People live in little rooms, crowded into barracks like soldiers—she is telling me this in simple images, the way one speaks to a child who has never before been asked to contemplate hypocrisy and injustice. The people are unhappy there and scared. There are even children—"little boys just like you"—who did nothing wrong but still they can't go home any-more and have to stay in the camp until my mother can find them a place to live where nobody will bother them anymore and they can be happy again. When she arrives, hundreds of people are gathered together in the camp's church to meet her, and she goes into it to tell them that she will help them get jobs and a safe new place to live. She goes to the front, smiling even though nobody smiles back. I can't understand why people won't smile back at my wonderful mother, who wants to help them. Then looking out at the unhappy people, she sees a little boy staring straight at her, locking onto her gaze, and then putting his fingers to the corners of his eyes and pulling them down until they are straight like hers, and laughing.

When I was small, a number of the Japanese-Americans my mother knew during the war still came to our house in Yonkers from time to time, before they left the East to return to their homes in California or Hawaii or the Pacific Northwest. I remembered Kenji Nogaki best of all: a dapper and affectionate man with the first mustache I'd ever encountered—a strange and wonderous thing that I thought only Kenji could produce—and who had a knack for making me laugh. Others are now only grainy images in old photographs: my mother's secretary Kathleen Iseri, a round-faced and ever-smiling George Kubota, Tom Sato and his buddies posing with bazookas in captured trenches in the south of France. There are pictures of Kenji Nogaki, too, resplendent in a homburg and double-breasted suit, a boutonniere in his lapel, and in another set of pictures with his brother Takeo's family picnicking somewhere in New Jersey. In one of these Takeo, slim like Kenji but more robust, pushes one of his tiny sons in an inner tube across the shallows of a pond. In another, a little boy peers with uneasy perplexity into my father's lens. In a third, Kenji is laughing, long fingers clapped to his cheek, obviously at a loss for words. My mother wrote in the album, "Kenji was embarrassed when we dropped in unexpectedly on his brother Takeo." These pictures are strangely fascinating to me, for when I look at them I can feel my mother's inescapable presence, hovering just out of the camera's sight like a ghost whose wit and vitality must, I feel, have given this scene the appealing warmth that glows on the faces of the people on their blankets in the grass. These pictures are also deeply deceptive, for they are devoid of any hint of the politics and history that are their harsh and unwritten text.

. . .

THE ATTACK ON PEARL HARBOR prompted widespread fears of an imminent Japanese attack on the West Coast. Rampant rumors warned that Japanese-American truck farmers, fishermen, gardeners, and domestics were a Fifth Column of saboteurs who had deliberately settled near military bases and other strategic facilities in preparation for the coming invasion. Twenty thousand Japanese in the San Francisco Bay Area were said to be "ready for organized action," when in fact there was a total of only thirteen thousand men, women, and children of Japanese ancestry there at the time. In February 1942, General John L. DeWitt, who headed the Western Defense Command, urged President Roosevelt to order evacuation of all Japanese-Americans from the coastal areas, declaring, "A Jap's a Jap. There is no way to determine their loyalty . . . It makes no difference whether he is an American; theoretically he is still a Japanese and you can't change him."

News from the Pacific warfront lent a semblance of credibility to Americans' fears. The Japanese army had overrun large parts of China, and had invaded Malaya, the Dutch East Indies, and the Philippines. Hong Kong and Singapore had fallen. The only Allied fleet in the western Pacific had been destroyed in the battle of the Java Sea. American defenses in the Philippines were collapsing. Japanese bombs were falling on Australia. The President, preoccupied with the deteriorating military situation, had little attention for the constitutional questions involved, and in March he ordered all Japanese-Americans removed from California, Oregon, Washington, and parts of Arizona. By November more than one hundred and ten thousand men, women, and children, two-thirds of them nisei, or American-born United States citizens, and none of them accused of any crime, had been forced to leave their homes, property, and businesses for internment in what it is difficult to avoid calling concentration camps.

In the early 1940s the coarsest sort of racism was still woven deep into the folds of the American mind. Few Americans saw anything unusual in the barring of blacks and members of other minority groups from jobs, restaurants, hotels, playgrounds, swimming pools, theaters, barber shops, and many stores and other facilities, and not only in the South. Months after Pearl Harbor isolationist congressmen were still openly blaming the war on "international Jewish bankers." In popular publications Japanese were typically caricatured as sinister apes, with feral eyes and claws instead of hands. Even as staunch a liberal as my father instinctively thought of the attack on Pearl Harbor in terms of skin color and race. But my mother, despite her hatred of fascism, even knowing that Americans would now have to fight the Japanese in a war whose end no one could yet foresee, remarkably, did not. In such a climate there was scant concern for the rights of uprooted Japanese-Americans. The conservative columnist Westbrook Pegler declared: "The Japanese in California should be under guard to the last man and woman right now and to hell with habeas corpus until the danger is over." Another popular newspaperman, Henry McLemore, wrote: "Herd 'em up, pack 'em off and give 'em the inside room in the Badlands. Let 'em be pinched, hurt, hungry and dead up against it."

After weeks or months in assembly centers evacuees were assigned to one of ten "relocation centers" in isolated areas in the Mountain States, the Southwest, and Arkansas. Typically each camp consisted of a square mile of tar-papered barracks, mess halls, schools, hospitals, stores, and administration buildings. Families of up to six were housed in a standard single room twenty by twenty-five feet in size that was furnished with a stove and cots and blankets, but that lacked running water or provision for cooking. Unlike concentration camps in Germany and the Soviet Union, these had churches, schoolrooms, libraries, and recreational facilities, and inmates elected their own leaders and managed many of the camp's affairs themselves, including the growing and processing of food that suited Japanese taste. Still, military police patrolled the camps' barbed-wire perimeters, manned guard towers, and carried on a degree of surveillance that few other Americans have ever had to endure in their own country. Takeo Nogaki's sons would eventually show me the 1943 yearbook that their parents had brought away from the Minidoka relocation center in Idaho. It was a bizarre thing, designed and bound like a high-school yearbook, showing the inmates playing at the rituals of American small-town life as if the barbed wire and MPs meant nothing at all. There were pictures of the camp's glee club, a swing band called the Harmonaires, Miss Ise Inuzuka who had been voted the "Sweetheart of Minidoka," and the like. "Familiar scenes and home and friends were left behind when evacuation took place," the text proclaimed, burying pain in breeziness. "Their hearts were young and afraid. Yet they could understand their government's action. . . ."

It soon became evident to the War Relocation Authority, the agency that was created to run the camps, that the evacuation had been unnecessary. In May 1942 Japanese expansion in the southwest Pacific was halted at the Battle of the Coral Sea, and a month later the imperial navy suffered a crippling defeat in the Battle of Midway, making it clear to American military planners that Japanese forces would never be able to mount an invasion of the United States. "Once the implications of the Midway battle were clear (although never publicly acknowledged)," Page Smith, a historian of the evacuation, has written, "the whole evacuation, an enormously complicated and expensive undertaking (without taking into account its human cost), became a huge embarrassment. But no one at this point could put Humpty-Dumpty together again."

The WRA's director, a career bureaucrat from the Department of Agriculture named Dillon Myer, defended the agency in public, although he was privately convinced that "loyalty could not flourish in an atmosphere of restriction and discriminatory segregation." Conditions in the camps were already distressing. A WRA official who toured the camps in the summer of 1942 reported that although the general facilities were adequate, the social and psychological situation was abysmal. Normal social controls were breaking down. People of all ages were idle much of the time, and there were serious conflicts between Japanese nationalist and pro-American factions. The sensible policy was to get the evacuees out of the centers as soon as possible. The original plan to resettle them in the inland West was derailed by violent local opposition. Governor Nels Smith of

Wyoming warned that if evacuees were allowed to buy land in his state, "there would be Japs hanging from every pine tree." Relocation was also opposed by many of the evacuees themselves, who saw it as an attempt by the government to evade the responsibility of caring for them by turning them out into a hostile Caucasian world. Myer believed, however, that hostility toward Japanese-Americans was chiefly due to their numbers on the West Coast and that if they could be redistributed around the country they would eventually be absorbed into the general population. The WRA began looking toward the more cosmopolitan East.

MY MOTHER'S WAR began on October 20, 1942, when she was hired as secretary to the director of the WRA's new Eastern Area Office in Manhattan. On the application that she submitted, apparently a standard one for government service during the war, she stated that she was willing to travel "constantly," if required, and to accept a posting "in any allied country." She added, "Although I list only 3 languages (Italian, 'fluent'; French, 'good'; and Spanish, 'fair') I have the necessary basic training in Latin, Greek, and general linguistics to make it possible for me to acquire with some rapidity a working vocabulary in such languages as may be required for a particular project." Her resolve was never tested, for she remained in the New York area throughout the war, but it left me puzzled. What about my father? What was he supposed to do if she was packed off to "any allied country"? My father, in his memoir, says only, "I never knew why she left her job at NYU." Even allowing for his fading memory, this is an odd admission: either he didn't care why my mother left her beloved Classics Department or, more likely, he believed that it was none of his business, accepting that whole provinces of her life were to remain closed to him.

Why, then, did she join the WRA? There is no suggestion in anything she left behind that it was because of a falling out with Casper Kraemer, whom she listed as the primary reference on her application. I doubt that her motive was money. Although the starting salary of thirty-four dollars and sixty-nine cents a week that the WRA would pay her represented a significant raise over the twenty-three dollars per week that she was earning as secretary of the Classics Department, she probably had additional income from freelance research and editing that she performed for Kraemer and other professors. She may have been inspired in part by a sense of patriotic duty, thinking of her uncle Jimmie Madigan, who had been gassed in France during the First World War, of her mother rolling bandages for the wounded during the Spanish-American War, of the fictional stories that Maddy presented as fact about her father's Civil War exploits.

I found the nearest thing to an explanation in my mother's own words in a news story in the *Newark Sunday Call* of August 27, 1944. The story reads, "Miss Madigan"—throughout the war and in her Indian work she would use her maiden name—"joined WRA as soon as it was organized. She had no previous contact with Japanese. 'I was interested in their problem, just as a citizen of a democracy,' she explained. 'I wanted to help them find opportunities to work as free citizens. Since this thing has started I've been convinced the final result may benefit the Japanese-Americans by bringing more of them to the East." At first reading, this sounds somewhat impersonal, an echo of the WRA's official policy. But I think that it also reflected her deeply held feelings. It took courage for anyone to publicly help ethnic Japanese in any way at all while American soldiers were dying in the South Pacific and when vengeful racial hostility was still widespread at home. In Arizona, for example, a state law banned commercial dealings with interned Japanese-Americans, down to the sale of even cigarettes and toothpaste, without the transaction first being publicly advertised. In Missouri, public schools refused admittance to resettlers' children. As late as 1944 even Fiorello LaGuardia, New York's famously liberal mayor, would protest the WRA's plan to, as he put it, "dump" former internees wholesale in the city. "This ought to be stopped at once," LaGuardia declared in an open letter to President Roosevelt. "If it was necessary to evacuate them from their homes and originally put them in a concentration camp, what justification is there for turning them loose in Eastern cities at this time?" My mother's nisei friend George Kubota told me when I reached him by phone at his home in Hawaii, "What happened to Japanese-Americans had a great effect on her. She felt very sorry for us. I told her, 'It's not your fault. We're victims of circumstance.' But deep down she was very angry. She had a deep sense of moral outrage."

The WRA's records are housed in the National Archives on Pennsylvania Avenue in Washington, D.C. Sitting at an oak desk beneath its lofty coffered ceiling in the fourth-floor research room one afternoon, I worked my way through boxes of rough wartime foolscap that was now orange with age, searching for my mother's voice, like a thread of metal running through the heaps of bureaucratic slag. Newsletters that she wrote for distribution to the relocation centers in the West had headlines like "Employer Champions Resettlers," and "Issei Pioneers Morris County," and they are are always upbeat and encouraging: "Joe Munemasa Amano of Poston [a relocation center] is rapidly becoming a dairyman, to the delight of his employer, Charles Doscher of the Mount Vernon Dairy Farm in Clinton, N.J." Others told me that New Jersey employers were looking for a chemist with experience in fluorescent powders, dental technicians, chipping-hammer operators, spot welders, refrigeration mechanics, a pastry chef for $7.37 per day, stenographers for $25 per week, candle makers, truck drivers, and radio mechanics and roofers, and a graduate accountant with tax experience. There were letters to her from foundries and chemical manufacturers, and a shop selling bridal gowns, and the Waldorf-Astoria, and chicken farmers. She was there in yellowing news clips, reminding that former internees were American citizens, and had suffered, and needed help. I could discern her expressive turns of phrase in the speeches that she wrote for her boss Robert Cullum, the Eastern Area director of the WRA, to deliver on radio: "We learn to live at lower temperatures in our homes, we restrain our restless desire to use our cars, our wives haunt the groceries for a stick of butter or a pound of red meat." And: "We have through selective service taken millions of young men from the pursuit of their ambitions and are training them in the paramount but sterile arts of war."

The arts of war wrought their sterile purpose in the most personal way possible for my parents in the summer of 1943. My father's brother Arnie had joined in the Army Air Corps in January 1942. He was twenty-four when he enlisted, the baby of the family. For more than a year he had been shuttled among airfields in Arkansas, Alabama, Ohio, Wisconsin, and Texas, expressing constant frustration, in the letters he wrote home, that he was not earning enough extra flight pay to save money for the farm he wanted to buy in upstate New York. When he washed out of basic training in power planes, he decided to continue with gliders. Gliders were still relatively untried as a weapon, having only rarely been flown in combat: in an assault several gliders would be linked together by cables and towed by a power plane to the area of attack, then released to be flown down by their pilots into the designated landing zone. Arnie wrote, "Didn't care much for these little ships, but they're sort of fun." In early 1943 Arnie was overseas, in Tunisia. Although he probably did not know it at the time, since such information was top secret, he was to be part of Operation Ladbroke, the first wave of the airborne component in the invasion of Sicily. Twenty-eight of the one hundred and thirty-seven British gliders allocated to the operation were piloted by American volunteers. One of them was Arnie, craving flight pay, no doubt dreaming of that farm in Pine Plains. On July 9, the day of the assault, he wrote at the end of his last letter, "Think nothing of it if I don't write for a wee while." He was probably dead even before the letter left Tunisia.

The army suppressed news of the debacle in which Arnie died. Off the coast of Sicily his squadron was mistaken for enemy planes by jumpy Allied naval gunners. A recent document prepared by veterans of the Sixty-second Troop Carrier Group, to which Arnie was attached, tells what happened. "All hell broke loose as ships directly under our flight path began firing on us and shooting up star shells on little parachutes, the better to see us." This firing soon broke up Arnie's formation. Only the lead planes carried navigators. The rest became badly lost. "We had to wander up and down the east coast looking for landmarks in the quarter-moonlight." Most of the gliders were released too high and far offshore. "To make a long story short, seventy-three of the gliders fell into the sea and many of their men were drowned."

My father rarely spoke about Arnie's death. In his memoir of these years he talks mainly about boilers and air conditioners, which he was now installing and repairing and overhauling, mainly in the Bronx and Manhattan, and about "open-type compressors that had an awkward tendency to break their flat spring valves." He was finally called up by the draft in the spring of 1943. "In the event," he writes. "I was rejected and declared 4F. This was because of spots on my lungs which the examiner felt indicated TB. I could have told them otherwise, that they were more likely the result of the severe bronchitis I had when I was about four years old, but I did not think of it at the time. I am not sure whether I would have volunteered the info or whether it would have made any difference."

By the latter half of 1943 the number of Japanese-American internees in the relocation camps was dropping by an average ten thousand a month, a process that was facilitated by the growing shortage of labor in the Midwest and East. (As if to leave no humiliation unplumbed, before departing from the camps resettlers had to fill out questionnaires that included such questions as, "Will you assist in the general resettlement program by staying away from large groups of Japanese?" and "Will you try to develop such American habits which will cause you to be accepted readily into American social groups?") What had begun in the West as a military operation, in the East became transformed into a social-welfare strategy whose implementers, including my mother, spoke of "rebuilding the evacuee's sense of security," "reinvesting him with a sense of personal dignity," "allaying his feelings of uselessness," and "inculcating in him a feeling of rightful belonging."

IN AUGUST 1944 my mother was appointed director of the new Newark branch of the WRA, with offices in the imposing Royal Insurance Company building on Washington Place. From it she could look out through tall fan-shaped windows past the bronze statues of Columbus, Jose Artigas, the "National Hero of the Republic of Uruguay," and Seth Boyden, the inventor of patent leather, into a white working-class city of four hundred and thirty thousand that, long before the race riots of the 1960s that would make it a national byword for urban crisis, was thriving on war contracts for zippers, tents, telephone equipment, and warships, which were built in ship-yards on the Hackensack River. The dry thirty-eight-page Final Report on the work of the Newark office that she submitted when the WRA was liquidated at the end of 1945 yields scant sense of the woman who wrote it. It does tell me that her official responsibilities included "formation of policy, making of contacts with state agencies, work in field for promotion of agricultural opportunities, supervision of staff members . . . preparation of publicity for centers and for local press and of other public relations material; reception, placement of, and obtaining of welfare or other assistance for resettlers." Through the report's impersonal prose I can sometimes catch a glimpse of her, recruiting women from the Ridgewood Chamber of Commerce and the Ramapo Valley Cooperative and the Family Welfare Association of Paterson to serve on a committee to help resettlers adjust, creating a state council on resettlement, investigating salaries for gardeners and nurserymen, organizing an exhibit of art by Japanese-Americans that will tour the East Coast. The report occasionally betrays her impatience with the bureaucracy of which she was a part, taking ironic note, for instance, of the ludicrous competition for resettlers among rival WRA offices. In one place she playfully describes the "anarchistic, if frequently effective, performance by staff members [of the Newark office]. The loose administration was attributable partly to a certain light-hearted disregard of the Newark office on the part of the supervisory area staff, and attributable partly to reluctance to exercise self-discipline on the part of the Newark District staff itself."

My mother's main concern was finding work and housing for the "resettlers." (In official lingo they were no longer "evacuees" or suspect subversives, but something that evoked pioneers and homesteaders, *real Americans*.) When resettlers arrived in the New York area they had been on the train anywhere from two to five days, sitting up nights, changing stations, keeping track of luggage, taking care of children, finally ending months or years of segregated confinement to step suddenly into the confusing welter of Manhattan, wounded in their dignity, stripped of property, fearful of the future. George Kubota told me, "I will forever be grateful to your mother for what she did for me. Her job was taking care of strays like me who turned up in New York. When I first got to the city I went straight from the train station to the War Relocation office in the Empire State Building—I just looked for the tallest building. She was very gracious and helpful and found me a place to stay. She befriended me. On Christmas Eve she and Harold invited me to their apartment, and I got so drunk they put me under the shower—oh, I got so drunk! After that it was a joke every time I went to visit them. They'd always say, 'George, we're going to have to put you under the shower again!' Most of the time we just sat around the apartment and talked about books and Hawaii and the war. She was the most remarkable woman I ever met." What, I asked, was so remarkable about her. Kubota paused for a while before answering and then said that she had "a rapport," and then that that wasn't quite it either, or just that she felt such a sense of responsibility for what had happened to Japanese-Americans, but something more than that, an extraordinary ability to establish trust and a bond. "She had a real interest in the person she was talking to. She wasn't prejudiced at all. I've met a lot of people in my life. You know who's faking. She wasn't."

IN THE FILES of the Newark office I found a single, glancing reference to the trip to Arkansas that she had told me about when I was small. Rohwer was one of the two internment camps in that state. Apparently my mother went there early in February 1945, probably to make a pitch for relocation to New Jersey. The mocking boy and the atmosphere of rage and the staring faces are unrecorded, surviving now only in my own memory. I felt unreasonably annoyed and frustrated that there was nothing more. I wondered as I searched futilely through box after box of files why, when there was so much else that was new and intriguing about my mother's involvement with the WRA, this particular trip, this particular narrative, was so important. Then I realized—looking out from the National Archives up Eighth Street toward the Grecian colonnade of the National Gallery, a classical perspective that my mother would have admired—that it had been there in the sandbox, listening to her tell me about the trip to Rohwer, that I first realized that my mother was not like the other mothers I knew, that she had done things whose meaning could not be explained in terms of the familiar patterns of life on Mayfair Road. I understood, of course, as she intended me to, that making fun of people was hurtful and wrong, and I also understood, though less clearly, that the people in the church had stared at her because they were angry, and in some still vaguer way that they were angry because they had been made helpless and fearful. Much later in my life, when I thought about this story, as I did surprisingly often, I realized that in telling it to me my mother was also mocking herself in a way, letting me see her through the eyes of the little boy, and to see as he did the ridiculousness of her round eyes and white skin and pale hair. I can see now that it was then also, listening to this story, and puzzling over it in later years that I began to understand that differentness was something that I needn't be afraid of, and the fact that I would always seem different to someone, indeed not just different but strange, and that sometimes that would scare me as I think it had her, but that if I stood up in front of the crowd, as it were, as she had, I would be rewarded somehow, with respect, or understanding, or at least an *interesting experience.*

SOUNDS OF CHILDREN on swings, of lawn mowers, of someone hosing a car sift into the Nogakis' kitchen in Bergenfield. The familiar sounds are deceptive, arguing that nothing out of the ordinary could ever have happened to the elderly man and woman and the two balding men in jeans and polo shirts, now in their fifties, who sit across the table from me, pecking at almond cookies and marshmallow squares baked with Rice Krispies. The families that my mother had worked so hard to resettle scattered after the war, some among the towns and farms of rural New Jersey, others across the Hudson to New York or, like George Kubota, back to the homes they had left in the West. But the Nogakis were not hard to find. A nisei journalist I knew had found me the name of a businessman active in Japanese-American civic groups. This man knew Kenji and Takeo Nogaki, and he told me that they had died but that Takeo's sons and his wife, Florence, still lived in northern New Jersey. Florence dislikes remembering the war. Later her sons will tell me that she nearly broke down and cried after we talked. "It was a pretty frightening experience," she says. "We had to do what they said. How could we oppose them?" We eat cookies for a while and then talk about how built-up Bergenfield had gotten since the war, and how there used to be blackberry patches and brambles and woods where there are houses now. Then Florence says, "Well, I guess we proved ourselves. That's a funny way to put it, when you think about it though. What did we have to prove? It was really a very strange time, an unbalanced time in our lives. Deep down we still clung to the idea that we were Americans, not Japanese. We thought, why are they doing this to us?"

When I ask about Kenji, the Nogakis tell me that he married an Australian nurse he met in a hospital in New York and went back with her to Australia and died there in 1980. Rodger, a risk analyst for the insurance industry, says, "Kenji could talk about anything—dance, sports, opera, classical music, Julius Caesar." It was the kind of brightness and eclecticism that always appealed to my mother. "He was a funny person," Rodger continues. "He had a bow tie and he'd make it go up and down with his Adam's apple." I remember this suddenly. My father did exactly the same thing. Had he learned it from Kenji, or Kenji from him?

I asked Florence to tell me what happened to the family during the war. She said that Takeo, though American-born like herself, was the branch manager of a Japanese bank in Seattle. The day after Pearl

Harbor, Takeo found FBI agents at the bank with padlocks. They told him that the federal government had ordered all Japanese banks in the country to be closed. The Nogakis had kept all their savings in the bank, and they were left with nothing to pay the mortgage on their home, or the payments on their car and appliances. Takeo finally found a job delivering coal in sacks on his back. Then, in March of 1942, the Nogakis were told to pack what they could carry and report to an assembly center at the Puyallup fairgrounds, where they were billeted for a month in a horse stall before being sent to the Minidoka Relocation Camp in Idaho. Rodger remembers that when his mother baked him a cake for his fifth birthday a soldier methodically cut it to bits in front of him with his bayonet, searching for weapons.

Near the end of the war the Nogakis bought a house in Bergenfield, just north of Newark, and only a few blocks from the newer tract house in which we sit. "I remember like yesterday the day we moved in," says Rodger, who was eight years old then. "Everyone in the neighborhood was out looking at us, lining the sides of the street. Nobody said anything. There were no Asians in town. People used to spit at me. They'd tell me, 'Get off my sidewalk.' I'd go to swimming pools and they'd turn me away. One of my teachers called me 'Jap' and 'chink' and 'gook.' He said, 'You know, I killed your people over there.' By the time I got to high school, I was the toughest kid in town."

In contrast to Kenji, Takeo was an authoritarian. "He wanted all of his sons to be perfect so that no one would ever cast any aspersion on any other Japanese-Americans," Rodger says. Every Saturday morning he led his sons down to the basement and beat them with a razor strop for the sins they had committed during the week. Sometimes neighborhood children would gather at the basement windows to watch. "He knew that every Japanese who followed in this town would be judged by the impression we made. You see, we didn't want to be Japanese. We thought of ourselves as white. But he said, You'll always stand out, you'll always be different. He used to say, 'You do ten things right and one thing wrong, and people will remember the one wrong thing because we're different. We've got to do ten things right and then another ten."

John Iwatsu, Florence's brother, interrupts him, his voice frail and sarcastic. "You'll never be an American with your Japanese face." During the war Iwatsu was fired by the architectural firm he worked for, interned, and finally relocated to New York. He is unforgiving.

"It's different now," Brian says. Brian is an insurance agent in Fort Lee and has done well. Like every one of Takeo's sons—another brother became a teacher, and two others military officers, including the first Japanese-American to graduate from the Air Force Academy—Brian married a non-Japanese, and he takes pride in having in-laws of mixed Irish, Swedish, and Italian extraction. "We're an embodiment of what America is all about," he says.

The old man sniffs. "You're giving too much credit to the United States."

Turning to me, edging away from the argument, Rodger says, "My parents were beaten people when they came out of the camp. The WRA kept them from going off the deep end. We owe them a lot. They encouraged us to start over. If we'd gone back to the West Coast, we'd all have married Asians. Coming east made us develop a new perspective on our identity."

We swap old photos in silence—the Nogakis' snapshots of the Brooklyn hotel where they lived when they first came to New York, and my father's of that long-ago day at the pond. I want news of the ghost, of that invisible presence in the picture that, it soon becomes clear, is visible only to me. "What did she say that day?" I ask. "Was she nice? Was she funny? Did you like her?" I want the piece of her that she left with the Nogakis that day. I want to take it away and hold it close and make it part of me. But of course Takeo's boys were scarcely more than infants, and Florence—I can see her there in one of the pictures, mostly hidden behind Kenji's creased slacks, a young mother no doubt grateful for a quiet moment—says she just doesn't remember my mother at all. Kenji was their link to her, and Kenji is dead. His road into my mother's past is closed now, washed out, erased from the map.

"Take a look at this," Brian tells the others, holding up the picture, in which Takeo can be seen pushing him gently through the shallows, reassuring him, one imagines, that the water and the strangers with the camera will do him no harm. "It's a rare moment," he says wistfully. "It's almost as if he was being tender. I don't believe that I ever pleased him with anything."

I sensed that the argument between the younger Nogakis and John Iwatsu was one that had taken place many times before, one that was in equal parts generational, political, and historical, an irreconcilable standoff between the past and the present. It also seemed to me that their argument was, in its own way, as much a legacy of my mother's work for the WRA as the letters to labor-starved foundries and truck-farmers and the yellowing press releases. Takeo Nogaki's rage and John Iwatsu's bitterness seemed to give the lie to the WRA's belief that it was "rebuilding the evacuee's sense of security" and "inculcating in him a feeling of rightful belonging." But Takeo's sons reflected the WRA's idealism after all: they were successful, less "Japanese" than their parents, assimilated. This may well have been my mother's hope too, at least to the extent that a term that is today equated by some with cultural genocide was the liberal doctrine of the 1940s and a precursor of racial integration and the civil rights initiatives of later decades.

During her years with the WRA I can see her becoming the woman I will know as my mother, as she enters a larger, less interior, more political world, discovering that she can talk to anyone—evacuated nisei, club women, chicken farmers—that she possesses a talent for organizing things, that there are ways other than protest politics to harness moral outrage. I can also see that there is something more than politics and idealism and professionalism at work in the extraordinary commitment that she brought to what could have been merely a functionary's role: a visceral sense of the vulnerability that lay hidden beneath the surface of other people's lives, and of the ease with which the dependent and helpless could be humiliated and hurt, as if she had herself once lived in a strange skin, or had been made vulnerable and mocked and demeaned, helpless as a bug or a toy soldier at the hands of fierce boys.

IN AUGUST 1945 a B-25 bomber lost in a fog over New York City crashed into the Empire State Building. My mother told me how one of the bomber's engines penetrated the building at the level of its seventy-ninth floor, passing completely through the building and severing several elevators, how she was there, in the WRA's regional office, that day and had no idea what had happened, only that there had been a catastrophe, that the elevators had ceased to work, and that the building was full of smoke. Everyone would have to walk down the crowded and smoke-filled stairwells to the street. She was terrified, sure that the building would burn and that she would be trapped and that she would die before she could get out. Miraculously, there was no panic, and in the event few people were killed. Had more of the plane entered the building or had the flaming engine remained inside, or had the thousands of people inside the building that day panicked as they crowded the stairwells, my mother's life might well have ended there, a would-be poet, a minor government bureaucrat remembered for her better-than-average sense of justice, and childless.

My father photographed the Empire State Building after the crash. I still have several of his pictures. There are, of course, no people in them.

7

WITH THE END of gas rationing in 1945, like millions of other Americans, my parents took to the highways. For both of them it was really the first time since before the Depression and possibly the first time in their lives that they were able to travel freely. They drove to the Berkshires, New Hampshire, and Maine, the Adirondacks, and then, in 1946, south to Gettysburg and the Smoky Mountains and Virginia and Tennessee. My father photographed trains, trestles, car barns, railroad cuts, suspension bridges, old canals, and covered bridges. Occasionally my mother can be seen pretending to tug an abandoned plow through a field or posing on a mountain road or reclining on a boulder to give perspective. The pictures do not show it, of course, but she is thinking about babies. *I can almost hear myself in the wings of your life now, a player about to enter, soon to howl and puke and nuzzle my way into your life. But it is not quite my time yet. These are other, strange infant voices that I hear, the not-mes, the might-have-beens.*

My mother felt a great pressure to bear children. In a sonnet written as early as the mid-1930s she expressed a fear of barrenness:

> *When thinking of the women of my clan*
> *Whom not a cudgel or a threat or bribe*
> *Could bring to kneel before a living man*
> *Beyond the inmost councils of the tribe,*
> *And when I think upon my fertile breed,*
> *And of my father fallen back to dust,*
> *With no tall sons to recreate his seed,*
> *And how his daughter has betrayed the trust,*
> *Then I am sick of this bad heart*
> *That wears the honor of my people thin*
> *And lets a stranger rip their pride apart,*
> *Not fit to serve my black-eyed father's kin*
> *And never like to sell his couch again*
> *For house and deities such as I profane.*

She became pregnant for the first time in 1945. Sometime during her third month my father got a call that she was in trouble. He hurried home from the Bronx and rushed her to the hospital, but by the time they arrived the miscarriage had already occurred. Then the following year she lost twins. One evening a few months into this second pregnancy she began to experience pains. "The elevator was out of order and we were on the fourth floor," Harold writes in his memoir. "LaVerne was not allowed to walk, so I enlisted Bill, the super, to help. We put her on a chair and carried her down to the car. Then, after traveling a few blocks, I found that my brakes were almost useless, and we were in a hurry. With one hand on the wheel and the other on the emergency brake handle we made pretty good time, but we were still too late." I cannot know what these losses meant to her, what kind of challenge to her womanhood or to her marriage the threat of childlessness might have represented. She rarely alluded to these events within my hearing, and never in a way that revealed her feelings. However, an Indian friend who knew my mother in the years just before her death told me that she had mentioned it often. The woman said to me, "LaVerne wanted a baby so badly that she was afraid she would steal one from somebody. She was terrified that she would really do it."

Early in 1947 my mother became pregnant for the third time. The contractions began while she was carving the Hallowe'en pumpkin. My great-aunt Nancy, a pious Catholic, who was in the apartment at the time, was quoted ever afterward as having exclaimed, "He'll either be a devil or a saint," depending on whether the birth occurred before or after midnight and therefore fell on All Souls' Day or All Saints' Day. This time nothing went wrong. My father got her downstairs and drove her to Gotham Hospital on the East Side, across the street from the Carlyle Hotel. Like many men of the era, perhaps, he passed most of the night in a bar nearby, leaving my birth entirely to the doctors and slowly getting drunk. Fortunately for Aunt Nancy's peace of mind, I was delivered the next morning, November 1st, All Saints' Day.

In the spring of 1948, as my father puts it in his memoir, "LaVerne began the campaign for 'a house in the country.' " They looked first in New Jersey, and then in Westchester County. Perhaps it was Catherine Ruth Smith who put them onto the house on Mayfair Road. Yonkers would soon begin an economic decline that by the 1970s would leave it raddled with slums, crime, and racial conflict.

But none of this was evident in 1948. Large carpet mills, the Otis Elevator plant, and a sugar refinery employed large numbers of workers of mostly Polish, Irish, Italian, and Ukrainian extraction, who lived in tenement neighborhoods surrounding what was still, in the 1950s, when I knew it, a lively urban core. Even before the Second World War, more affluent suburbs had begun to grow up on the northern and eastern edges of the city, especially along the routes or the New York Central Railroad and the Saw Mill and Bronx River parkways, and after the war they expanded at a rapid rate. However, Yonkers always lacked the cachet of neighboring communities like Bronxville and Scarsdale. "This city of 300,000 was considered, by Westchester standards 'sort of second-rate,' " my father wrote, "but the house came with a four percent mortgage, and from the back windows we could see the Putnam Line trains of the New York Central Railroad steaming (as they still did then) to and from New York City."

My father's memoir ends here. The last thing he talks about is the difficulty of repairing the controls of early air conditioners, and the way that compressors were hermetically sealed with their motors in a steel shell and were often unrepairable too, and how even open-type compressors had an awkward tendency to break their flat spring valves, and how when they broke it required finesse to replace the lead head-gaskets whose clearances were measured in ten-thousandths of an inch. Perhaps he intended to write more, or perhaps the deepening emotional uncertainties of his marriage to my mother finally got the better of him, demanding more truth than he could face and finally defeating his preoccupation with the verities of nuts and bolts. Or perhaps he just got tired of writing, or decided that he had no more to say, or no longer found satisfaction in remembering the past and just let it slip from his grip.

Part Three

❧

Indian Lady

To be is to have been, and to project our messy, malleable past into our unknown future.

—DAVID LOWENTHAL
  The Past Is a Foreign Country

MEMORIES OF MY FIRST YEARS have a disembodied quality, like myth, in which time and space are conflated, undisturbed by self-consciousness or reason. The child I see in them is both me and not-me, a doppelgänger in whom I recognize myself but who is also a stranger I do not know at all.

In one of my earliest memories my mother is pushing me in a stroller up the avenue at the end of our street, then all the way up the hill, then up the steep flagstone steps that go on up the hill where it is too steep for the avenue to continue. The steps are so steep that they go up into the sky and beyond, so high that surely if we keep going I must eventually fall off and fall away into a void of space below. But she will not let me fall. When I get to the last step, I am on the top of the world and I can see everything there is.

In another I am making my way through a sea of tall grass without end and I am afloat in it, buoyed by my mother's hand. No one exists in all the world but us. The smell of grass is so sweet that I can taste it on my tongue. A creature is coming wonderfully toward us through the grass, roaring, making the tall grass disappear. The tractor's driver stops and leans down and asks if I want a ride. Sitting on his lap now, I am making the grass fall down, making the sweetness, making the wonderful sound. Then I see a tiny fir tree ahead in the grass and that the tractor will kill it. I cry to my mother to make everything stop. We go home running and find a trowel and come back to the field, and carefully she digs the tree up and we carry it home in our arms and plant it in our front yard. Day after day I watch it, trying to catch it growing. I will watch it for years as we, the little tree and I, race onward toward some unforeseen destination.

In still another I find rocks in the driveway and make them friends. They wait for me every day and love me when I come to see them. If I step on them, they cry. I collect the rocks whose secret names I know and put them to the side, out of harm's way. But there are so many of them! I am so afraid of stepping on them that for a long time I avoid the driveway. I show them only to my mother because I know that even though she says nothing she will understand. When my father paves the driveway I know they are in pain and crying underneath, but no one can hear them anymore, and finally they die.

There are books everywhere, stacked on tables, propped open with empty drinking glasses and paperweights and packs of cigarettes, stuck in alcoves next to the beds, rising in lofty ranges and massifs up the walls of the living room. Even before I can read, their colored bindings—the maroon of the Everyman Shakespeare, the silvery palm fronds on Ovid and Augustine, the green-jacketed *Tristram Shandy*, the squat *Moby Dick* with the whale on its spine—hold the promise of secret worlds where only my mother can lead me. Like a tiny mountaineer I scale the shelves like cliffs until, looking down and suddenly terrified, I cry out for her to save me.

In another memory it is summer and I stand shirtless on cinder blocks on the terrace behind the house, my arm flung in the air, shouting, *"Patres conscripti!"* and then, "Friends, Romans, countrymen, lend me your ears!" I shout it over and over and over, and my mother laughs gaily with her head flung back against the canvas of the lawn chair. Still laughing, she praises me in Latin words that I crave to understand. I think, when I know Latin I will be her.

At bedtime she tells me stories from the Odyssey and the Iliad and King Arthur's Round Table, and as I drift off to sleep, it is my mother whom I see in the armor of Athena descending upon the Trojan plain, or as the lovely Guinevere, or, when she has read to me from the Arabian Nights, as Scheherezade, spinner of wonderful tales without end.

A family at the top of the hill keeps a pet monkey named Oscar in a little house like a birdhouse mounted on a pole. My mother often takes me to see him. Then one day he is gone, and I can't understand why and beg over and over to see him, crying when he will not come out, until finally my mother tells me that he is dead and will never come back. I beg her to tell me how long she will live, to tell me that she will live forever. Finally she says, "How long doesn't matter. I'd rather a short exciting life than a long dull one." For a long time afterward whenever I see a monkey I think, *My mother will die.*

No longer is LaVerne Madigan a half-stranger excavated from news archives and yellowing photos; she is *my mother.* She is at the center of everything, indistinguishable in my earliest murky memories from my own infant self, inseparable from our street, from the ambience of rooms, from the feeling of certain hours of the day, and thus from time itself. She is infused like a vapor into everything I know. She is the bedrock, the Precambrian, upon which everything rests.

IN PICTURES from this time my mother usually wears a plain print dress and her hair pulled back from her forehead and face and fastened in a bun at the back of her head. I never really noticed before how much, especially now as she neared her forties, approaching the age at which her father died, she came to resemble him, now dead twenty years. Perhaps it gave her pleasure to be reminded that she still carried a part of him—the broadness of his face, the loftiness of his brow, the very waves in his hair—with her always. Or, perhaps, looking into the mirror was like looking into a death foretold. *Now, when I look into my own mirror, I see your blue eyes, your white skin, the waves that were yours and your father's before you in my own thinning hair: I see my own death.* But morbid reflection of that sort was not really her nature. These were good years for her. She was building a home, raising the child for whom she had longed. In the backyard she was creating what would eventually become a magnificent garden, a work of art, a symphony of aroma and color that would eventually enfold the small yard like a medieval tapestry.

Photographs of the garden during our first years in Yonkers barely hint at what is to come, showing just a scattering of hollyhocks and foxgloves and a low-clinging blur that is probably portulaca. For that matter, all the pictures of the neighborhood that I have

from that time convey an impression of emptiness, of a place still unformed. Lawns are tentative and sparse, shrubbery obviously freshly
planted. There is nothing strange about this, of course, since the
houses on our side of Mayfair Road were quite new, having been
built only a year or two earlier in the first wave of postwar suburban
development. Our own house stands nakedly on its plot, indistinguishable from the Beebes' and Gassmans' almost identical houses on
either side, and looking north from my backyard it is possible to see
across six or seven open lots, clear to the corner of Odell Avenue.

Today when I visit the neighborhood I feel the present as but a
thin curtain through which I catch fleeting glimpses of the hidden,
truer text of the past. There is a neat, trim look to things: lawns are
mowed, hedges snipped, brickwork pointed, yards picked up, shady
places filled in with ivy or pachysandra. Most of the houses have
added colored vinyl siding over the almost universal white shingling
that I remember. And there are black and Asian faces now. Although
probably fewer people live in the neighborhood than when I was a
child—everyone had young children then, it seemed—it feels more
crowded, even claustrophobic. What was raw and unformed in the
pictures taken half a century ago has now been filled in, improved,
completed. Spare lots have been built up. Here and there, decks and
swimming pools have been added, a luxury beyond imagining in the
early 1950s. And there are more fences now, more barriers, reflections of a society that has become more defensive and divided, more
protective of space, more fearful perhaps. Then we scampered indis-
criminately from yard to yard, slipping through hedges, hurtling
across lawns, swinging in clumps from neighbors' trees, fighting wars
with broomsticks and twigs for guns, recognizing no boundaries,
claiming everything as our own. No one seemed to mind.

Someone has now planted a vegetable garden of tomatoes, cu-
cumbers, squash, and corn where our house stood. The maple tree
that bathed the front yard in deep shade is gone, along with the little
fir that we saved that day long ago. There is, of course, no trace of
my mother's magnificent rose garden; it disappeared long ago, when
the four-family house was built on our back lot. Dense brush has

overgrown the field beyond the Gassmans' house, where I once tried to dig a tunnel to China, where I buried "time capsules" of bottle-caps, ticket stubs, scribbled messages to the future, and unloved toys, and where my friends and I excavated foxholes for our wars, carrying out savage ambushes and hurling ourselves against each other in desperate hand-to-hand combat, reenacting the landings at Tarawa and Iwo Jima and Normandy, the war of our parents, which extended its glamor of duty and violent death in a noble cause the length of our childhood. The bigger field, on the other side of Bretton Road, where I saw the tractor, has been named Kenneth Kardash Park after a boy I knew who was motivated more than I was by those notions of duty and nobility and was killed in Vietnam. There are swings, a slide, contraptions on springs for toddlers to ride, and all around the park chain-link fences (everywhere more fences), making it impossible to chase flies now into neighbors' yards. But on summer days kids still laze in the shade, luxuriating in boredom and the limitless horizons of time, too languorous to throw a ball or swing a bat or climb on a bike, or to go home, half-narcotized by the sweet, insinuating smell of new-mown grass.

We lived only a few miles north of New York City, yet certain aspects of our life in Yonkers now seem remarkable and quaint. Families left the doors of their homes unlocked when they went out, and their keys in their parked cars. We bought staples like bread and milk at a general store on Odell Avenue, but much of what we needed came to our door. Fresh vegetables arrived three times a week in a horse-drawn wagon driven by an Italian who announced himself by jingling a string of bells over red alps of beets and radishes, and green ones of cabbage and lettuce. The knife grinder came in a wagon, too; of him I remember nothing but bony hands, the hands of a pirate or a wild Irish chieftain, pressing against the grinding wheel mounted in the wagon's bed ordinary household knives that in those fearsome hands suddenly became weapons fit for fanatical attacks and the slicing of helpless throats. Fish was delivered by a man in a black panel truck that looked to me like a fish, long and low and swimming down the street and disgorging the fish man himself in a smock stained with smashed silvery fish scales and blood. For important shopping we took a trolley down Nepperhan Avenue past the vast carpet mills to Getty Square, now a wasteland of empty shopfronts, discount joints, and parking lots, but then alive with stores that remain with me less as visual images than as collages of remembered scents: a department store that was a magical amalgam of perfumes and new leather and linen; the five-and-ten that smelled of liver and onions and popcorn and camphor.

Before television, in the evenings my mother would play music for me on the Victrola: Josh White and Leadbelly, and Tom Glazer and the Weavers, and the symphonic recordings of Leopold Stokowski—Mozart, Beethoven, and Tchaikovsky—and Italian opera, which she loved most of all. (With the arrival of TV, Puccini and Verdi would, to my mother's dismay, quickly give way to the rest of the family's demands for Jimmie Durante, Jackie Gleason, and Milton Berle.) On Sunday afternoons we got in my father's patched-together prewar Chevy and drove to a pond in Scarsdale where I could feed the ducks, or to a café that was in a log cabin in Armonk where they made cinnamon doughnuts, or cruised up the Saw Mill River Parkway to Hawthorne Circle and back down the Bronx River Parkway, making a game of trying to spot woodchucks and deer. My father always drove, my mother in the front alongside him, smoking, talking politics and searching for interesting things to point out to me. How restless she must have been traveling at my father's cautious pace: years later, when I rode with her in the West, I saw how she loved big powerful cars and the open road, and disliked riding when anyone else was behind the wheel, and that when left to herself she drove fearlessly and fast, and how with a cigarette between her lips and a thermos of fresh coffee by her side and someplace new to go, she looked happier than I ever saw her anywhere.

I can see my father driving us on summer evenings to buy dough-nuts, or ice cream at Schrafft's in Scarsdale, or Chinese take-out from the place on Central Avenue. I can also see him—perhaps the quint-essential image—at his basement worktable, bent over a vise, work-ing obscurely at lengths of copper pipe or galvanized sheeting, or in

the Hephaestean glow of a blow torch that throws into grotesque relief the rows of his tools neatly suspended from hooks over the table.
But for the most part he rarely appears in my early memories. I often
have a sense of his presence, but no image at all. It is as if he has been
airbrushed out of the picture like some fallen Communist potentate.
When I do see him it is usually fleetingly, a walk-on without lines in
my mother's drama. Perhaps he was actually away a lot in those
years, installing boilers and air conditioners in the city. But I think
that the truth is that he has just fallen out of my memory. The cruelty
of this forgetting leaves me almost breathless, astonished at the way
in which someone who was present every day, whose life was so in-
tertwined with mine—*my father, after all!*—could simply disappear
like this, as if by some sinister sleight-of-hand. If even a father can be
lost so easily, how much else has seeped away without a trace? Just
the thought terrifies me beyond belief.

On Sunday mornings my mother usually slept late and my father
would take me along in the car when he drove Maddy to mass at St.
Anthony's on Nepperhan Avenue. We would buy the papers at Barbalette's—the *Times* and *Herald Tribune* for my mother, the *Daily
News* and the *Journal-American* for my father—and wait out the
mass at the Lighthouse, my father's favorite bar, named for the miniature lighthouse on its roof, a local attraction that was just the right
size for a little boy, I would think, if he could ever get up there. When
I told my father that I wanted to live there someday he would laugh
and give me nickels to play the pinball machines while he drank rye
and read the funnies. When I got bored, he put me on the stool next
to his and set up ginger ales for me while he drank. There was magic
in the dimness and in the male smell of the place, and in the rows of
bottles that glowed behind the bar and that reminded me of the
books that filled the walls of our home: the books were my mother's
mysteries, the bottles my father's, runes to which only he held the key.
In all those years it is only on Sunday mornings at the Lighthouse that
I see us together in a world of men, without my mother, the only
place where I can see with certainty that I once loved him without
restraint.

Religion belonged to my grandmother, and I associated it inextricably with illness, boredom, and gloom. In spite of my parents' atheism, I thought of us, vaguely, as Roman Catholic, which meant to me something like saying that we were Irish or Norwegian, depending on which of my parents' families we happened to be talking about, implying not much more than a sense of origins rather than loyalty to any particular doctrine, much less to Rome, or for that matter even belief in God. My mother told me that when I was old enough to decide for myself, it was my own business what I chose to believe in and that what mattered in life was telling the truth and sticking to principles and helping the underdog, not trust in priests and myths. Only Maddy's room, the room that would become mine years later, after her departure for the nursing home, after my mother's death, hinted at a religious presence in our home. It always seemed darker than the rest of the house, the effect, I think, mainly of much heavy old furniture that must have been handsome in its day—the furniture of the Washington Street house, of her truncated marriage, of the eminent golf-playing, Elks-leading Dr. Madigan. When I was sick, it was always to this room that I was taken and where I sweated out fevers and passed muzzy, bored days recuperating in a bed so high that I imagined myself afloat on the high seas in a Spanish galleon. Maddy fed me cinnamon toast and sat on the bed and played Parcheesi and Chinese checkers with me, and told me her stories about her father's adventures in the Civil War and Gilded Age New York and the house on Shore Road. When she left me alone, I would stare in my feverish drowse at the strange calendar that marked off Fridays with pictures of fish and the tacked-up mass cards and the old Bible that Maddy's father had brought from Ireland, and finally, inexorably, though I hated to look at it, at the tortured corpse on the cross that hung on the wall opposite the bed, and I would feel a sickening terror that what the bad men had done to him would someday be done to me.

Four or five times a year my mother would perplex me by taking me to mass at St. Anthony's with Maddy. What were we doing there, got up in Sunday clothes like the Francks and the Campanellas, and the *real* Catholics? Was it possible that from time to time my mother lost confidence in her unbelief and actually needed some kind of spiritual reassurance? Or were these trips to church impulsive exercises in nostalgia that evoked pleasant memories of the frescoed Christ that throughout her pious childhood had descended toward her from the spellbindingly blue ceiling of Sacred Heart? Or were they empty gestures to placate Maddy's distress that I was not being raised a Catholic at all? If my mother ever told me the reason, I have forgotten it. Nothing much remains except a vague impression of boredom and of my knees aching from the unfamiliar routine of prayer. But for almost half a century I have preserved the image of her elegant white gloves, snug-fitting so that the shape of her fine, small hands showed clearly beneath fabric that was as soft as a cat to the touch, clasping and unclasping in what was either prayer or worry, like furtive white birds in the nest of her lap.

My mother was probably the most sophisticated and the best-educated woman in our neighborhood. Although she got along well with everyone, I can't help but believe that on some plane she must have felt alien and isolated. Yet she never complained or spoke slightingly of our neighbors, except when questions of politics or race intervened. Somehow she had acquired an emotional self-sufficiency that enabled her to live at ease with her differentness, to not mind not fitting in. She did try, without much luck, to cultivate the few foreigners in the neighborhood: the Swiss who worked for the UN and lived on Bretton Road, an Australian couple who had a daughter in my school, and the von Bleikens, who came from South Africa and lived up the street from us. Of these, only the von Bleikens seemed to work out for a while, perhaps because they had a boy around my age. Mrs. von Bleiken was a dark, exotic-looking woman who dressed in what I seem to remember as silky, sinuous clothing that accentuated the impression of foreignness. The father, a boisterous near-giant, liked to recount tall tales about his exploits in Africa and before that in Russia, from which his family had escaped after the Revolution. Rennie was an excitable boy, rougher than the rest of us but also bigger and more spontaneous, and therefore often a leader in our play, the one who wouldn't hesitate to pilfer something to play with from the forbidden sanctum of a parent's bedroom or to try to start up the family car on a lark.

The von Bleikens lived in one of the larger houses on the block, faced with stucco and set behind a huge maple that was often the focus of our games. One day we were playing with the new boy who had moved in next door, and Rennie said, pointing to me, "You be the cowboy and we'll be the Indians and we'll tie you up." I can easily see now that what happened next was a ploy to impress the new boy, to coopt him, to startle him into the obedience that Rennie obviously knew that he could expect from me. But it was also a betrayal, my first evidence that friendship could not completely be trusted and that the placid and familiar surface of my childish world might conceal undreamed-of terrors. I said nothing as the two boys tied me to the maple with laundry line and began piling leaves around my feet. Somewhere Rennie had gotten matches. Had he planned it all beforehand? I stood helplessly against the tree, paralyzed with fear and trust as he set fire to the leaves. I could see my mother in our yard far away down the block. Rennie followed my eyes and said, "If you say anything, we'll kill you." I fought back tears and promised, sure that I was going to die anyway, like the poor man on the cross, but I was determined to do it bravely, like a marine, and then began to cry anyway and begged to be released while Rennie lit more matches under the smoldering leaves. Finally, contrite or simply bored, he and the other boy let me go, and I fled down the street to my mother, climbing into her arms with relief, knowing that my world had somehow changed for the worse and knowing, too, that having discovered that I was a coward at heart, I would preserve my vow of silence forever.

2

AROUND THIS TIME the first black family moved into the neighborhood. Probably they were professional people since they bought one of the better homes, a large brick house on Delaware Road. This was long before there was any local legislation barring discrimination and there was soon anxious talk about "blockbusting" and about how something had to be *done*. A crisis meeting was held at the community center on Saw Mill River Road. My parents went along with everyone else. My mother told me afterward that terrible things had been said, that people said that the Negroes had to be gotten out, and that there had been shouting, and words spoken that she would not repeat. It was hard to visualize my playmates' parents behaving this way. Had Mr. Jetter been one of the shouting people, or the Collinses, or Mr. Franck, or the doctor who lived on Odell Avenue? My mother told me that of all the people at the meeting she was the only one who spoke up for the new people. She would have told the neighbors to their faces what they were, and I know that she wouldn't have been shy about it or pulled punches. She would not have been shrill or polemical; rather, as I sometimes saw for myself in later years, when she faced bigots who had underestimated her because of her size and her sex, she would at first probably have been anecdotal or witty, seducing them into complacency, and then cut them dead, making it quite clear how deeply she held them in contempt. But that night, just an angry little woman who didn't fit in, she was finally shouted down or walked out in disgust. Eventually the Negro family was somehow forced to move, or simply made to feel so unwelcome that they left on their own. My mother tried to explain to me what had happened. But I didn't really understand the neighbors' rage, or what difference it made whether the Negro family stayed or left, or whether my mother stood up for them or not; in those days, Delaware Road—five blocks from my house—was another world, and what happened there was as remote for me as if it were happening in China. I did somehow understand that my mother, because she wouldn't keep her thoughts to herself and wasn't afraid of making a scene and didn't care what the neighbors called her, had done something heroic.

By the time we moved to Yonkers, the postwar Red scare was in full swing. The threat of another world war was palpable as the wartime amity between the United States and the Soviet Union dissipated as the Soviets consolidated power in Eastern Europe, suppressing opposition, and making it hard for all but ideologically blindered Americans to recognize the totalitarian nature of Communism. In Western Europe huge, well-organized Communist parties seemed poised to overwhelm the unstable democracies of France and Italy. Communist partisans were engaged in a bloody civil war for control of Greece. Russian and American tanks had come close to confronting each other in Iran. In China, communist armies were on the brink of defeating Nationalist forces that had been heavily and expensively supplied by the United States. Americans' anxiety that the United States was losing control of the peace approached panic when it became apparent, in 1949, that the Soviet Union had an atomic bomb. Membership in the Communist Party USA had swelled to its peak of one hundred thousand during the War, and it had taken a prominent role in support of the war effort, in addition to its less public one in some labor unions and civil-rights groups and organizations concerned with promoting friendly relations with the Soviet Union. Although the Party's actual influence on government was insignificant, the American Legion, the Hearst newspapers, the Catholic Church, and right-wing Republicans were encouraging Americans with ever greater stridency to believe that both their national and personal security were in imminent peril from Communists who were boring secretly at every American institution, like a virus that corrupted all it touched. Disagreement with established policy was increasingly viewed with distrust, and vigorous dissent as disloyalty.

It became clear in the 1946 Congressional elections that Redbaiting paid off at the polls when Richard Nixon and other Republicans defeated liberal Democrats by alleging links between Communism, the New Deal, and FDR. The House Un-American Activities Committee, a political watering hole for what was probably the worst collection of bigots, reactionaries, and opportunists ever to grace the halls of Congress, was already hard at work hunting for alleged subversives and determined to find them wherever it looked. In an effort to counter the Republican charge of being "soft on Communism," the Truman administration instituted a pervasive regime of background investigation that was intended to certify the loyalty of government employees. While employees theoretically had the right to hear the charges against them, accusers could in fact withhold anything they designated as secret, including their own identities. Many who were accused and later dismissed from their jobs were guilty of nothing more than having belonged to liberal organizations that were merely alleged to have had Communist affiliations. In 1948 the government indicted the entire national board of the Communist Party under the Smith Act, arguing that although they had done nothing to actually subvert the government, the simple fact of belonging to the Communist Party made them part of a conspiracy to do so in the future; they were eventually sentenced to five years in prison each. That summer—*Were you still unpacking from the move from the city? Planting the first seedlings in your garden? Painting the new dining room that red that you would always hate?*— a reformed Communist named Whittaker Chambers, now a *Time* magazine editor, testified before HUAC that Alger Hiss, a former New Dealer and diplomat and now the respected head of the Carnegie Endowment for International Peace, had turned over government documents to the Soviets in the 1930s, an accusation that eventually led to his conviction and imprisonment for perjury, a denouement that convinced Americans both that Communism had insinuated itself into the very core of the American elite and that even the mighty could be destroyed by the rising tide of anti-Communism.

My mother had committed herself to the Communist Party, perhaps even loved it once, if briefly, with all the seriousness that she brought to everything in which she believed; when she understood the Party's essential opportunism and its slavish promotion of Soviet interests, she rejected it and, to the best of my knowledge, never looked back with even a trace of regret. She knew from her own experience that the Party deserved much of the distrust with which it was increasingly viewed even by liberals. She was never a bleeding heart—it was a term she used with disdain—and she believed that the country had a duty to protect itself where protection was necessary.

But she also believed unequivocally that what people thought was their own business and that they had the right to express it however they pleased, and that suppressing their voices was a worse crime, or at least a greater danger to the nation, than facile talk of revolution, and that democracy was in greater danger from the actions of American zealots than it was from Soviet espionage.

She was deeply though quietly patriotic: she saw to it that we hung out a flag on national holidays and folded it with precision when we took it down, and she never lost her fundamental confidence in American institutions, though it was sorely tested in those years. She had a clarity of political values, an *uprightness*, that seems almost antiquated today in this era of slack convictions and airbrushed ethics. She would have been influenced, certainly, by her father's civic-mindedness and, later, by the radical activism of the 1930s; but at the root of her politics, I think, lay a vision of democracy as a matter of personal honor that came, at least in part, from her intimate knowledge of the classical world, and particularly her love for the vibrant democracy of fifth-century Athens, when responsibility for every political decision fell equally upon each free man, so that being true to oneself permitted no escape from decision, and decision none from action. Years later, when I read Thucydides, I recognized something of her in the words that Pericles spoke over the Athenian dead of the Peloponnesian War: "In the business before them they thought fit to act boldly and trust in themselves. Thus choosing to die resisting, rather than to live submitting, they fled only from dishonour, but met danger face to face. . . ."

Like many Americans who hoped that the end of the war would bring a return to the progressive policies of the New Deal, in which, my mother believed, fairness and generosity of spirit had ennobled Americans and led them to their own better nature, she was dismayed by the onset of the Cold War and the virulent politics that it had ignited. She hoped fervently for Adlai Stevenson's election in 1952, believing that he would put an end to the witch-hunting, demagoguery, and invasions of civil liberties. A few days after his defeat she would write, in a letter to Oliver LaFarge, the president of the Association on American Indian Affairs, where she was by then working: "Roosevelt was already in office when I had my first vote, and it took me until this November fourth to realize what democracy demands of those who believe in it as a form of government. My heart didn't ache like this when I was a maiden writing sonnets."

The panicky mood rippled steadily outward from Washington. When Julius and Ethel Rosenberg were arrested in 1950 as key participants in a Soviet spy ring that had channeled atomic secrets to the Soviet Union, it seemed to justify the anti-Communists' warnings. Genuine concern over Communist influence had already prompted the CIO, the NAACP, the Urban League, and other liberal organizations to expel Communist-dominated affiliates. The American Federation of Teachers voted against allowing Communists to teach. School systems around the country began requiring loyalty oaths and firing tenured faculty who took the fifth amendment when accused of Communist Party membership. The School Librarians Association of New York ordered library shelves stripped of books by the novelist Howard Fast and other "subversive" authors, regardless of the content of what they had written. Businesses hired former FBI agents to investigate the politics of their employees. In Peekskill, New York, a short drive from our home in Yonkers, a mob led by the American Legion attacked the audience at a concert by the black Communist singer Paul Robeson. Political discourse became increasingly poisonous. After a friend of Alger Hiss committed suicide by throwing himself from a window, Congressman Karl Mundt of South Dakota answered a reporter's request for more names of Communists by replying, "We'll name them as soon as they jump out of windows."

I knew Joseph McCarthy's name before I could ride a tricycle. For a time I thought of it as something I could call someone when I wanted to hurt his feelings: "You dirty McCarthy!" Like "Alger Hiss" and "the Rosenbergs," whose names were also staples of dinnertable conversation in our home, it was further evidence that things could go deeply wrong in the adult world. It was a word that would turn my mother's lilting voice suddenly harsh and my father's profane. Even my Irish Catholic grandmother spoke of the Irish Catholic

McCarthy with the kind of sneer that she reserved for the Orange-men and the ill-bred. It was on February 9, 1950 that the junior sen-ator from Wisconsin famously declared in a speech to the Women's Republican Club in Wheeling, West Virginia, making it all up as he went along, that he held in his hand a list of the names of two hun-dred and five Communist spies who were "shaping the policies of the State Department." In the course of his four-year rampage, Mc-Carthy alleged massive Communist infiltration not only of the State Department, but of other branches of the government, the Protestant clergy, and the army, attacked his critics variously as "left-wing bleeding hearts," "egg-sucking phony liberals," and "communists and queers," and denounced the Roosevelt and Truman years as "twenty years of treason." Apart from the China scholar Owen Lat-timore, whom, with no evidence at all, he claimed to be the "top Russian agent" in the United States, he never identified a single sub-versive. When a committee of his fellow senators concluded that his charges were a "fraud and a hoax perpetrated on the Senate of the United States and the American people," McCarthy dismissed their report as a "sign to the traitorous Communists and fellow travelers in our Government that they need have no fear of exposure," and continued his smears unabated until he overreached by taking on the army in 1954. By then, McCarthy and other senate and congressional committees had launched no fewer than eighty-five separate investi-gations into alleged domestic Communist influence. It has been esti-mated that, in all, several thousand Americans lost their jobs, the great majority of them guilty of no wrongdoing, a few hundred were jailed, and two—the Rosenbergs—were executed for espionage.

In 1952, to my mother's unending shame I suspect, NYU became the first private university in the nation to actually invite the investi-gation of its faculty by interested federal committees. That October my mother's one-time departmental advisor Edwin Berry Burgum would take the fifth amendment before the Senate Sub-Committee on Internal Security. Three hours after his appearance he was fired from his position by NYU's chancellor. Later he would be sentenced to a year in jail for contempt of Congress.

Neither my mother nor my father could have been in much danger of investigation, since she did not even return to work until late
1951 and he was a part-owner of the heating service company for
which he worked. Their membership in the Communist Party had
been comparatively brief, and there is no evidence that either of them
played a prominent role; nor is there a record of either of them having been investigated by the FBI. Yet the paranoia of the time reached
even into our home on Mayfair Road. One day my parents went up
to the attic and cleaned out what was left of their days in the Party.
In his old age my father told me: "We decided to get rid of that stuff.
You didn't want to have it around in those years." In my imagination
the scene has a furtive quality. I see it taking place at night after I have
been put to bed, although it could just as easily have happened on
some sunny Saturday morning while I watched cartoons on TV. I see
them squatting on pieces of plywood thrown down over the rafters,
their heads bent under the slant of the roof. They search through old
suitcases and packing crates and folders, picking out clippings and
poems, and photos and addresses that I would now give anything to
see, whatever records still remained of what they did and who they
knew. They also got rid of the sets of Marx and Lenin that everyone
in the party had been pressured to buy, hardcovers most of them, a
costly investment in the depths of the Depression, overlooking only
the single stray volume of Lenin's works that I stumbled upon years
after my mother's death. My father took everything but the books
down to the backyard, where he burned it in the barrel that we used
for paper waste. He put the books in the trunk of the two-tone Chevy
and drove them away to a dump, perhaps in the Bronx or Queens,
somewhere far away.

*Can you really have done this? I remember you as utterly fear-
less, uncowed by anyone or anything, unswayed by something as
fickle as public opinion. I look at the photos of us—you and me—on
those sunny afternoons in our still-tentative backyard: laughing,
wide-eyed, I am totally absorbed with the camera and you, barely
conscious that I even exist outside your love, never imagining that I
cohabit in your thoughts with Alger Hiss and the Rosenbergs, and the*

howlings of Karl Mundt and McCarthy. The child who still lives somewhere deep in my heart cries out with all the self-absorption of the infant I see in the pictures that it was I—only I!—who provided you a respite from the poison abroad in the world. Perhaps I at least reminded you that there would, after all, be a future and that I would grow up into an age less mad than this one.

The day the Rosenbergs were executed at Sing Sing, not far north of where we lived, we drove for some reason to a little stand that we liked on Saw Mill River Road and bought hot dogs for dinner. (Maddy and my father must have been there, but I see only my mother and me, and the Greek who ran the stand, sweating in a white apron and cap.) Standing alongside the Chevy eating our franks, my mother said that there was no need to have killed the Rosenbergs, that it would have been enough to have put them in jail until they served their term, and then let them go to Russia if they wanted to go. They deserved mercy, not because she believed they were innocent, because she didn't, but because their execution was vicious and unnecessary, and shamed the country, and shamed her as an American. How much of what I remember she actually said then and how much is the residue of later conversations I don't know, but I have always thought of that muggy June evening on Saw Mill River Road as the first time that I began to grasp the idea that punishment for wrongdoing could be worse than the crime itself, that it could irrevocably taint the punisher, and that a country that was remorseless in its quest for vengeance could eventually destroy what was best in itself.

My mother wrote a sonnet around this time called "Ballade of the Golden Age." In it I see her as if she were here before me now, looking out the window of her bedroom, where she wrote, toward Saw Mill River Road and the tracks of the New York Central, a yellow legal pad on her knees, smoking and feeling dreadful for America and fleeing temporarily into the hard Attic sunlight that she always dreamed of but was never fated to feel in the flesh, and to which she always returned in her imagination when her way in life was no longer clear:

Assuredly, there was a golden time
For us upon the earth. A breed forlorn
As we are now must have survived a prime
When to be born a man was to be born
The best of animals, with eyelids worn
Wide open and a sweet clean mouth to say
A private truth out plainly as a horn.

3

ONE MORNING in the autumn of 1951 my mother went back to work. She had been hired as assistant to the executive director of the Association on American Indian Affairs, which had its office on East Eighty-sixth Street in New York City. The Association, as everyone called it, had been founded in 1930, and in the early 1950s it was the only important independent advocate for Indian rights in the country. Its small but influential membership of twenty-five thousand was composed mainly of anthropologists, former government officials, and others with a personal or professional interest in Indian affairs. The Association saw itself, in the words of its president, the respected Pulitzer prize-winning author Oliver LaFarge, who had led it since 1933, as "a sober and impartial fact-finding institution" that defined its role as "public education, guidance of the federal and state governments in their administrative handling of Indian matters, or, when necessary, opposition to them, and guidance and stimulation of the Indians themselves in various forms of self-help and self-advancement."

The then-executive director of the Association, Alexander Lesser, recorded his first impressions of my mother in a letter to LaFarge. Lesser had been seeking an assistant who would be capable of shouldering at least some of the Association's policy work. "I feel sure that her loyalties are to people, especially minorities, and not administrators. My only fear in her case is that her intellectual abilities are too great for the dirty work side of the job. Miss Madigan is the first new employee I've ever had who came in on her own Saturday of her first week to study over some of the files and think through what must be done to straighten them out. Incidentally she has started at $80 per week as against [another candidate's] $90, itself a recommendation of her real interest in what we do rather than a mere job." In less than four years, she would have Lesser's job and be leading the Association into an era of creative activism that would be indelibly stamped with her character; for the first time she would also have a field of action wide enough to match her ambition.

I never thought much about my mother's decision to return to work. I always took it for granted as something incidental to the political influence and celebrity that to my childish imagination seemed preordained. But there was nothing commonplace about it at all in an era when popular magazines typically portrayed career women as miserable and emotionally empty, and glorified dutiful mothers and wives. The authors of a popular psychology book of the time entitled "Modern Woman: The Lost Sex" asserted that feminism "was a deep illness" and declared that "the independent woman is a contradiction in terms." My father's memoir has nothing to say about this except his characteristically matter-of-fact comment that "I think she always planned to go back to work." I don't think that we needed the money; my father's business was doing well. And she had me, a child not quite four years old. Perhaps the limitations of our neighborhood finally got to her; or perhaps she felt starved for the independence that she had yielded when the War Relocation Administration was liquidated, and that was something that no woman could then take for granted. In France, Simone de Beauvoir had recently published *The Second Sex,* the most influential feminist work of its era. When I was six or seven, I would notice the American edition, with its mysterious title, lying for a long time on my mother's bedside table. "It is through gainful employment that woman has traversed most of the distance that separated her from the male; and nothing else can guarantee her liberty in practice," de Beauvoir wrote. "Once she ceases to be a parasite, the system based on her dependence crumbles; between her and the universe there is no longer any need for a masculine mediator." Did my mother need to read this in order to understand where she stood in the male world? More likely it only confirmed what she already knew. She was far ahead of her time in her assumption that she deserved a career of her own, and the right to participate in the larger world and make her own mark on it, and that her family could be expected to accommodate it.

The image of that unseasonably warm autumn morning is still clear. My mother and I stand facing each other at the bottom of the driveway. She puts her hands on my shoulders and kneels to reach my level. She has on the pert green pillbox hat that I love, which she wears in every early memory that I associate with her work, the quintessential symbol of the mother who is now different from all other mothers, the only one who goes away into the great world on the train every morning with the neighborhood dads. (Sometime later she will give me this hat to keep; I will put it on and think, *I'm going to New York to help the Indians.*) Holding me, she tells me that she will be leaving me every day but that she will always come back, so I shouldn't be afraid. She is obviously worried that I will bawl and beg her to stay. Of course I could not imagine, any more than she probably could, that from this moment on she would never again belong to me in quite the same way, that she would be drawn inexorably away from us all, year by year, toward Rosebud and Cherokee and Macy, and a hundred other places where Indians lived and that would, in their way, finally consume her. She lifted the green veil from the lower part of her face, kissed me, and left.

THE ARCHIVES of the Association on American Indian Affairs are stored on the top floor of Seeley G. Mudd Library at Princeton University. They were deposited there helter-skelter in the 1980s, at a time when the Association was in decline and moving to smaller, less expensive quarters in Manhattan. (A victim of the racially polarized politics of Indian country, it has since removed whites from its board and shrunk to a small office in rural South Dakota.) Until the files were catalogued recently, they remained as the Association had left them, a vast jumble of cardboard boxes in such disorder that it made research in them painfully frustrating. In my work on an earlier book on contemporary Indians I had used the archive only sparingly and with an acute, almost physical, discomfort that had nothing to do with the chaotic state of the files themselves. I felt overwhelmed by my mother's presence and uneasy at what I might discover. I stuck to the dry prose of policy, self-consciously avoiding the pursuit of references to her for fear that I would find a woman whom I did not recognize, fearing that I might discover mediocrity and irrelevance, someone whose achievements I had magnified through childhood fantasy and who would now seem small and second-rate.

But if there is any monument to my mother it is this archive, where everything she believed in for the last decade of her life lies contained in the four hundred file boxes that rest in silent shadow on metal shelves alongside those (she would have been pleased) of the American Civil Liberties Union. These thousands, these tens and hundreds of thousands, of papers are her own papyri, filled with reports that are in their own way as hauntingly filled with the spirit of their time and place as those of the camel merchants and clerics and fig farmers of sixth-century Syria that she deciphered as an undergraduate at NYU. It took me a long time to come back to Mudd Library. I knew I would find my mother there, and that there more than anywhere else my memory would be forced up against the documentary record. Inescapably I would see how much of her I had invented, how much might turn out to be a figment of wishful imagination, an idol burnished by guilt, remorse, and nostalgia.

It was a dank autumn day. The New Jersey sky was gray and dimensionless and wet, the air blustery. Shoppers on Nassau Street were flogged relentlessly by a sodden wind that slapped collars into faces and turned umbrellas inside out. Through the library's picture windows I watched students pressing forward against the wind, and wet trees shorn of leaves that careered away into mist. Apart from myself and a tall bald man bent like a question mark over another of the plain wooden tables that were set aside for researchers, there was no one else there. I was surrounded by mounting stacks of manila folders, memoranda, reports, newsletters, correspondence, photographs, wads of sheets from yellow legal pads. As I read, hour after hour, I felt my mother rising around me like a tide, drowning me in her incredible energy, her brilliance. Here she was briefing Edmund Wilson on the Iroquois, and here warning the Secretary of the Interior that he was expected to keep his word to a group of Alaskan natives ("I am sure you do not want the Eskimos to be answered equivocally"), and here cajoling the governor of Florida into releasing land to Indians squatting in the Everglades, and here trading witticisms with Margaret Mead, and here planning a pot luck dinner with Indian friends in Nebraska. Familiar places percolated from the pages: Rocky Boys, Cattaraugus, Fort Berthold, Shishmaref, resonating so intensely that they seemed to take on material existence, as if I could take them in my hands and hug them to my breast. Pages were still stained with spilled coffee from the cup that was always at her elbow. Instinctively I sniffed and, as if stumbling into some long-hidden crevice in my memory, the aroma of freshly brewed Martinson's seemed to swarm through the room. There were innumerable handwritten letters scrawled in her vigorous, racing script. There were countless reports—boiling vats of ideas—filled with plans for economic enterprises, the protection of reservation law and order, stockraising programs, tribal farms, arts-and-crafts factories, even the herding of reindeer on native land in Alaska. In newspaper articles from Oklahoma, Alaska, New York, Washington, the Dakotas, Miss LaVerne Madigan was always *saying . . . declaring . . . commenting . . . warning . . .* There were hundreds of letters to humble people: advising an Indian parent whose son had become discouraged about applying to college, or promising to find fifty dollars to repair a fieldworker's car. I even found myself here. In September 1952 she wrote to her old WRA boss Bob Cullum, "Fergus entered kindergarten this year. He keeps his own counsel and won't tell us anything about it except that one of his classmates looks like a pumpkin with gray hair." In another letter to Cullum, from 1954, she described a trip that she took me on to Massachusetts, my first alone with her: "We went to Boston to visit Lexington, Bunker Hill, North Church, Salem, Ply-

mouth and other places which, happily, can be seen with restored idealism when one is accompanied by a little boy."

I found many items that recorded her delight in tribal customs
and beliefs. She wrote to LaFarge from the Northern Cheyenne reservation in Montana, "Tonight on the way to a meeting I was hurried
past a spot identified as a medicine man's grave. The old boy came
out of it the day he was buried, walked around the reservation for
several days, and then vanished under his mound of earth. His reason? To show people what he could do. On the way home from the
same meeting we hurried past a second place, on the highway, where
it was said practically every Cheyenne had seen a phantom car that
goes before drivers and tries to lure them into the thirty-foot gully. I
checked, and just about everybody did see it." She added wryly, "I
think I shall spot a leprechaun tomorrow night. The Cheyenne
spooks need cheering up."

Other writings revealed an extraordinary ability to step into the
psyche of ordinary Indians and to understand the maze of contradic-
tions that shaped their attitudes toward whites. "Whites must be
stingy by nature. That is why they always have money for groceries,
money in the bank, money to send their children to school. Whites
know how to manage their lives, and they are ugly; when they are
angry their blood goes up to their heads and their faces flash on and
off like traffic lights. They know how to do what they want to do,
and they hate Indians. That white teacher gave pieces of pie to the
Omaha boys and four of them got sick; she must have tried to poison them. Whites are not really bad, but they always know what to
do. They are better than Omahas."

She also had a deep, instinctive empathy with the bitterness of
conquered and frustrated people, understanding that the Indian
problem was not just one of administration and better provision of
federal services, but something that went to the heart of American
democracy. "The problem is that of what a democracy is to do with
elements of conquered peoples who do not admit to conquest," she
wrote to LaFarge, on the familiar yellow foolscap, at a time when it
appeared that Communist agents were attempting to penetrate Indian

organizations and manipulate them in ways that would benefit Soviet propaganda. "Almost as great a danger, I think, lies in the fact that intolerable as this may be to us in our national self-image, our democracy is impure to the extent that the people we conquered do not accept it as their democracy—and to that extent we are corrupted by a hidden colonialism (hidden from ourselves, I mean). We owe it to our children to make [our democracy] as nearly perfect as we can—this is not a mere exercise in political idealism . . . As long as the corruption, the colonialism, is there, or until the implacable colonials die out, we shall have spiritually desperate people among us who are subvertible by the spiritually base."

Occasionally there were letters that showed something of the grit that kept her going. In July 1961 she wrote to Dallas Little Head, a Cheyenne friend who was apparently deeply discouraged by the slow pace of change, "I think I understand you but perhaps I do not. I think your whole heart and soul is in what you are doing. You are giving your whole self. Because it means so much to you, you feel terribly discouraged whenever something goes a little bit wrong, and you get terribly worried about failure. What can I say to you, my friend? Only this. Next time you are disheartened and afraid and angry, think of me. I feel like that sometimes, too, but I never threaten to resign and I never will. I believe that a better time is coming for the Cheyenne, and I believe that the work we are doing will make that time come. When some foolish Cheyennes say bad things, or when real leaders like you and Mr. Woodenlegs get discouraged, I feel tired and afraid too. I feel like running out. But I don't run out. I am still here."

Boxes of photos revealed faces that for thirty-five years had lain like ancient palimpsests deep in the well of my memory: William Whirlwind Horse, John Woodenlegs, John Stands in Timber, Alfreda Janis, Buddy Gilpin, Ella Irving, Guy Okakok. There was LaFarge with his long, handsome face and long torso, and long arms and long hands, and hollow-cheeked angularity, and tight Yankee lips. There was, of course, her face, too. In a quintessential image of her later years she sat amid a panorama of folding metal chairs, next to La-

Farge, at a meeting that had just ended or was just about to begin, dressed in a short-sleeved cotton jacket that hung with suave Manhattan elegance over her shoulders, and several pieces of Navajo jewelry, tilting her head as she had for photographs since that day on the steps of Sacred Heart School in Mount Vernon, pulling off a white glove. There was a look of thoughtful expectancy in her eyes and the ghost of a smile on her lips; she was stylish, alert. It was an image of a woman at the center of things, a woman in charge.

In these thousands and thousands of pages I at last saw the mother that I remembered: the "Indian lady" as she was known, fondly or not so fondly, to many who knew her in Washington and the West, the hard-headed idealist, the woman who made things happen, who was always boiling over with ideas, who enjoyed power and used it well, who loved the people for whom she wielded it, who knew how to move good but uncertain men toward the achievable. As I read, I saw her growing in political acuteness, seizing issues and making them her own, creating order out of political chaos, challenging moral equivocation. Forty years later I could still feel her optimism, her self-confidence, the thrill of a new sphere of politics being created upon the somnolent colonial landscape of Indian country: "It is predictable that the positive forces released in the Indian communities will rapidly become self-sustaining or win local Indian and non-Indian support. The most important force released has been self-sustaining from the start, for that force is the faith of the Indian people in their strength to direct their own lives."

I HAVE NO EVIDENCE that my mother knew much about Indians before she joined the Association. But she quickly learned that the human panorama of Indian country in the 1950s was a dismal one. In the course of four centuries of European settlement the native population of North America had fallen from two million or more in 1492 to a low of two hundred and fifty thousand at the turn of the twentieth century, mostly as a result of imported infectious diseases against which Indians had little resistance. So stark was the rate of their disappearance that nineteenth-century Americans expected Indians to die away completely within a generation or two. The collapse had catastrophic consequences beyond the sheer number of dead; it wrought havoc upon each community's ability to defend itself, to reproduce, to replenish its food supply, and to sustain its spiritual life. The demoralized survivors remained at the margins of American society, isolated on reservations and dependent on subsidies from a government that, as a matter of policy, ignored their leaders, suppressed their religions, and bullied them to live like white Americans.

By the end of the Second World War the Indian population had recovered somewhat to about half a million, divided among some three hundred tribes ranging from a few dozen members to several tens of thousands. Nearly all of them lived in a state of appalling destitution. Rates of infant mortality, suicide, homicide, alcoholism, and infectious diseases far surpassed those of other Americans. Little news about Indians was reported in the national press, apart from features about rodeos and the like. A rare exception was a story that appeared in *Time* in the autumn of 1947, reporting that between twenty-five thousand and thirty thousand Navajos in Arizona were close to starvation; the story matter-of-factly added that "by January, if the winter was hard, there would be snowdrifts on the reservation and many of the children and old men would be dead." Occasional brief periods of reform had attempted to alleviate the worst aspects of reservation life, though never with lasting success. The most recent such period, initiated during the administration of Franklin Roosevelt, had halted the sale of tribal lands and provided for the election of tribal governments with limited powers, although they remained under the tight control of the Bureau of Indian Affairs, which was commonly referred to as the BIA or simply the Bureau, and its local superintendents, who continued to run tribal affairs like colonial governors. This era was just coming to an end when my mother joined the Association on American Indian Affairs.

In another of the abrupt reversals of policy that has characterized the federal approach to Indian affairs, the Truman administration embraced a program of mass relocation of Indians to the cities, culminating a long-standing strain of policy making that held that Indians could only be saved from poverty and hopelessness by shedding their tribal identity and abandoning the reservation. My mother may well have been attracted to the Association precisely because she recognized this as a restatement of the policy that the WRA had carried out with Japanese-Americans during the latter part of the war, although she probably did not yet understand that an exodus of Indians would finally wipe out already fragile tribal communities. However, her emotions must have been aroused as she read about the Association's investigations into the case of the three Indian boys in Idaho who had been sentenced to fifty-six years in prison for stealing a sheep, and about the two North Dakota white men who received ninety days in jail apiece for "disorderly conduct" after stabbing an Indian to death, and the white man in Nebraska who got a two-year suspended sentence for bashing an Indian's head in with a baseball bat in an unprovoked attack, and the South Dakota policeman, who was never prosecuted after he shot an Indian who failed to stop when ordered, and then ran up and finished him off as he lay wounded in the gutter.

Pressure to solve the "Indian problem" once and for all accelerated after the Republican victory in the 1952 elections. New bills, which had the strong support of Western cattle interests and which passed both houses of congress without any attempt to ascertain the wishes of Indians themselves, called for the outright termination of Indian tribes, the abolition of tribal governments, and the break-up of reservations into private property. In spite of the official lip service that was paid to the idea of democracy, federal policy was overtly hostile to the consent of the governed when it came to Indian communities, allowing its agents to flagrantly override the will of tribal governments as they saw fit. In one case that preoccupied the association at the time my mother joined, the BIA was refusing to permit a tribe in Nevada to hire its own lawyer with its own money to protect its legal fishing rights on its own reservation. Elsewhere, when the commissioner of Indian affairs traveled to reservations, tribal leaders typically were not allowed to meet him with their attorneys, minutes of meetings were not made available to tribal members, and tribal council resolutions approving the speedy termination of their own tribe were prepared in advance by BIA staffers and handed to the council members.

Although it would be overshadowed by the better-reported struggle of black Americans, this would become one of the great civil-rights battles of the era. Indian rights, however, meant not only equal treatment under the law, but also the freedom to refuse to assimilate, to remain aloof from white America. "Reservations are not prison camps but the remainder of a homeland," my mother would write in a 1952 memo to Lesser, perhaps for a speech or press release, and perhaps explaining these things to herself for the first time. "Indian tribes entering treaties with the United States did not think they were signing away their right to be Indian. The sense of sovereigness which the Indians had about themselves and which can be inferred from the very existence of treaties has to underlie any Indian rights which exist today side by side with equal rights for Indians, which are different." The Association, almost alone, vigorously opposed termination, arguing that the federal government had a duty to retain its responsibility to the Indians until they had achieved, as a minimum, the standard of living of their non-Indian neighbors, and that it should be left to Indians to integrate themselves at a pace controlled by their own readiness to take the necessary steps. The Association's concerns were well-founded. In California, when state jurisdiction became immediately effective, the authorities promptly started arresting Indians for exercising their ancient right of hunting and fishing on their own land. Elsewhere, when tribes were terminated thousands of impoverished Indians poured onto county welfare rolls.

LaFarge's prominence and his pedigree had lent the Association a certain moral force virtually from the beginning. A product of Groton and Harvard, grandson of the the painter John LaFarge, and a lineal descendant of Benjamin Franklin, he had been trained as an anthropologist, and had done fieldwork in Central America and the Southwest before becoming a writer. He was lionized after his first novel, *Laughing Boy*, a romance set in Navajo country and the first serious novel to cast Indians as its protagonists, won the 1930 Pulitzer Prize for literature, having been picked over *A Farewell to Arms, Look Homeward Angel,* and *Dodsworth.* But by the 1950s his work was out of fashion, and his correspondence with the Association from his home in Santa Fe, where he worked, reflects a continuing anxiety over money and security until his death in 1963, at the age of sixty-one. He was, his obituary stated, "a tough and salty [man], not always easy to get along with and very hard to please," but "he was always on the side of people who needed help." He admired my mother's classical education and her eagerness to learn, and his confidence in her abilities grew over time. In return, she admired him for his intellect, his sense of justice, his knowledge of Indians, and perhaps, I suspect, because he was a writer living a life that she once wanted for herself. Preparing for her first field trip to the Southwest, she waxes enthusiastic "especially [for] the part in your company. I can see you as a sort of Virgil leading Dante." There would have been irony in this remark, but I think not much.

I learned from LaFarge's biographer, Robert Hecht, that one of my mother's secretaries, Lillian Pollock, was still alive. I found her at the age of ninety-two living on West Twenty-eighth Street, in Manhattan. Tiny and spry and smiling at me from beneath a tuft of white hair, she told me right off that she hadn't been feeling well, that she'd been mugged in the lobby of her building a few weeks before, "the first time anything like that happened to me, and he knocked me down and afterward I couldn't get myself up again, and now I don't like to go downstairs unless I have to." Then she showed me picture after picture of granddaughters and nieces and nephews who lived in Florida. After that she went into the bedroom and came back with a white envelope that she had saved since 1962 and gave it to me. Inside was a copy of my mother's obituary from the *New York Times.*

"Your mother was what I call a real Yankee Doodle," Pollock said. "She was a real bread-and-butter, meat-and-potatoes lady. She was the most brilliant person, but she never threw her Phi Beta Kappa in anyone's face, though she could have. She wasn't like a boss. No job in the office was too petty for her. To even the most humdrum tasks she brought a kind of restlessness, a zealous desire to get things done. At the same time, she was curiously modest, getting people to do things by indirection rather than by demand. She was willing to listen to you." We talked for a while about how it had seemed to me, especially in her last years, my mother was always in motion, on her way to Washington or the reservations, never resting, never taking a vacation without returning from it with a cargo of reports and a stack of legal pads filled with jotted plans and ideas, and about how, I thought, she must have been incredibly strong to have kept it up the way she did. "I don't know where her strength came from," Pollock said. "She didn't talk about things like that." Then she added something that puzzled me. "LaVerne always had a smile. Once she said, 'I could be the sickest person in the world and no one would know it.' She meant because it never showed on her face."

I had never thought of my mother as someone who calculatedly masked her emotions. Naïvely, I had never thought of her as anything more or less than she appeared to be, a complicated woman surely, but clear and direct, prizing honesty above all. Of course she was the product of an age when it was considered rude, if not irresponsible, to allow private concerns to intrude into the public or professional realm. But still, her remark had stuck with Pollock all these years. It hinted at something more than just professional dignity: deliberate concealment, an ease with facade.

Pollock gave me a phone number in Brooklyn for Sylvia Hermelin, who did fund-raising for the Association during my mother's tenure. I remembered Hermelin vaguely but quite fondly because every year around Hanukkah she sent home a chocolate-filled dreidel for me, the only seasonal present that I was allowed to open before Christmas morning and that I played with on Christmas Eve, filled with anticipation for the day to come. When I reached her, she said that she was on the committee that was building a Holocaust memorial in her neighborhood and had to be on her way to it but that she'd be happy to tell me what she could. "It was always something new with LaVerne," she said. "She always came in with one batch of books and left at the end of the day with a different batch of books.

She was always trying to absorb things. The more she knew, the more she wanted to know. Al Lesser was a brilliant man, but mostly he just sat at his desk. He didn't mingle with the people. She did. It wasn't just a job to her. Until she started traveling, no one did. She was excited about it. When she came back from one she was always full of ideas, and she got us excited, too. The Indians weren't just names anymore. Before she came, you never saw them. Now they'd come to New York, you'd meet them, and you got to see the person behind the name. She didn't give a darn about the average way of life. What she was concerned about was what she could do for other people. She didn't worry about hours. She worked on her vacations. She'd come in when she wasn't feeling well. She always had to be accomplishing something. She delved into it and until she got what she wanted from it—I don't mean for herself, but for the Association, for the Indians—she wouldn't stop. She didn't give a damn about her personal self."

My mother had only been on the job a few months when Lesser left on vacation, informing LaFarge that "Miss Madigan will be in charge and I have ever increasing confidence in her abilities and discretion." In August 1952 she made her first of many field trips for the Association, driving with me and Maddy to western New York, where she met with members of the Seneca and Tuscarora tribes to canvass their feelings about the imminent extension of state criminal and civil jurisdiction over their reservations. Nothing much remains to me from this trip except the thunder of Niagara Falls and the vague impression of a dark and eerie place that may have been an old fort on Lake Ontario, and a peculiarly persistent and troubling memory—more an image, really—whose sense of import never faded although its identifying details long ago melted away. I am standing in a vast open place, clutching my mother's hand. We are waiting for something momentous to happen, perhaps for someone to come, who never does. The atmosphere is one of intense expectation and disappointment. That's all. This image always gave me a sense of vertigo: the tiny child lost in all that empty space, and the strange feeling that everything else has fallen completely away, leaving only my mother and me, and our disembodied hope. Over time I lost the sense that this even reflected a real event that had taken place in the physical world and came to think of it as the residue of a dream or fantasy. Then a few years ago I found myself in the small city of Salamanca on the Seneca reservation, where I stayed for a few days in a hotel across the street from a disused railroad station. Looking out the window at this scene it struck me instantly that this was the place in my memory: that the vast open place I remembered was simply the station parking lot, and that my mother and I were waiting there for my father to arrive. Since my mother had the car, naturally he was coming by rail to meet us, at what was then still a major railroad junction, just the sort of place that he, with his lifelong fascination with trains, would love. We waited and waited but for some reason he failed to come. But it is just as possible that he arrived after all and that my memory long ago rewrote the script, finding the wait and the anxiety, the disappointment at a train that may have been delayed an hour or two more memorable, more interesting, than the anticlimax of his arrival.

My mother was apparently the only person in the office who got along with the unstable Lesser. Lillian Pollock told me, "We were all scared of him. We thought he was *meshuga*. He'd be shouting at the top of his voice when he came in in the morning. If he couldn't reach someone on the phone, he would scream and start pulling the phone out of the wall. LaVerne would flap her hand to him to keep it down. She wasn't afraid of anybody. She'd say, 'Go up on the roof—you could send smoke signals.' " Whether from her competence alone, her willingness to stand up to him, or some ability to calm and reassure (which, curiously enough, is not something that I associate with her at all), or most likely, a combination of these things, she won and kept Lesser's confidence and that of the board of directors, who grew increasingly anxious as Lesser's state of mind deteriorated.

In time it became abundantly clear that it was my mother who was actually running the New York office. Lesser had become very erratic and almost impossible to work with. He would call board members up in the middle of the night to rant about his problems, and couldn't stop talking. Corinna Smith, a wealthy and influential member, complained to LaFarge that at a private lunch with her in Manhattan Lesser had "shrieked" for two hours "in the manner comparable to McCarthy's tactics . . . He kept yelling 'I, I, I' until I was completely exhausted." My mother told Smith that the office "was in a condition of chaos because of Lesser being so upset that he cannot get down to the immediate work required." LaFarge worried that Lesser was crippling the Association at a time of particular crisis in Indian affairs. "We are looked on as the national authority on this subject, the Indians consider us their principal friend and champion, and we are in danger of being unable to deliver because we are overextended," he wrote diplomatically to one board member. "Above all, our Executive Director, Dr. Lesser, is so overloaded that he is swamped, and cannot give adequate attention to any one of the many phases of our work." More bluntly, he told Smith in a private letter that in his opinion the executive director was "pretty close to psychopathic." By 1955 a majority of the board had turned against him. "We are going to have to ditch the man before he destroys us," LaFarge warned them. Lesser was induced to resign at the end of June 1955. My mother was officially appointed executive director early the following year. The new mood around the New York office was palpable. Writing to LaFarge in a voice whose proud, combative ring I can still hear, she declared, "Suddenly from an organization which agitates we are emerging as an organization which acts."

After the spring of 1957, when LaFarge, a prodigious smoker, underwent an operation for the removal of a lung, leadership of the Association passed firmly into my mother's hands. For the rest of her life the Association would be the most visible, most forceful, and most creative Indian-rights organization in the United States. My mother's reports from these years show a woman who is almost constantly in motion, who is exhilarated by the exercise of power and by the knowledge that she is having an effect. LaFarge tells her warmly, "You have been, of necessity, dashing about the nation putting out brush fires—or starting them." She is on her way to Florida to persuade the governor to put land in trust for the Miccosukees, and to upstate New York at the invitation of Iroquois nationalists who want her to communicate their views to Washington, and to Washington where the commissioner of Indian affairs wants her to put his agenda on the desk of the secretary of the interior, whom he has been unable to get an appointment with for a year, and to Mississippi to try to unseat a hard-core segregationist who is superintendent of the Choctaw Agency, and to a weekend with Edmund Wilson at his place in the Adirondacks, where he has asked her to read his manuscript of "Apologies to the Iroquois" ("His whole thesis is unsound from start to finish"), and to Montana to advise Cheyennes who want to repurchase lost parts of their fragmented reservation. Her energy is inexhaustible; in a letter to LaFarge, she describes herself humorously as "this report factory named LaVerne Madigan. . . . I dreamed for a moment about an IBM thinking machine which could be fed field notes and grind out narrative reports and sound policy recommendations. Of course, I would kill myself if this could be done."

4

IT IS IN THESE YEARS, then, the last six years of my mother's life, that I see us, my mother and me, with the greatest sharpness and fixity, cut like a frieze in stone: heroic mother and adoring son. Memory insists that it was in these years that our relationship reached its ideal state of mutual understanding and shared adventure, and it was always in these years that, in my imagination, I took refuge during difficult periods in my life. It was only years later, with hindsight, that I could see that the center of my mother's life was shifting toward Indian country and away from our home and family. "I feel on safe, familiar ground in the oddest corners of the United States," she wrote to her friend Harry Forbes, an influential member of the Association's board, in 1959 from Billings, Montana. "As I drove in here from the airport tonight, I was thinking, 'Well, home again!' "

I was excited about her new work. After all, she was working with *Indians*, and to a suburban boy growing up in the Golden Age of Hollywood Westerns the word summoned up fecund imagery of frontier adventure and couldn't help but thrill. After she became executive director of the Association, she traveled increasingly often, sometimes for weeks at a time. Her phone calls would come in the night long-distance—still an exciting event then, requiring pre-arrangement and a special operator, and patience with connections that sometimes took hours to make—from places with names like Wind River and Rocky Boys and Chadron that from the perspective of Mayfair Road seemed as unimaginably exotic as Timbuktu. When she came home there would be a kind of glow about her, a vividness, and she would always have something strange for me in her suitcase, a bone flute or a painted medicine pouch or arrowheads, proof that she had been to a world utterly unlike ours and that she promised me that I could, with her, one day enter, too.

I spent more time with Maddy now. After school, we would sit on the living room sofa and watch the soap operas that she adored, or play cards and Chinese checkers, and she would tell me stories about Ireland, or at least the handed-down Ireland that she had never seen, an Ireland of martyred patriots and diabolical Orangemen, and so green that when we went for drives on Sunday afternoons and I saw fields or forests that looked greener than others I would ask, "Is that as green as Ireland?" My mother's Irishness was a point of pride and a source, perhaps, of her easy wit and joy in combat. But it was, at its root, I think, a cerebral thing; determined to give me an Irish name, she chose one not from the familiar catalogue of Celtic saints, but instead a warrior's from the poetry of William Butler Yeats. But it was my grandmother's vague and fabulous Ireland that survived for years in my imagination, fostering a sense of Irishness that, after three generations in the United States, had little real meaning in the suburban world where we lived, yet seemed somehow as significant, and ineffable, as my memories of my own infancy, and that forever remained infused with the mood of those languorous afternoons, and the soap operas, and the Chinese checkers.

I would listen to Maddy, enveloped in her remembering, as she told me over and over about James Patrick Farrell's "escape" from Ireland, and his supposed adventures in the Civil War, and about his "brother's" Louisiana plantation, and how she had rolled bandages for troops at Fort Hamilton in the Spanish-American War, and about the pillared mansion where she grew up overlooking the Narrows, and about her life there that was so much grander than our own in Yonkers, hinting at connections to the Harrimans and Astors, and to other grandees of the Gilded Age. These stories, I know now, were a muddle of fantasy, wishful thinking and only occasional truth. Still, it was from them that I first grasped the idea of the past in a personal way, and understood that when I was born I had entered a world that was already old but that could be made real again through the power of memory. From Maddy I learned that the past was a place I could go any time, a foreign country where I always knew the landscape and the language, and in which, whenever I wished, I could disappear.

I can see now, however, that for Maddy these stories were not about history at all, or at least not particularly, but about a deep hurt that she could express to me in no other way, for nearly all of them carried a pointed subtext of unhappiness: most of all in her own childhood, with its persecution by the seven imaginary brothers. (Or, perhaps, I now wonder, by a drunken and sadistic father?) Even in her seventies she was still asking for pity. "We're pals, aren't we?" she would often ask as we sat in front of the TV, eating our cinnamon toast. She would try to hug me and I would instinctively pull away, never understanding her craving for intimacy, love, and approval. It's impossible to say when she began to behave oddly, or whether, perhaps, the strangeness had been there for a long time but had just been better concealed. But finally it became so glaring that it could no longer be ignored.

My father, perhaps prompted by my mother, who recognized that Maddy was less fit to take care of me, now from time to time initiated expeditions that years earlier might have drawn us closer together but that now felt false and strained and were almost always fiascos: a fishing expedition on Long Island Sound, though neither of us liked fishing, or a Saturday matinee at the movies, watching a film that neither of us enjoyed. We would ride home in silence, both of us

bruised and irritable, never understanding the lasting price that
would be paid, by both of us, for saying nothing at all. But days like
this were few and then, after a while, there were no more.

There were changes in the neighborhood. Most of the woods that
remained were cut down to make room for new houses. The steam
engines on the Putnam Line were replaced with diesels, and then pas-
senger service was discontinued altogether and my mother and the
neighborhood men who used to ride it to the city took to automobiles, big new luxurious models, for the daily commute. One of the
country's first shopping centers was built a few miles from us on Central Avenue, and the commercial center of Yonkers began to run to
seed. When a modern supermarket opened on Nepperhan Avenue,
the vegetable man bought a truck and tried to compete for a while,
and then ceased coming around at all. The advent of stainless steel
put the knife grinder out of business. Television increasingly took
over our evenings, or at least mine and my father's and Maddy's, replacing the gusty discussion of politics that my mother loved and
that, before she traveled so much, used to go on at the table long after
dinner was over.

Like many children of the 1950s, I was growing up with the utterly unquestioned conviction that the suburban world I knew was
eternal, safe, and complete, as if history had existed simply in order
to bring into being the complacent quietude of Mayfair Road. My
mother must have seen the danger in this, and she did her best to un-
dermine it. She took me with her on her travels as often as she could,
first to the Southwest, and to Nebraska and the Dakotas the next
year, and then to Oklahoma and Florida and North Carolina, and
then to Montana and the Pacific Northwest, and to Mississippi, and
to Alaska. To most of these places, we returned together several
times, and to a few of them, particularly Nebraska and South Dakota
and Alaska, many times. I loved being with her on the road, watching the ever-receding horizon, often not caring when or even whether
we got where we were going, just enjoying the humming of the car
on the open road like a great mechanical cocoon, and having my
mother beside me and no one to bother us, and the vast prairie out

the window all around us, and the feeling that nothing, ever, could make me happier. I fell in love with the open West at my first sight of it, that first summer of 1956, driving through Arizona and New Mexico, across land hued in a multitude of reds and yellows that I had never seen in the earth before, and nearly empty of people, and so devoid of trees that when I did see one it seemed like something wondrous and inimitable beneath the impossibly vast sky; and after that, and after seeing for the first time what my mother was really doing, and how the people she was working with lived, in shacks and falling-down cabins and sometimes abandoned cars, and how so many of them had a grim, beaten look that I had never seen on the faces of people in Westchester, Yonkers was never quite the same again. Although I could not have articulated it then, if anyone had asked me, I was beginning to grasp the remarkable security of the way we lived at home, and to feel that it was perhaps no more deserved than was the horrific poverty that I saw, though usually at a safe distance, on the reservations. It wasn't guilt that I felt, since I could see for myself that my mother was working as hard as she could to do something for the Omahas, and the Sioux, and the Choctaws, and the Cherokees, and the Navajos, and all the other Indians I met; rather, I felt—and I imagine that it is something like what my mother felt—a seeping discomfort with the ordinariness, the predictability, the sheer *easiness* of our suburban world, and I knew without knowing just what I wanted in my life that I wanted something more, and that my mother would eventually lead me there.

5

"THERE REALLY WAS no other voice before LaVerne to make sure that Indians had something to say," Betty Rosenthal told me. I found Rosenthal—properly, Dr. Elizabeth Clark Rosenthal; anthropologist, child of missionary parents and raised among Indians in South Dakota, and the only surviving member of my mother's board of directors—living in Santa Fe, and in her late seventies still immersed in

native issues. "LaVerne was a brilliant director. She had an instant instinct for it. She identified with people in a way that no one else had
from the day she got there. She went against the inner atmosphere of
the Association, which had always helped the Indians as a sort of
'distant dowager' program. But LaVerne really cared about these per-
sons themselves. She loved them and they her. I don't mean collec-
tively; I mean individually, really being friends on an even basis. It
wasn't just a feeling for people's hurt, which you could sense that she
felt. It was a deeper common human thing that she really lived. At the
same time, she was a ball of fire. There were always new ideas. We'd
have one, and then another would come out of it, and then another
from that one. That whole period was like an enchanted forest."

My mother's most immediate concern was the concerted federal
attempt to liquidate the "Indian problem" by terminating the tribes.
It was one of the most inglorious periods in American political history. "Every device of obstruction with which a powerful arm of government could block and bewilder ill-educated poor people was
brought into play, justified to the public by half-truths, misrepresen-
tations, and plain lying," my mother wrote. This attack upon Indian
communities was being carried out through an array of superficially
unrelated congressional acts, BIA measures, and state laws. In some
areas tribes were denied the power to repurchase lost tribal land with
their own tribal money. For years, in one instance, the BIA had actually prevented the Cheyennes from using their funds to buy back a
tract of former tribal land that came up for sale. My mother wrote,
"The senseless aggression of the United States via the Bureau against
this little community makes me think of those old one-reel Charlie
Chaplin comedies. Charlie would be walking down the street happily
toward some pleasant destination, when inevitably that huge man
with the bulging eyes would charge at him, grab him up by the collar and shake him until his teeth rattled, stamp on Charlie's hat and
break his cane." Elsewhere BIA administrators practiced outright de-
ception, telling tribes falsely that since they were slated for termination they would benefit by terminating themselves. On some
reservations, states were refusing to enforce law and order, leaving

Indians utterly without police protection while the federal and state governments bickered over financial responsibility for reservations that, it was assumed, would soon disappear. "Some Indian Bureau officials and anthropologists question the fitness of certain of the Plains Indian groups to survive even though they have the will to do so," my mother wrote in an essay in the Association's newsletter. "The questions arise: can a democracy wash its hands of any of its children? Can it remain a democracy if it allows a community of its people to die out when that community desires to live?"

While the Association's two brilliant young lawyers, Richard Schifter and Arthur Lazarus, lobbied aggressively to reverse termination, my mother proposed a fresh way of thinking about Indians, no longer as the alien inhabitants of isolated entities known as reservations, but as American citizens with a distinctive way of life and the right to live it as they chose in their own communities. She demanded real self-government for tribal people who for generations had been made to feel incompetent to set their own goals: "The exercise of political authority in their own immediate community-level affairs is the only method man has yet discovered whereby a people may show that it has community purpose, and to carry out that purpose."

Under her leadership the Association lobbied for an aid program for American Indians modeled on the United States foreign-aid program then being offered to developing nations abroad, calling for a commitment of technical guidance and financial assistance based on the tribes' assessment of their own needs, the maximum development of tribal natural resources and agricultural production, a longterm commitment to vocational, technical, and professional education, and respect for Indian culture and identity. Although it was not until years after my mother's death that the federal government made a commitment to this kind of support, it was her work that laid the groundwork for what came later. She set up the first curriculum workshops to remove stereotypes of Indians from school texts and to develop new teaching materials for the public schools that would include Indian culture and history. She committed the Association to putting up funds for the legal defense of Indians who were convicted after unfair trials and sponsoring the first law course ever for tribal judges. In the face of opposition from Christian missionaries, many of whom still regarded traditional Indian religious practices as forms of "devil worship," she urged that peyote men be given a place in interdenominational church services.

The concrete embodiment of her thinking was a program to which she gave the deliberately corny, unthreatening title of "We Shake Hands," after the Lakota symbol for friendship. It was intended from the start as a pilot program for the revitalization and empowerment of Indian communities across the country. She put the problem this way in a long article entitled "Indian Survival in the Great Plains" that she wrote for the September 1957 issue of the Association's magazine *Indian Affairs*: "The question is being decided by our generation whether the Indian people of the Great Plains shall survive with self-esteem in communities simultaneously Indian and American, or whether they shall survive as landless individuals—forlornly reproducing themselves where their lands used to lie or migrating desolately from camp to camp."

The We Shake Hands program was a radical departure from anything that had ever been done before in Indian Country, and it was far ahead of its time. The question to be tested, as my mother put it, was whether "an Indian community on the death list had the will to survive and, given an opportunity, would act on it." The idea was to develop a core of local, civic-minded individuals, rather than a mass movement, and to provide both the Indians and non-Indians of the region with a sense of being fellow citizens in their home counties and states. In the process Indians would also gain access to the local non-Indian allies they would need in the struggle to survive as communities. The Association did not directly fund economic-development programs, for which it lacked the resources. Rather, it supplied funds for local, mixed Indian-and-white organizations, which planned development for themselves. It was the first time in American history that the initiative for an Indian program was to be left to the Indians themselves and that whites who wanted to help would be expected to follow the Indians' leadership.

After a hundred years of paternalistic rule even Indians had come to believe that the absence of power to act in their own interest was an Indian cultural characteristic. My mother believed that, at least to some extent, it was less important what Indians actually accomplished than that they accomplished it themselves. "In the United States only in war time is the average citizen asked to sacrifice his individual good for the commonweal," she wrote, "but . . . our Indian citizens are asked to decide day after ordinary day between food on the table and survival of their tribal community. The average white American can serve his country merely by being no worse than average. The Plains Indian can serve his people only by being a hero." We Shake Hands "is an action which, in order to fulfill itself, must liberate all of the imprisoned forces of change in the Indian community," she wrote. "It is not, therefore, a race relations action simply. It is, depending upon what the seeker seeks, an action in colonial self-assertion, in ethnic community survival, or in rural community development. It is, almost incredibly, an action by the Indian people to resist federal programs to terminate their communities through land-sales and dispersal of population—an action whereby the Indian people themselves began to take back from the Bureau of Indian Affairs the basic political power." Tribal leaders "began the action with a feeling of awe at the might of the federal power which was then pitted against their community's power of survival, and a feeling of awe at themselves for exposing their people to they knew not what impossible tests of competence to act on their own behalf, and to they knew not what Kafkaesque retribution if they failed."

My mother selected as the two main laboratories for this ambitious experiment the Omaha Indian reservation, seventy-five miles north of the city of Omaha, in Nebraska, and the Pine Ridge reservation of the Oglala Sioux, in western South Dakota. Federal officials had glibly cited the Omahas as the most culturally disintegrated, socially ill, morally ruined, and least fit to endure among the nation's tribes. Most of the tribe's one thousand or so members lived in decaying farmhouses and shacks around Macy, the tribe's main town, which my mother described after her first visit there, in early 1957, as "the forlornest, most ramshackle Indian community to be found anywhere in the Great Plains." There had been no law enforcement on the reservation since 1953, and society had completely broken down. On the weekend before her first visit there had been a stabbing, an Indian-white gang fight, a rape and a kidnapping, and a man was beaten to death by a gang of drunks, all in the center of town. "Any visitor who spent a week in Macy . . . could not fail to hear the endless, obsessive gossip about adultery and dishonesty. He could not fail to see drunken parents, neglected children, youthful violence sometimes ending in bloodshed, and deliberate cruelty to animals." She reported that nearly everyone lived in homes that lacked running water and often even electricity. Broken windows were stuffed with paper to block the winter chill. Typically a husband, a wife, three or four children, and perhaps one or more grandparents would be eating, sleeping, and living in a single room. When children had been delivered to school, the husband would stand around on the streets of Macy until it was time to take them home again. The mother might sit with other women on a bench in the general store, watching her husband closely through the store's window. "Her jealousy is the only occupation she has." Superstition was widespread. People exchanged tales about a hill that screamed and a phantom horse that was often heard but never seen galloping along the roads, about a dog that turned itself into an old man and of a strange erotic creature they called the Deer Woman, who seduced young men and left them mad. As citizens the Omahas were "politically inert but perpetually disgruntled." Their greatest woes, she thought, were "the desperate, grinding, debasing need for money, and the tragic lack of understanding of government as the means by which the people act in community. Elected officials were so poor that they frequently embezzled, or pilfered, minuscule amounts from the tribal funds."

The Association had been invited onto the reservation by the tribe's young, newly elected leaders. Of these, my mother developed the closest relationship of all with Pauline Tyndall, the tribe's first elected female official ever, and a woman who concealed beneath the compliant manner that was expected of her in a male-dominated society a quality of steady and implacable determination that impressed itself on me even as a child. She was, in my mother's words, "educated and book-loving, public spirited and eager for social change," much more literate than non-Indians in the surrounding communities, and she found it cruelly difficult not to be recognized as an individual by whites. The tribe's chairman, Wayne "Buddy" Gilpin, was also rare among the Omahas at that time, having had a year of vocational training plus several months of business school.

I remember Gilpin well: a severe man, all bones and lankiness and jet-black, sleekly groomed hair. Although his English was imperfect, he expressed himself with a certain homespun dignity. In response to the BIA's decision to terminate the tribe as an alleged "efficiency measure," he declared that the Omahas were "just waking up" to their helplessness, "just rubbing their eyes," adding, "I say, most humbly, to the respected officials, that cheaper administration, even better administration, is not everything. The good and happiness of the people is everything. I knew my Omaha people would be afraid when they heard the Bureau of Indian Affairs was thinking of making a great change in their lives. It is a poor life, but it is the only one they have to live. The only changes that will not frighten my Omaha people are the changes they make themselves."

THROUGHOUT 1957 and 1958 my mother virtually commuted to Nebraska. At first many of the Omahas were suspicious of her motives. But she faced hostility with aplomb. After one raucous meeting she drily wrote in her report, "Angry, decisive questions came so thick and fast that the writer raised a sandwich to her mouth a hundred times but never did have a chance to eat it." With her support, however, Tyndall and Gilpin formed for the first time on the reservation voluntary citizens' committees around dissatisfaction with the county school board, farm prices, and federal Indian policy. Soon they were producing an economic-development program, applying for federal loans, committing tribal money to the repurchase of former tribal lands. Some women formed a branch of the PTA. Others went to church more regularly. Young people, "coming upon the idea of group recreation like a new continent," my mother wrote, persuaded the tribal council to buy a juke box and Coke machine and held dances every night. The Omaha Junior Tribal Council invited non-Indian 4-H clubs from the surrounding area to visit them at Macy. They also arranged for an advanced course in public speaking and for adult courses in business English and composition. They began talking, for the first time, about starting a course in Omaha language and history. The tribal council introduced the primary election and the secret ballot for the first time and began talking, hesitantly, about opening the tribal records to all who wanted to see. Ordinary people began to pay more attention to their personal grooming, their homes, their children's attendance at school, school-board and county elections, and violations of their civil rights by law-enforcement officers. "The pent-up forces of social change burst forth in such a Niagara that the Indian people who live in [Macy] have been speeded to a comprehension of what is taking place and are inviting leaders from other Indian areas to visit their town as if their community experience were a visible tourist attraction," my mother wrote, adding that Tyndall, "a fascinated observer of human behavior in and out of Macy, peers into the Omaha community, as a chemist peers into a retort he has put on the bunsen burner, and reports excitedly, 'It's happening!' Perhaps what made the difference to the Omahas was the fact that for the first time they felt like part of the United States and the state of Nebraska, and not like a colony of cultural lepers exiled on Mars."

ONCE MY MOTHER LEFT ME for a few days at the farm of one of her Omaha friends while she went away to a conference. She intended this as a treat, I think, a chance to get to know a couple of Indian boys about my age, her friend's sons, and to explore a landscape that, in spite of its poverty, she truly loved. But it is also possible that she meant it as something more than that, something that would toughen me, prepare me better for the harsh world in which Indians and, increasingly, my mother lived.

The farm was a poor and depressing place in the middle of rolling hills of corn, several miles from Macy. The old clapboard house showed no trace of whatever color it had originally been painted. There were no books in the house or comic books, no radio or television, no window of any kind into the America of the 1950s. The older boy, Mike, was a stolid sort of boy about my own age; Alvin, who was a few years younger, was permanently crusted with grime and wore nothing but a dirty T-shirt.

My first day there, Mike showed me the cornfields and the mudhole where they swam in summer, and the smokehouse out back where they cured meat. "That's where my dad beats me when I'm bad," he said. "That's the strap he uses." He pointed to an old strip of leather. The darkness of the old smokehouse and the stale smell and the strap frightened me. I said that I had never been beaten in my life, but I don't think Mike believed me.

I was bored and anxious, and after only a few days had passed, I began to imagine that I had been there for weeks. The vast ocean of corn seemed strangely sinister and claustrophobic to me, and disturbing fantasies flooded through my head. What if I had to spend my life here? How often would I be taken to the smokehouse and beaten? What if my mother never came back? At night, in the swaybacked bed where I had been put with the two boys, I lay awake for hours, rigid with fear, worrying that my clothes were going to be taken away from me, that I would be left naked in the tidal fields of corn.

I had been to many reservations before this. But it was not until now that poverty penetrated my consciousness in a personal way, in the boys' solemnity and their fear of the strap and the awful loneliness of the place, and realizing that there was nowhere to escape to, that this was simply *it*, the alpha and the omega of nowhere. Memory tells me that for days on end I stood for hours in the dusty road, staring through the corn, willing my mother's car to appear. This cannot literally be true. But the image is indelible: the red-haired boy filled with fear and helplessness, and hating what he felt, ashamed of wanting his mother, and thinking that she would be disappointed in him if she found out that he wasn't a Viking at all. And I thought: *I will never tell you how scared I am.*

When my mother's rental car finally appeared through the corn-fields to take me away I promised myself that I would never give her reason to leave me behind again.

Like the mental pictures of us together on the Arctic shore, and at the conference at Tanana, and speeding through the night across the prairie, this image is a paradigmatic one. Unlike the others, how-ever, which speak to me of intimacy and pride, and the thrill of a shared journey into the unknown, this image speaks to me of fear and shame, of my almost complete lack of self-sufficiency. I see, in this petrified boy in the red Nebraska dust, a boy who has nothing to go home to any longer—that although he will not understand it for a few more years yet, home has become his mother alone, and that without her he is utterly lost.

THE PINE RIDGE SIOUX RESERVATION was more typical of the larger na-tive communities on the Great Plains. It was more populous than the Omaha reservation, and much more isolated, ninety miles across empty, rolling prairie from the nearest city. I remembered it as a rough and ready place, where families with too many children and not enough clothes or food lived in shacks and abandoned cars and little one-room log houses without running water or electricity. Still, to a young boy, the Old West still seemed amazingly alive there, where Indians my age knew more about cattle and horses than they did about what was on TV, which many of them had never yet seen, and the men were saturnine and tall and long-legged and narrow in the hips, as if nature had crafted them perfectly to fit a horse. Pine Ridge was famous as the site of the tragic 1890 Wounded Knee mas-sacre and as the homeland of the clans of Red Cloud and Crazy Horse, and in the 1950s memories of the frontier wars were still vivid and close. It was a very bleak time for the people at Pine Ridge. My mother wrote: "The Oglala Sioux are losing their land at the rate of 80 acres a day; long unemployment is making the people unemployable, and the Oglala future seems to lie over the edge of a cliff." A joint declaration of the tribal government and We Shake Hands stated that "two-thirds of the [1,875 families] on the reservation constitute a chronic problem of poverty, disease and social maladjustment, as reflected in broken homes, alcoholism, and a disturbing crime rate." In small towns near the reservation violence against Indians was rampant and went virtually unpunished. "The Indians, with justification," wrote my mother, "live in a state of helpless fury" over such abuses. At the same time, she was aghast at the Indians' ignorance of their most basic constitutional rights. "The Indians themselves, including the chairman of the committee, showed complete confusion about how to proceed," she wrote. "I discovered on this visit [in May 1961] that none of them knows with certainty what civil rights are nor what protections the Constitution affords. As Moses Two Bulls put it, 'Something tells us when our rights are violated and we protest, but we never saw the Bill of Rights.' "

My mother never doubted that even a community as ravaged as Pine Ridge could be stabilized and made productive for its people, but she was also hard-headed in her assessment of what was possible. She knew that because of its isolation, its lack of valuable resources, and the low level of education, the chances of it becoming self-sufficient were virtually nil. So, in contrast to the Omahas, who, my mother believed, could achieve complete autonomy, the goal of We Shake Hands at Pine Ridge was to determine how much political "self-realization"—my mother's favored term—a community inescapably dependent on federal programs could reasonably achieve. Essentially she foresaw a future in which the people of Pine Ridge would request programs that they needed and participate in their administration, rather than passively submit to whatever the government chose to give them.

As she had in Nebraska, she organized a network of white academics, women's clubs and church groups that would serve as a liaison and as advocates for the Sioux at the state and county levels. Working with the tribe's chairman William Whirlwind Horse and with Alfreda Janis, a member of the tribal council, one of the many exceptionally dynamic women who gravitated toward my mother, she also initiated a series of mass meetings in small towns around the reservation. I have transcripts of some of these meetings. "The Oglala Sioux fought bloody battles to win the land that is called the Pine Ridge reservation," she reminded the assembled Yellow Bulls, and Looks Twices, and Red Clouds, and Kicking Bears, and Runs Againsts, and scores of others who had come together in a community hall in the hamlet of Allen, the first gathering of this kind to be held on the reservation, in October of 1959. "They could have left this reservation to go to other parts of America where jobs are plentiful and white neighbors are friendlier. But instead they chose to stay on the reservation that has become their homeland. They have chosen poverty and ill-health and loneliness sooner than leave the place where they can be Oglala Sioux together. . . . The land of the Oglala Sioux is disappearing from under their feet. But if they plan to keep what is left of their land, our organization will fight for the plan the Oglala Sioux make. And if the Oglala Sioux people make a plan for living a decent life on their land, our organization will fight for that plan too. . . . I am sincere when I say that you Oglala Sioux people and not I should be talking. The philosophy of our organization—and we think this should be the philosophy of the Federal Government—is to find out what the Indians want to do and try to help them do it."

Out of these meetings grew an economic-development plan that included a land-repurchase program to accommodate the growing population, ideas for agricultural development and tourism, a public-works program, a youth program modeled on the New Deal's Civilian Conservation Corps, and aid to small businesses; all this was conceived years before Lyndon Johnson's Great Society initiatives made such programs a common part of federally funded community development. There were also ideas for a pageant based on the epic of Sioux history, and for the establishment of an independent civil-rights committee, and for adult education. Young people started up a junior tribal council, and women under the leadership of my mother's friend Ella Irving founded an interracial branch of the League of

Women Voters, the first ever in the United States to be chartered on an Indian reservation. In response to this, candidates running for Congress and for state and county positions for the first time bothered to come to the reservation to present their views and to meet Indian voters. "[We Shake Hands] is the one and only organization that has done things that the Indian people feel they are a part of," Alfreda Janis, by now the local coordinator of We Shake Hands, wrote to my mother. "More and more they come to me and say will your organization help us with this problem? My answer to this is will you try to help yourself & then together maybe we can find an answer to do away with this problem. For the first time they are treated as individuals."

There was, in those last years of the 1950s and the first years of the 1960s, an atmosphere of excitement and political ferment at Pine Ridge, a glimmering that new and important things might be accomplished. In her description of an encounter with an impoverished family my mother captured the fragility of this hope: "An Oglala family I know camp, for lack of a home, by the highway outside of Rushville, Nebraska, on the border of their reservation. I went to look for them one day after a heavy snowstorm. The air was so cold that it hurt to breathe it, and the wind blew the fallen snow in clouds over the prairie. I had to squint to see my friends through the whiteness. They came out of their tent behind the billboard. The mother butchered meat on an old crate and the father chopped wood. He was a big lord of a man with a frostbitten, intelligent face and hopeless eyes. He leaned for a moment on the long handle of his axe and said, 'I guess you know what we are trying to do for ourselves.' He did not say any more, and neither did I. Both of us had the superstitious feeling that to state our expectation of better things was to doom it."

I often traveled to Pine Ridge with my mother, usually for a few days at a time, occasionally for a week or more. Curiously, considering all that was happening at the time, the memory that remains most vivid for me is a particularly painful one. It was 1958, when I was ten years old, and I was to be given an Indian name by Ella Irving's father Ben, in a public ceremony at the midsummer powwow, which was held in a circular enclosure on the prairie outside Pine Ridge village. My mother and Ella and Alfreda Janis stood around me as Ben dressed me, settling a splendid headdress on my head and tying a fan-like feathered bustle around my waist and connecting it to my wrists with an arrangement of cords so that I, or at least a dancer who knew what he was doing, would be able to manipulate the bustle as I danced. Ben, incongruously dressed (for a powwow) in a suit and tie, took my hand and led me out in front of the multitude, many of them feathered and in buckskins, like a mass reincarnation of another age, and declared that he was giving me the name of his uncle Rocky Bear, and by giving it making me a member of his family. He was honoring me, of course, but also my mother, and the Association, linking his and his family's honor to her work at Pine Ridge. Drums were beating. Men were chanting Lakota phrases that I couldn't understand. I was expected to dance alone around the circle but, shy even with people I knew, I was now frozen by self-consciousness, acutely aware of how preposterous I must look with my red hair and whiter-than-white skin and freckles and all the feathers. I just stood there unable to move. Then people began to laugh, whether in sympathy or embarrassment, or because I really looked as ridiculous as I felt, I didn't know. Get going! Ben whispered. But I couldn't move. The laughter grew louder. Finally Ben gave me a hard push and I lurched forward and danced, faking it, as anyone could see, agonizingly aware of my clumsiness, feeling that I had failed my mother terribly, that I lacked the courage that she wanted to see in me, and lacked her wonderful ability to join effortlessly—so it seemed to me—in whatever was happening around her, and to take joy in it, and to make it part of her, and to seem instantly as if she belonged. I don't remember what happened afterward. I suppose that my mother must have hugged me and praised me, as parents do at such times, but no matter what she said I was sure that she was as ashamed of me as I was of myself, that I had let her down unforgivably in front of everyone.

6

WHILE ALL THIS was taking place on the northern plains, my mother was simultaneously engaged in a complicated strategy to win federal recognition for the Miccosukee Indians in southern Florida. Apart from the few along the Tamiami Trail west of Miami, the Miccosukees lived as their ancestors had for generations, in open thatched dwellings called *chickees*, scattered across an archipelago of islets hidden amid the sawgrass and mangroves of the Everglades between the highway and Lake Okeechobee. "One, perhaps the most beautiful of these," my mother wrote, "could be found only by an Indian who knew his way home across the apparently trackless swamp. It is solidly walled by banana trees, in fruit, and within the green circle four *chickees* stand on ground that has been swept clean." When she arrives, by airboat, two small boys dressed in knee-length purple and yellow gowns are wrestling, while a barefooted grandmother sews beneath Spanish moss and a young wife "with beads piled from shoulder to chin," cooks at an open fire; the grandfather has not been among white men for ten years. "Human waste vanishes into the teeming swamp. Out of it, to the sound of many wings, a flock of pure white ibis wheels up and over the island." Few Miccosukees owned more than a few clothes, a mattress and some cooking pots, worth perhaps twenty-five dollars in all, by my mother's reckoning. Some raised cattle, while others earned occasional wages as unskilled laborers and as guides to sportsmen, or by catching frogs, whose legs were a staple on Florida menus. Women worked from dawn to dark stitching the intricate strips of many-colored cloth that went into the skirts and jackets that they sold to tourists along the Tamiami Trail. "Independence is as important as life to these Indians, and the laziness of dependent people is unknown among them," my mother wrote.

The Miccosukees were closely related to the Seminoles, who referred to them as the "ones who never came in" after the Indians' defeat by the United States Army in the 1830s. They claimed the watery wilderness where they lived on the ground that they had never surrendered it, but because they had never signed a treaty or been recognized as an official tribe they had no legal standing and therefore no way to prevent the drainage projects that promised to soon encroach on the Everglades and that would benefit giant farms, cattle ranches, and developers. There was good reason to fear that if the Miccosukees did not acquire title to their land within the next year or two, they would see the time when they would be unwelcome on it, even as squatters. While older Miccosukees rejected any contact at all with government, younger leaders were hoping to work out a formula whereby the Miccosukees might have some kind of protection of their land-rights without diminishing their status in their own eyes as an unvanquished people.

My mother's first tense encounter with the Miccosukees must have taken place either late in 1958 or early in 1959, because by March she was already meeting on friendly terms with the younger tribal leaders. Her first goal was to see that the Miccosukees permanently obtained the right to use their land as they wished, and her second, because it was the best way to ensure the first, was to obtain federal recognition for the tribe. "I made it crystal clear that we would do everything in our power to try to get them the land." The business about them being a sovereign nation, she also told them "was alright if it made them feel important but would not get them any closer to settling the land question." My mother was convinced that at least part of the problem lay in the machinations of the tribe's Miami lawyer, a white man whom she believed to be linked to a larger (if ultimately ineffective) Communist effort to infiltrate tribal self-determination movements. "I think it is incorrect to define the problem as that of communist agitation of Indians," she wrote to Oliver LaFarge. "The communist thing comes second. If we, as a nation, do not find some way in which to let whatever rankling aspiration they have pass out of existence through fulfillment they will probably look to the Martians next. The fact that the Hopis, Miccosukees, and Iroquois seem to be expressing themselves in the Union

Square manner indicates exploitation of their spiritual resistance to conquest, but not that the resistance itself is inauthentic."

Florida Governor Leroy Collins, a liberal Democrat, was inclined to help the Miccosukees, but he was not eager to hand over a vast tract of state land to a reclusive group of Indians who were not recognized by Washington and who were openly consorting with Cuban Communists. The tribe's lawyer had encouraged the Miccosukees to approach several foreign embassies to draw attention to their cause and was now urging them to undertake a tour of South American capitals where they would denounce the United States and finally settle in Cuba, where the new revolutionary government had offered to provide them with land. In the summer of 1959 a Miccosukee delegation did in fact turn up in Cuba, where they received VIP treatment, being whisked through the streets of Havana in a fleet of flag-decked Cadillacs escorted by machine-gun-toting guerrillas. According to the *Miami Herald*, the Miccosukees presented Castro with a declaration written on buckskin praising his "victory over tyranny and oppression" and giving the revolutionary government formal "recognition." In return, Castro formally recognized the "duly constituted government of the sovereign Miccosukee Seminole nation."

In the records of the negotiations that followed the Indians' return to Florida I can see perhaps more vividly than anywhere else the political deftness that my mother had honed in her years with the Association. She pilots her way through this political maze with unflagging confidence. She is behind the scenes everywhere, teasing compromise and commitment from suspicious and uncertain people, both in Washington and Florida; curiously enough, the Miccosukees on their islets in the Everglades and the bureaucrats of the BIA are like mirror images of each other, both of them hobbled by distrust and pride and by the inertia of tradition on the Indians' part and the inertia of bureaucratic habit on Washington's. She bluntly tells the Indians that the trip to Cuba was a disaster: "It wrecked all you ever did to get land for the Miccosukees, and it wrecked the work we did." At the same time, determined to keep the negotiations alive, with deliberately disarming self-mockery she cajoles the Florida attorney general, who is deeply distrustful of the Miccosukees' motives, "I think of myself as a good debater, until I try to change a lawyer's opinion. Then I always find that I cannot fight a steel blade with a wooden sword—and I always end up, as I do now, by appealing to the completely immaterial, completely wonderful sense of what is compassionate, honorable and good."

Through the rest of that year and the next my mother traveled regularly to Florida, often at very short notice. She was in almost constant contact with the Miccosukees, the Association's lawyers, the BIA, the Department of the Interior, and the Florida governor's office. She knew that the state was willing to give the land to the Miccosukees if the federal government had a plan to administer it. But there was little enthusiasm for this in a Bureau that was spiritually, if no longer publicly, committed to termination and dispersal, not to the creation of more tribes. Although Assistant Secretary of the Interior Roger Ernst was sympathetic, my mother felt that strategically it was essential to win the support of Commissioner of Indian Affairs Glenn L. Emmons, a man for whose intellect she had faint regard. How she choreographed the solution to this conundrum is a fascinating cameo of bureaucratic intrigue. First she called Emmons and asked if the Bureau had worked up a program for the Miccosukees, knowing quite well that it hadn't. "He wondered if I had any ideas," she reported. "I said I'd telephone in a proposal the next day. . . . I wrote up the attached proposal in the small hours of the next morning, checked it for feasibility with the superintendent of the Seminole Agency and with [Association lawyer] Art Lazarus, and then read it to Ernst over the telephone. We agreed that I should 'give' it to Emmons and let him tell Ernst about it as if it were his idea." Basically, the plan called for Florida to turn two hundred thousand acres of the Everglades over to the federal government, which would recognize the Miccosukees, allow them to manage the land like any other duly constituted tribe, and enable them to receive the services enjoyed by other tribes. My mother next called a member of the Florida state cabinet, which had to approve such a transaction, and urged him to look favorably on "Emmons's" plan, and then did the same with the Florida attorney general. She reported, "[The attorney general] hesitated and then asked, 'What do you think we ought to do?' I said, 'Give the Miccosukees the land.' "

However, reluctant to promote an idea that had originated with the Association, Emmons failed to press the plan with vigor. In April the cabinet finally acted, but the result was disappointing. At a meeting to which no Indians or their allies had been invited, the cabinet voted to set aside just a fraction of the land that the Indians wanted, and even that would be administered by the cabinet itself instead of the Miccosukees, with the state retaining the right to take it back whenever it saw fit. Furious, my mother tracked down a senior official of the Interior Department at home on the weekend. "I told him not to waste his time trying to make the record look good, because it would look disgraceful when we told the whole story—as we would." That night she went home and mapped out a pressure campaign. She alerted the Miccosukees and their white friends, journalists in Florida and New York, and even asked Arthur Sulzberger of the *New York Times*, a member of the Association's board, to arrange an introduction to the American ambassador to Cuba, who was then in Washington temporarily, with a view to having the State Department impress on the Secretary of the Interior that issues of international consequence were at stake. Soon the Florida governor's office was flooded with telegrams urging that the state turn over the land and administration to the Indians.

In July my mother's strategy began to pay off, when the Interior Department declared the Miccosukees to be a "duly recognized Indian tribe." It remained now to bring the Florida cabinet into line. My mother prepared a revised plan of action for the Miccosukees; this time Ernst himself presented it to the Secretary of the Interior, Fred A. Seaton, as his own. She recorded the following vignette in a memo to members of the Association's board. "According to Ernst, Mr. Seaton said such things as: 'What do you think Miss Madigan wants? Do you mean to say you haven't settled it with Florida yet? Oh, if you are going to Tallahassee Monday, why wasn't Miss Madigan informed?' " Seaton then met personally with my mother and asked her to travel with Ernst to Tallahassee, where he was to present "his" plan to the Florida cabinet. "I told him that this was to be the Department's meeting, but that I would change my travel plans if he thought it important. He said, 'I hate to ask you to do that, but I would like you to be there and then report back to me with Roger. Roger will have to sit around with the governor, but you can move around and talk to people and hear things Roger won't hear.' " My mother added, "I thought it would be kittenish to seek further assurance. I said I would go to Tallahassee."

In October 1961, as a result of the Association's steady pressure, the state finally agreed to transfer the two hundred thousand acres to the United States, and ultimately to the Miccosukees, in accordance with the plan that my mother had created more than a year before. The historic decision was reached in a palmetto-thatched *chickee* in a Miccosukee camp on the Tamiami Trail, where members of the Panther, Otter, and Bird clans, the guardians of Miccosukee tradition, had gathered with representatives of the Interior Department and the state of Florida, and of course my mother, against a backdrop of mountainous white clouds, cobalt sky, and trackless swamp.

THE MICCOSUKEE INITIATIVE was just one of several that took the Association into the South for the first time. "I have never been busier," my mother wrote to Harry Forbes in the autumn of 1960. "[But] if you think we are busy now, wait until you see what is ahead. I am positive, judging from Indian stirrings in Mississippi, Louisiana and North Carolina, that we are entering a period in which all those forgotten southern groups, which have no protection from the federal government and are subjected to severe racial discrimination, are going to stand up and fight—probably in the courts. The explosion of appeals for help will come as soon as word gets about that we are handling the Lumbee case." The Lumbees, a racially mixed North Carolina group of obscure origin, was seeking, and today still continues to seek federal recognition as an Indian tribe. "Our activity will be popular as long as the southern Indians are 3/4 or so Indian and 1/4 white," my mother continued. "When the 1/4 turns out to be Negro instead of white, we shall not be so popular."

Segregation was a way of life throughout the South, and it was inescapable for anyone traveling there, including those who, like my mother, loathed it with an intensity that she reserved for nothing else I knew. Hateful though this was to her, we stayed in "whites only" motels and ate in "whites only" restaurants; to do otherwise was only to invite trouble. Once, on the Tamiami Trail we stopped at a diner that had an entrance for blacks at one end and for whites at the other, and a fence of chickenwire dividing the two sections in the middle, allowing only the counterman to pass between them behind the counter. When my mother's meal came, she sat looking at it, trying to eat and failing, and finally saying it would make her sick to eat anything in a place where Negroes had to eat like animals in a cage.

Among the Southern Indians my mother's most intense involvement was with the Mississippi Choctaws, the descendants of those who had refused to migrate West under federal pressure in the 1830s and who had lived in isolation ever since, near Philadelphia, in east-central Mississippi. Although they had federal recognition and a small reservation, the Choctaws were on no one's mental map of Indian country, and they were administered by a BIA staff comprised entirely of white southerners who held their jobs as a result of political patronage and who, one unguardedly told my mother, "think the Indians are one step lower than Negroes." Choctaws were forced to use segregated restaurants, bars, and public facilities, and were not permitted to work in local factories. Many lived almost completely outside the money economy, surviving as best they could by hiring themselves out as field hands and migrant laborers. Rather than send their children to black schools, many declined to send their children to school at all. Efforts to enroll them in white schools were frustrated by the BIA's own local officials, who repeatedly told the Choctaws that integration was impossible and that the ultimate solution for the tribe was dispersal.

In 1957 the Association discovered that a BIA labor contract for

the Choctaw area specifically omitted the federally required antidis-
crimination clause. The Association's lawyers successfully protested
to the bureau and ensured that the contract was made to conform.
"This action, good in itself," my mother wrote, "took place in a vacuum, in that the Choctaws were totally unaware of the unfairness of
the contract in its original form and of our intervention to change it.
They were unaware of the existence of organizations to defend Indian
rights, and were probably unaware of the very concept of Indian
rights." Troubled by the Association's neglect of the Choctaws, in
1958 she wrote to the chairman of the tribe, telling him about the Association's purpose and asking whether a field reporter would be welcome to visit the reservation. The letter was never answered. Two
years later, in 1960, she learned the reason when she met the by then
former chairman in Washington. He told her that he had never received the letter, even though he had been alerted that it was coming.
"He said that the letter was probably delivered to the agency, and
that the Superintendent 'lost' it after opening and reading it. He said
that mail which reaches him through the Agency frequently arrives in
opened envelopes."

The new tribal chairman, Phillip Martin, was a burly man, then
in his thirties, with a massive Indian face, who had trained to be an
electrician but had had difficulty finding employment because of the
discriminatory policies of the agency. My mother was impressed with
him from their first meeting. "Mr. Martin has a superb intelligence,
his ideas come rapidly, and his expression of them is always well-
organized." He had also traveled in the larger world, having served
in the Army in Europe and Asia; at the end of the Second World War
he had seen Germans foraging for food in garbage cans and had also
seen them pick themselves up and start rebuilding their country from
the wreckage, and he thought that Indians ought to be able to do the
same. My mother reported, "[The Choctaws] said they realize that in
the past nothing ever improved for them because they never came out
in the open where we could see them looking for help. Now, they
said, they are out and they are not going back into hiding. No change
that comes can be a change for the worse, they said."

Martin asked my mother to accompany a delegation of the tribe's leaders on a round of visits to the Department of the Interior and the BIA where, with their new assertiveness, they intended to ask for economic-development aid and for the transfer of their superintendent, Paul Vance. She promised to find time in her already densely packed schedule to fly to Washington to meet them. To the Choctaws' dismay, however, they were thwarted in their plan to come to Washington alone. Vance and the BIA's area director for the South, Paul Fickinger, were aware that complaints were to be registered against them, had insisted on going also, and on including themselves in appointments with officials made for the delegates.

My mother reported with sly humor what happened when these two came face to face with her at the Interior Department.

The Choctaws told Fickinger and Vance at the last minute that I was to join them before they went into the conference room, and these characters were peering uncertainly down the long, long corridor as I approached. Vance is a tall, blonde, pale, slender man in his forties, with a blandly handsome face, worried eyes and nervous hands. Fickinger is below middle height, dough-colored, blind in one eye, and well into his fifties. The Choctaw chairman [Phillip Martin] introduced us, and all three of the delegates wore broader smiles than mere courtesy demanded. Vance looked as if he thought I were going to accuse him of a crime, and openly showed relief when I shook hands and said something cheerful about the weather. The Choctaws stood about dead-pan, but their glances were flashing forth between Fickinger and Vance, and the chairman said later that they would describe the officials' discomfiture in their report to the tribe. Clearly, this was a thing that could only happen in the North, and they will tell every detail in Mississippi. . . . As we entered the conference room, Mr. Martin asked whether I had noticed the beaded ties Fickinger and Vance were wearing. "They would not be caught dead wearing those on the reservation," he said. "They took those out of their suitcases in Washington."

After conferring with the BIA's education staff, the Choctaws were scheduled to see the Assistant Secretary of the Interior. "Mr. Ernst's secretary called the conference room to say that he was ready to see the Choctaws and me. Fickinger and Vance looked at each other helplessly, having imagined they were included in all of the Choctaws' Washington appointments," my mother reported. "Mr. Ernst had planned to spend about ten minutes with the delegation, but was taken by their dignity, wit and intelligence and spent an hour." Despite Ernst's personal interest, the majority view at the BIA was still that nothing should be done to encourage continuation of the Choctaw community. In a letter that the tribe sent to Secretary of the Interior Seaton but that was actually composed by my mother and that clearly reflected her views, she wrote, "History and statistics show that the Mississippi Choctaws are not going anywhere. . . . The Bureau of Indian Affairs and we Choctaws agree that our situation is tragic and no self-respecting human beings should go on living in it. Our agreement ends there. Our Choctaw goal is to change the situation. The Bureau's goal for the Choctaws is for us to run away from it. We do not think the Bureau of Indian Affairs should be allowed to substitute their goal for ours. That is termination against our will, the policy you said should not be forced on any tribe."

Until her death my mother worked tirelessly to bring some form of economic development to the Choctaws and to unseat Vance. The secret of this racist mediocrity's remarkable staying power only came clear when she learned that he was married to the niece of the powerful segregationist Senator James Eastland, whose influence increased when the new Democratic administration took office in 1961. Despite her own frustration, she continued to urge the Choctaws not to give in to cynicism or hopelessness, and to trust that the government would eventually do the right thing. The flawed men and the bigots would one day be gone, she tried to reassure them, and policies would someday change; the very process of pressing for change would teach the tribe how to move their enemies and win allies and how to discover their own power.

7

IN 1960, WE SHAKE HANDS and most of the Association's other projects were suddenly dwarfed by what my mother perceived to be a gathering crisis in Alaska. One of the Association's Washington lawyers, Arthur Lazarus, had pointed out that Alaskan statehood, approved by Congress the previous year, had abruptly put the status of all Alaska's natives—Inupiat (or Eskimos), Indians and Aleuts— into question. "The Association needs a policy on Alaska," my mother wrote. "No one has one now; and if an issue were to come up, the Natives could lose important rights or property while we looked frantically for a set of principles on which to stand." She recognized that Alaska would mean a political battle on a scale far beyond any that the Association had entered into before, and it was only with some difficulty that she was able to convince the board of directors to take it on. "I may be guilty of insubordination in taking up the Alaskan issues, but I am willing to face the consequences," she wrote to Harry Forbes, who was perhaps her closest ally on the board. Quite unperceived by the state's natives, there were immense political pressures coming to bear from mining interests, from the new state's congressional delegation, and from white Alaskans to open the entire state to development.

Still an archaeologist at heart, my mother unearthed the almost forgotten provisions of the Alaska Purchase Act of 1867, in which the United States explicitly promised to respect aboriginal rights to land and hunting. While those rights were basic to the future security and well-being of the state's Eskimos and Indians, they had never been clearly defined or generally recognized. Although the political feeling of the Alaskan natives was essentially one of complete independence and self-sufficiency, they had never developed a theory of sovereignty, because armed conflict with the United States and dispossession of their land never forced them to. For the most part, they took little notice of politics outside their own village; one Inupiat told my mother that most had never thought much about the consequences of state-hood and had supported it because "they wanted to be nice and friendly."

My mother took me with her on her first trip to Alaska in June 1960. The week that we spent in Alaska was, for me, one of unending marvels: I saw moose in the wild, climbed in a glacier, ate caribou burgers, flew in a seaplane, saw the sun circle the horizon on the summer solstice, and rode in a dog sled across the frozen Arctic Ocean. My mother's ultimate destination was Barrow, the northernmost town in the United States, a straggling sprawl of shacks and quonset huts that, although it had been a military base since the Second World War, still had about it the tentative quality of a hunters' camp. Several whales had been killed a week before we arrived and there was hardly a house that did not have baleen or the rib of a whale lying about somewhere, while teams of ferocious-looking sled dogs yelped and snarled where they were staked out in the sand. Everyone wore bright cotton summer parkas, mittens, and sealskin mukluks. We stayed in a hotel that had once been an army barracks and that had now been divided into small rooms and furnished with cots. The inside temperature (according to my mother's notes) was twenty degrees Fahrenheit, but still too warm for Inupiat visitors, who stripped down to their T-shirts when they came inside.

My mother loved the raw beauty of Barrow from the moment we landed:

From beyond the southern horizon flat, brown tundra stretches away toward the pole. The sea is flat like the tundra, except where the shore meets the ice-cap. There the ice has been pushed up into jagged mountains, perhaps five feet high, perhaps twenty feet. You cannot tell how tall they are because in that level place your sense of distance disappears. In June there is never any noon, for the sun, without rising or setting, travels endlessly in a circle below the zenith. It shines whitely in the white sky from four directions, but never from overhead. Because of this, long shadows are cast by the smallest things. The low wooden houses and shacks of the Eskimos cluster haphazardly at the edge of the ocean, weatherstained to brown that merges into the tundra behind the village and grey that merges into the sky and sea. Since there is always light, villagers can be seen at any hour, appearing and disappearing as they walk in and out among the houses on their way to some destination—hard to guess when the time is midnight. At 2 A.M. I saw big boys on the shore, practicing for the Fourth of July baseball game. Apparently the whole village never goes to sleep at this season of the year. Yet the sounds they make seem very small, and the silence seems enormous—perhaps because there are no cars. Roads cannot be built on the thin layer of grainy dirt that lies over the permafrost. The only motor-driven vehicle that is regularly seen is a little bus, with six-wheel drive, that makes the trip once a day during the summer months from Barrow to the airfield, running along the gritty Arctic beach.

More than to any other Native Americans, except perhaps her beloved Omahas and Sioux and Cheyennes, my mother was drawn to the Inupiat. "The men were deep-chested and powerfully-built," she wrote to LaFarge. "They should be, for all except those employed by the Army build their own hide-covered boats and hunt whales, seals, walrus and polar bear. They also go out to hunt caribou when the herds are spotted. Somewhere outside of every house lay the body of a white seal—its head bloody from the clubbing which killed it and its eyes wide open. A dead seal must be the limpest thing on earth. Outside some of the houses red-stained, butchered seal meat was piled up on the ground. It could not spoil because it had frozen naturally." She recognized that the Eskimos' straightforwardness made them exceedingly vulnerable to manipulation and betrayal by unscrupulous whites. "They say exactly what they mean, although they cannot always calculate the effect on others of their translated English."

In Barrow she met Guy Okakok, who would become her best friend and closest ally in Alaska. I remember a humorous and outgoing man, round-faced and weatherbeaten; a whale hunter part of the year, he was also a journalist who wrote a column on Barrow for the Fairbanks newspaper. He wrote my mother lively letters in which policy suggestions were interlaced with comments about daily life: "I have been away for weeks hunting, Bowhead Whales this fall. 3 whales were killed the very same day, but one sink. . . . Dog racing for 17 long miles was very good. One woman had an accident, one of the drivers somehow her mittens got caught on one of the dog traces and tangled her. Dogs were galloping partways all the time too. She is much better now, way I heard today. Anyway we have good Christmas."

After that first trip to Barrow, a sense of terrible urgency increasingly pervaded everything my mother thought about Alaska. She felt certain that unless the Association acted, statehood would prove to be a juggernaut that would accomplish in a few years the destruction that centuries of contact had wrought on the native peoples of the lower forty-eight states. I have a copy of a letter that she wrote to Guy Okakok a few months before her death. "Ever since I went to Barrow that first time, I knew the most important thing I could do in my whole life would be to help the Inupiat preserve their aboriginal rights and their freedom to live the way they want to live," she wrote. "It is not easy to make our Directors understand. Except for one man they have never been to Alaska, and they have never been close to the native people as I have, and it is almost impossible for them to imagine how time is running out so fast for the Inupiat. I think they are a little bit afraid that I make things sound worse than they really are; but they trust me, and so far they have approved all my proposals for work in Alaska. In about two weeks I am going to propose that the Association go out and try to raise about $200,000 for all-out work in Alaska and to speed up that work as much as we can. I am also going to propose that I personally should spend as much of my time as necessary on Alaska work, even if that means I must take time away from our work with Indians in the Lower 48. . . . Some of our Directors will worry when I make that proposal. One reason they will worry is that, as I said, they know the Indian situation, but they do not really understand how short the time is that the Inupiat have left. Another reason they will worry is that I am not strong enough to do all the field work I do and they are always afraid that I will collapse and everything will go to pieces. You understand me better than they do, because in your own way you do things that take all your strength and all your courage, and you like to live that way. If the time ever comes when you cannot live that way, I think you will not want to live at all. I feel the same way."

Alaska was already exhausting her. Sylvia Hermelin, my mother's assistant, told me over hot pastrami sandwiches one afternoon in a Greek luncheonette near her home in Brooklyn what it was like in the office during those years. "Your mother put herself under tremendous stress. Many times she came into the office and she'd been writing all night. So many times she was exhausted and ready to drop. But she just continued. She'd be sick and we'd tell her to go see a doctor, and she'd say, Who has time for the doctor? She took it all home with her, if you know what I mean. And the way she smoked! She'd light a cigarette and I'd say, 'You just finished one.' And LaVerne would say, 'No I didn't.' But it was right there in the ashtray. That too, the cigarettes, it didn't calm her. She puffed one after another. She'd come in with one in her hand in the morning, and she'd be smoking one at lunch. She always had one in her hand. We'd tell her, 'Don't take it all so seriously.' But, no, she couldn't do that."

Working with an ever widening network of local Eskimo leaders, my mother became their key conduit of information, explaining Washington's thinking and the machinations of white Alaskan politicians to people whose isolation, in today's era of the Internet and satellite communications, can scarcely be imagined. She felt that there was virtually no way for her to find out what people in the villages were really thinking unless she flew there herself and visited them personally, which she did in a series of trips that year and the next, traveling sometimes alone and sometimes with Guy Okakok by small chartered plane to Nome, Kotzebue, Shishmaref, Unalakleet, Kalskag, Bethel, King Island, Anuktuvuk Pass, Barter Island, Point Hope, and a host of other minuscule, far-flung Inupiat towns. She was heartened by the response she met everywhere. "The Eskimos have appeared acquiescent only because they were totally uninformed, but their leaders are extremely intelligent and sophisticated and, in a good sense, hard," she wrote. "They jumped at our offer to make it possible for them to meet to organize themselves to act on their own behalf."

Through her contacts in Washington she learned that the Atomic Energy Commission was preparing to set off a nuclear blast on the Arctic coast near the Inupiat village of Point Hope on the Chukchi Sea, allegedly to explore the use of nuclear energy for excavating new harbors. It would be an explosion fourteen times greater than that at Hiroshima and was likely to scatter poisonous strontium 90 over a vast area, infecting fish, flora, and eventually the caribou, upon which the Eskimos depended as a primary food source. She ascertained (the government had never bothered to ask) that springs used by Inupiat hunters lay less than five miles from the blast site and that radioactive snow blown horizontally across the tundra would be inhaled by hunters and travelers and by the inhabitants of igloos that were used for long periods as dwellings during storms.

She convinced the Association to aggressively oppose the project on the ground that unsettled native rights were involved, and that the Bureau of Land Management had no authority to turn over to the AEC land subject to native claim. There is a transcript of the hearing that was held in Washington, where she bluntly confronted the government's spokesmen and scientists:

Q [LaVERNE MADIGAN]: The Eskimos have a potential claim to Cape Thompson and the whole surrounding area, and a definite basis for suit if damage is suffered. What plans exist for compensating the community and its members?

(The AEC people showed surprise and uncertainty. Obviously, the thought that Natives might have property rights had never occurred to them.)

A: What? We never heard anything about that. We are not lawyers. Our lawyer should be here. He probably does not know the answer or he would have told us before now. We just don't know.

As a result of her almost single-handed efforts the project was postponed indefinitely and, after her death and growing opposition from environmentalists and from the Soviet government, which was concerned about the effect that fallout from the explosion would have in Siberia, finally canceled.

My mother's work in Alaska climaxed with two historic native-rights conferences, held, respectively, by the Inupiat in November 1961 in Barrow, and by the Indians in June 1962 in Tanana, on the Yukon River. Organized in large part by my mother and funded by the Association, the conferences brought native representatives from the farthest reaches of the state into contact with each other for the first time. "Maybe the people will come to a meeting and say what they really think," she wrote to one of her native collaborators. "They should not say what white people want them to say. They should say the truth about what they feel." The Barrow conference was a great success, making clear to representatives from seventeen villages that had little or no contact with each other and were scattered across hundreds of miles of tundra that they shared the same problems and that by uniting they had at least a chance to shape their own future. The final document of the conference defined the Inupiat homeland in terms of both place and identity, as "our land around the whole Arctic world where we Inupiat live, our right to hunt our food any place and time of year as it has always been, our right to be brave independent people, like our grandfathers, our right to the minerals that belong to us in the land that we claim." It also recommended that all Inupiat villages be allowed to apply for reservation status, with full mineral and hunting rights, and called for a permanent organization that would protect aboriginal land rights and work collaboratively toward economic and social development.

Bland as these propositions sound today, they were revolutionary in 1961, and they eventually formed the basis for a comprehensive native claims settlement when the North Slope was opened for oil development at the end of the decade. Although it never came to pass, my mother also promoted the idea of creating a vast ecological reserve, an "Inupiat National Monument," in affiliation with similar reserves that might be created in other Arctic nations, with a view to preserving the traditional native way of life there undisturbed. She conceived the state's first native newspaper, the *Tundra Times*; although it did not begin publication until after her death, in the hands of her Inupiat colleague Howard Rock it became an important force enabling communities isolated around the vast state to communicate with each other and to coordinate a unified statewide native movement.

My mother had not planned to attend the Tanana conference in person, although she had spent months organizing it, feeling that natives should run the event themselves. She was also physically spent. On her last trip to Alaska, in April, a trip that had involved a great deal of bush travel, including an apparently hair-raising flight through a snowstorm from Nome to Fairbanks, she had broken her wrist, and had still not completely recovered. After her death Guy Okakok, who had been with her at the time, wrote of this event, "I was sure any woman won't want to travel, yet with broken wrist, they'd give up and go back home. But she didn't. She kept on. Yet she didn't want to give up her good work." Only a few days before the conference was to open, she received several panicky phone calls from her allies in Alaska. They told her that the Indians were increasingly frightened by the opposition that was building to native rights among white politicians, and they considered it urgent that she come. So she went after all, taking me with her. We left the old Idlewild airport in the dark, chasing the dawn across the continent until somewhere over the Alaska Range the sun finally burst forth to reveal a landscape that seemed to swallow the sky.

Since Tanana was inaccessible by road, the delegates—from wonderfully named places like Metlakatla, Chalkyitsik, Mentasta, Nenana, and Kaltag—came by small plane or by motorboat on the

Yukon or Tanana Rivers. Their numbers swamped the limited facilities available. People were camped everywhere, and packed, as we
were, into the home of the local Episcopal missionary. "I lived on
peanut butter sandwiches and coffee for two days," my mother drily
reported to the Association's board. "People who hate peanut butter
were really hungry by the end of the conference. The village had run
out of matches on the first day, and by the end of the second had run
out of cigarettes. A bush pilot, who liked what we were doing, recognized the crisis and dropped off two cartons of Winstons the following morning." As at Barrow, the delegates listened to speakers
from each village describe the particular problems faced by their
communities, then conducted a hearing on native land claims, and finally, on the third day, set up a permanent organization and adopted
a document that bluntly accused the state of invading and selling native land: "Our people always thought they owned the land where
they lived and hunted. We still feel it is ours. But we find that no one,
the state included, thinks we have a right to our homes or the land
where we hunt and fish." In the face of a strident backlash from other
Alaskans, the Indians demanded full land, hunting, and mineral
rights and the withdrawal of tracts of land around native villages
from the public domain. "The politicians and newspapers attacked
them viciously, and the Indian leaders and their local white friends
were at a loss as to how to handle the onslaught," my mother wrote
to Harry Forbes. "Luckily I was able to interpose the Association's
big bulk between them and their attackers. The result was that the Indians were delighted to know that we exist and stand by or in front
of them—and were also delighted to be the subject of heated controversy for the first time in their history. They said that no one ever noticed their existence before."

After the conference we flew back to Fairbanks and the next day,
which my mother had promised to spend with me alone, we drove
north to a ghost town in the forest where, as I remembered it, we
spent hours wandering happily among the ruins of log cabins and
rusting mining equipment and guessing at the function of abandoned
pieces of machinery that littered the ground. Until recently I remem-

bered the day best for the trophy that I came away with: an enormous snowshoe that I had found in one of the cabins, alongside a calendar dated 1936, and that I then proudly lugged through airports and on planes all the way back to New York. In one of the boxes in the archives at Princeton, however, I found a picture of my mother and me that was taken in the ghost town that day by a photographer who happened to be there and who sent it to her later in New York. It was probably the last picture taken of my mother. In it we are standing in front of a log cabin. I stand a little behind her and to her right, hands in pockets, looking uncharacteristically relaxed and self-possessed. Even here in the wilderness my mother is dressed handsomely in a tailored blouse and trousers, and a heavy cardigan woven with stylized caribou and other native designs. She had always been a compact woman, but I am struck here by the impression of slack flesh and of weight slipping out of control. I am even more startled by her face, which is turned away from me toward the camera. It is as if once she had turned away something that she carefully kept hidden from me had spilled out. She is trying to smile but fails. In this face, which now seems so unfamiliar, I see the deep print of pain and distress. Why do I not remember this? How could I not have noticed it? *What was wrong?*

FROM FAIRBANKS we flew to Seattle and then on to Billings, Montana. We rented a car and drove east across rolling prairie to Lame Deer, where the Cheyennes were expecting my mother, to honor her for the help she had given them in recovering land that had been lost to the tribe. Of this meeting my mother wrote to LaFarge, "The men's smiles and eyes were quick, flashing, happy, conspiratorial, triumphant and, I am certain, a bit fierce." The next night we followed my mother's friend John Woodenlegs, the tribe's chairman, to a place where a tepee had been set up near a stream and a stand of cottonwoods. Perhaps a dozen or so Cheyennes were already there, almost all of them men, and dressed like cowboys (which, in fact, most of them were), in jeans and boots and wide-brimmed hats.

Inside the tepee we sat down in a circle around a small open fire that had been built at the center of it. Faces were obscure in the dimness, and among them I recognized only Woodenlegs's and my mother's. She whispered to me, Just watch what they do and you do the same. An elderly man spoke slowly and at great length in Cheyenne. Several other men then spoke, one by one. After that, metal cups were passed around filled with tea that had been brewed from peyote, the hallucinogen whose consumption is the central sacrament of the Native American Church. The drink was so bitter that I thought I would vomit, and my mother whispered that it was the way it was supposed to taste and to buck up and drink it down like the men. After that, buttons of dried peyote were passed around and we picked them out and chewed them. Finally there was a third round of peyote, this time powdered and rolled with tobacco into cigarettes, and handed around. Through all this I was so preoccupied with fighting back nausea that I probably consumed very little peyote, for while one by one the others subsided into a reverie, in spite of my headache and my legs aching from sitting so long crosslegged, I drifted off into a fitful, dreamless sleep.

I woke at the sound of voices resuming. Most of the men spoke in Cheyenne. Woodenlegs translated what they said for my mother and me. As each man returned from his reverie he wove his vision into that of the man who had preceded him—each adding a visual detail, a few words, a nuance of feeling—into a sort of braided dream in which the image of my mother became the central character, a horseborne figure girded for battle like a Cheyenne woman warrior of the old times, fierce and determined and heroic, someone who, I understood both proudly and jealously, others needed as much as I did and whose world she filled as much as she did mine.

8

FOR A TIME after my mother's death I felt a childish resentment toward Indians for taking my mother away from me for so many years

of her short life, as if she had been made prisoner by them, like somebody in one of the old captivity narratives of the frontier. Eventually
this resentment subsided and I understood that if she was a captive of
anything it was of other people's trust in her, of their need for her. But
it was still almost thirty years before I could bring myself to return to
any of the reservations where she had worked. Then, in 1991, I began
a book about contemporary Indians, entitled *Killing the White Man's
Indian: Reinventing Native Americans at the End of the Twentieth
Century.* I came to see as I worked on it that it was the one thing that
I could still give to her after all these years, the kind of book that she
might have written had she lived, an honest and unblinking look at
the people to whom she had devoted her life. I planned originally to
write about her, too, by looking at the several communities I remembered best from my childhood and seeing how they had fared during
the intervening years. But I eventually decided against it, and instead
to write something more comprehensive and less personal, essentially
an exploration of where Indians fit in late-twentieth-century America, feeling that if my mother had been there to ask, she would have
told me that she wasn't the story and that I mustn't let her get in the
way of the Indians themselves.

In my book I tried to demythologize the ways in which Americans see Indians, arguing that if one is to make sense of what is going
on in Indian country, it is essential to see Indians neither as artifacts
left over from a lost heroic past nor as idealized stewards of the earth,
but as modern people struggling with present-day problems. Over a
period of four years I visited scores of reservations and interviewed
hundreds of men and women, including a few who had been close to
my mother. I found an Indian world that was radically changed from
the one that existed in 1962. Tribes were now powers to be reckoned
with in many parts of the country, with a degree of autonomy that no
one could imagine in the 1950s. It was clear that many of them
would play central roles in the way that the United States evolves in
the coming years. All but the smallest tribes policed their own reservations, maintained their own roads, managed their own natural
resources, economies, schools, and service delivery. On many reser-

vations the local branch of the BIA was now, in effect, a department of the tribal government. The Choctaws now presided over a small empire of tribal enterprises that were manufacturing, among other things, parts for Ford and Navistar and other national corporations. The once reclusive Miccosukees now operated a gambling casino outside Miami, and most of them had moved to new homes along the Tamiami Trail. The Warm Springs Tribe of Oregon owned three hydropower dams and was selling electricity to the state grid. The Salt River Pima-Maricopa Tribe of Arizona was selling water to the city of Phoenix, while the Pyramid Lake Paiute Tribe had veto power over the distribution of water in western Nevada, including the city of Reno. On many reservations tribal colleges were preserving and teaching tribal cultures that had been given up for dead. Almost everywhere, there was a vigorous revival of long-moribund native religions.

In this new Indian world people of my mother's generation had been largely forgotten. The radicalization of Indian politics in the 1970s had fostered a brand of tribal nationalism that typically defined whites as enemies and helped to keep Indians isolated from non-Indian communities with which they had much in common and—my mother had seen this forty years ago—with whom they might have made common cause. I couldn't help but wonder how much my mother's work had finally mattered. In the short run much of what she worked for died with her. The summer of her death she was planning two books on We Shake Hands, one by an anthropologist (she had Margaret Mead in mind) on the way that it had worked for the Omahas and Sioux, and the other showing how it might be exported as a technique to empower passive populations in economically depressed countries abroad. What impact these books might have had is pure speculation, because neither was ever written, and We Shake Hands did not survive long after her death. Others in the Association did not share the depth of her commitment to the program, or to the kind of labor-intensive community-action work in which she had invested so much. Nevertheless, We Shake Hands made countless civic-minded non-Indians and universities throughout the Great Plains alert to native concerns for the first time. More important, it jogged tribal councils into action on their own behalf; tribes began to fight bureau land sales, and to demand participation in federal programs, and to assert civil rights. Before its demise, tribes in more than a dozen states applied to the Association for We Shake Hands, and the men and women who participated in it often became the ones in their communities to craft and manage more lasting community-development programs when they became part of federal policy in the late 1960s. "She was a revolutionary," William Byler, my mother's immediate successor as executive director of the Association, told me one day, at his home in Washington. "She was tough and she knew what she wanted to do. She wanted to break the government's hold on the tribes. Her work had tremendous power in Indian communities, and she catalyzed a whole generation of activists, many of them women. From her, tribes began to get the confidence that they could set their own priorities, make their own plans. She helped them rediscover their sense of defiance."

In the brief six years that she led the Association, my mother changed the whole concept of Indian affairs. She had shifted the national discussion of the "Indian problem" away from termination to survival. Tribal self-realization was enshrined in federal policy by, of all people, Richard Nixon, whom she despised for his role in the Red-hunting hysteria of the early 1950s but who is universally honored in Indian country for declaring, in 1970, "The time has come to break decisively with the past and to create the conditions of a new era in which the Indian future is determined by Indian acts and Indian decisions." My mother had led Indians for the first time into Washington's corridors of power, where they were now familiar and respected, and skilled indeed at pressure-group politics. "She kind of woke us up to what we could do in government," Phillip Martin, the Choctaw chief, told me. She laid the groundwork for the protection of native lands in Alaska and had assisted many tribes in recovering lost lands in the lower forty-eight states. She also helped lay the foundations for tribal autonomy and the empowerment of native leaders, and for the revival of traditional culture. Arguably most important of all, she was the first national political figure to engage ordinary Indian people in identifying their own concerns and in making decisions for themselves, something so accepted today that few people remember that it even has a history. An Oglala Sioux woman who heard my mother when she was a girl in the 1950s and grew up to become a leading activist in her own right, once told me, "Your mother was the first person who ever came around here talking about civil rights." I can think of no way that my mother would rather have been remembered.

I was thinking about such things as I drove north from Denver on a sunny autumn afternoon in 1997, on my way to see my mother's friend Ella Irving at Pine Ridge. Having turned ninety-one that summer, Ella was still living in the tiny green cottage that had been her home for decades, near the village center. She was still the tall, raw-boned woman that I remembered, but heavier and stooped now, drawn down by the years. When she saw me at the door she tugged me through it and enfolded me in her long arms, pulling me back into the kitchen, where there was cowboy music on the radio, and she smoked and complained in her high-plains drawl about the break-ins. The pottery that she used to make was now highly prized by collectors and sold for hundreds of dollars apiece, but she had none left for herself. The last of it was destroyed when her kiln was vandalized a few years before. Her house had been broken into, too. "Some kids, I guess. They come in through the windows. I lost some of my clothes, my dresses. They took 'em just to be mean." From where we sat, drinking Coke, I could see the bedroom filled with plastic sacks of clothes saved up against some future need, perhaps reflecting the anxiety of someone who in earlier life knew great privation. Shelves were packed with photos of nieces, nephews, grandchildren, cousins and friends, color pictures of Pope John Paul II, medicines, and plastic buckets printed with the logo of the new tribal casino. "I just love that place!" Ella declared. "I always win."

Pine Ridge looked better than it did in the 1950s, but not much. Newish pink, lime-green, and salmon-colored HUD homes lined the ridges south of town, and near the crossroads there was now a supermarket owned by the tribe, and a big new Texaco station, and a Pizza Hut that looked as out of place as a spaceship among the shacks and jalopies. The modern tribal office building was already dilapidated. There was a tribal college up at Kyle now, and Ella told me that it was even drawing students from outside the reservation, and a lively tribal radio station. There was also a remarkable revival of Lakota religion, something totally unforeseen in my mother's day.

But the county in which the reservation lay was the poorest in the United States. Rates of alcoholism, suicide, and ill health were very high, and there was the pervasive impression of too many people with no money and too little to do. Hardly anyone had a job outside the tribal government and the Indian Health Service hospital on the hill north of town. Tribal politics was mired in factionalism. The chapter of the League of Women Voters that my mother had been so proud of became defunct long ago. "It just gave out," Ella said. "After your mother died, things just kind of fell apart. If she had lived, we could have kept it going. Today some of those people tell me we should have kept it going. I say, 'I told you that thirty-five years ago.' "

Ella talked for a while about a day that she once spent with my mother in the Black Hills and about a geode they had once admired together in a rock shop somewhere, and then about an impulsive drive they had made to Rapid City. "I thought she was a little bit reckless," Ella said, giggling girlishly. "When she wanted me to go up to Rapid with her I said, 'I've got no money.' But LaVerne said, 'Just come on.' " Characteristically, Ella said, my mother insisted on taking the cutoff across the rugged northwestern quadrant of the reservation to shorten the ninety-mile trip. The road was all gravel then. "It wasn't safe. Boy, she was pushing that car. I said, 'Don't travel too fast on gravel, it can grab your wheel.' But she didn't seem to hear me. She just kept right on going. That was the only time I ever tried to tell her anything." Ella roared with laughter. "She liked to go fast, that woman!"

Then she talked about her disappointment with the latest tribal elections, and about how hard it still was for decent people to get ahead, and then, making an interior connection of some kind that she didn't explain, said, "I'll tell you about LaVerne and the *yuwipi*," alluding to a rarely performed and often terrifying ceremony, in which the medicine man invokes the spirits of powerful animals. "It was always in the medicine man's house, a small house on the prairie. The doors were sealed and the windows were blocked until the room was pitch-black. The medicine man was bound in skins and tied up. He says, 'Anyone who don't believe, a snake will crawl on your back!' I was a Catholic and I was scared. You'd feel a buffalo, smell him, hear his feet, and his breath. Then there was a deer and an antelope. Sometimes the house shook. I was so scared I was ready to run, boy! LaVerne asked for it each time she was at Pine Ridge. Not for herself, because she wasn't like that. It was for the people, for the work, to give them strength."

I asked Ella whether she thought my mother believed in such things. Ella shrugged.

"I don't know," she replied. "She was open. She wanted to enter into what other people believed. She knew it would give strength to people—she knew that they believed in it—and that it would show that the Association was committed to their customs and not coming in to boss around everyone."

After that we sat for a while, not saying much, just being quiet together.

"I've got something planned for tomorrow," Ella finally said. An impish smile fluttered across her wrinkled lips. "I'm going to give you another Indian name—'Big Road.' You've lost the name you had," she said, meaning, I thought, that the boy it had been given to was now gone. "Big Road was my great-uncle, Mark. He's gone now and the name belongs to me to give, and I'm going to give it to you. Big Road was the medicine man who used to do the *yuwipis* for your mom."

Mark Big Road was named for the railroad that was laid across northern Nebraska at the time of his birth in the 1880s. It was the most remarkable event of the day, opening the region for the first time to the outer world and, Ella might have added, to ranching and farming and the pressure for settlement, and endless demands for more Indian land.

I had rented a hotel room across the state line in Chadron, Nebraska. Driving back there in the dark I remembered nights with my mother, speeding alone across the prairie through the night, and how I would lean my head against the cool window and watch the shadowy nightscape, the undulating black line of the prairie or the notched silhouette of a mesa against the amazing starry sky, and how luminous the stars would seem, and so startlingly clear, that their silence seemed preposterous, as if they should be pealing out symphonies over the prairie. Once in a while a pair of headlights would appear from out of the well of darkness and flash urgently by, like a tiny planet hurtling through the night. Now in my mind's eye I could still see my mother's face intent in the dim light of the dash, the two of us alone together in all the universe, complete.

Except for the Lakotas at Pine Ridge, the whole region had hemorrhaged population for years now, and towns like Chadron were emptying out. Once it had been an important railroad town from which the ranches and farms shipped their produce east, but now only an occasional grain train passed through. There were empty storefronts on the main street, and most of the ones that were still occupied had a tentative, struggling look. In the restaurant two men were talking about rodeos and about how one man's brother was once kicked in the head by a horse and his eye rolled out across the ground in front of everybody, although of course it was an artificial eye. At home, when my mother was away on her trips, I fell asleep at night dreaming of her in Chadron, or in Rosebud, Winner, Lame Deer, or Fort Berthold, or any one of a dozen other towns whose names would set off an almost unbearable yearning to be away with her once again on the open prairie. *Chadron*: it had lain embedded in my memory like a rune that even years after her death I could use to instantaneously invoke her, to bring her back from the dead. Now when I went for a walk after dinner I could feel her in the air around me like a gentle pollen.

The next morning I drove back to Pine Ridge. At White Clay bottle gangs were already pressed up against the walls of the bars, and on the road between there and the reservation I passed more rumpled men and women hitchhiking south to start their day's drinking. When I got to Ella's, she and Dick and Mona Hagen from down the road, and Ella's sister Arta, and Arta's daughter Nancy were sitting on metal lawn chairs and old sofas in Ella's living room. We drank Cokes and talked, waiting for Ella's nephew Mike, Jr., a chanter and a popular drummer on the powwow circuit, who was coming up from his home in Nebraska to sing. The mood was quintessentially Lakota, a mixture of casualness and gravity, of wisecracks and baseball caps and old jeans, and of intense latent emotion, like a heart swollen with tears. Mike, Jr., proved to be a handsome, powerfully built man of twenty-five or so, and he brought along his infant son, whom people passed around and hugged and petted while his father sang.

Ella levered herself up from her chair and stood in the kitchen doorway. Her flat voice thickened as she said, talking about me, "This boy's mom was cut down before her time. She was one of my best friends. She was family to me. She was my Elder Sister. That's my own name, and that's what we called her in Indian. I really miss her." She began to cry. "This boy is part of my family too. He never forgot me. I never forgot him. I want him to be part of my family. I'm giving him the name Big Road."

"There are a lot of songs," Mike, Jr., said to me. "I tried quite a few of them, but they didn't sound right. So I created this song for you. It belongs to you."

"*Canku tanka cokata maniwo, youonihan onicuwapi, anpetu ki le nitawayelo.*" Mike Jr.'s voice went on and on, nasal and infectious, swelling and receding. "*Canku tanka cokata maniwo, youonihan onicuwapi, anpetu ki le nitawayelo* . . . Big Road, step to the center, we are going to honor you. This day is yours."

I stood in the kitchen doorway with Ella, not thinking or trying to make sense of what I felt, letting Mike, Jr.'s, words soak into me. I felt a sense of long pent-up relief, as if a wall had cracked, a recog-

nition that I was inextricably linked to these people and that a place
had always remained for me here, though for all these years I had not
properly understood it and had been too afraid to tamper with the
past to come back.

The naming was a renewal of the family bond, acknowledging
that I was no longer Ella's father's symbolic son but her own, and that
I had come back, like someone who had been lost, and also that Ella's
loss, like my own, had been a terrible one that had never healed, and
that this healing was for her, in the way that made sense to her, as the
probing and questioning and gathering of facts and erasing of doubt
did for me, for both of us, a way of reweaving our lives, of recreat-
ing a connection in which my mother still lived.

Afterward we ate microwaved tacos and drank more Coke, and
sat and talked about Mike, Jr.'s, new baby and about the tribal casino
and how the tribe had made enough money from it to finally buy
street lamps for the town. Later on, after everyone else had left, Ella
shuffled into her bedroom and rummaged among the boxes of clothing. She came back with a small white envelope. In it were snapshots
of me at the 1958 powwow. There were pictures of my mother and
me dwarfed by Lakotas in magnificent buckskin costumes and feathers. In one picture I saw Ella, my mother, Alfreda, and Ella's father,
Ben, handing me the splendid headdress that I was to wear. In another, Ben was leading me, petrified with embarrassment, to the center of the circle. The pictures were, of course, in black and white and
were taken at night with a flash; figures in the foreground had a livid,
almost three-dimensional, presence, while those in the background—
men and women in buckskins and spectacular confections of feathers—seemed shadowy and insubstantial in the blackness. I didn't
want to recognize myself in my baggy chinos hiked up too high on
my waist and the plaid shirt buttoned to the neck, and the too-short
brush cut and crooked teeth. I looked terrified. The sheer nakedness
of my inadequacy to the situation I was in was all too obvious. I saw
a boy who was afraid of poverty and the sour smell of Indian houses,
and of kids like himself who had no clothes, and the gloom of the
reservations, and who couldn't ride well enough to save his mother:

the boy who was destined for catastrophe. I wasn't grateful for the pictures. It was only with some effort that I could thank Ella for them.

"You were afraid of the Indians," Ella said. She was smiling. I supposed that she was teasing.

"I was just afraid," I said.

I looked more closely at the photographs of us together. Ella, Alfreda, Ben: they were all smiling at me, all happy for me. How could I have missed that, while the memory of my shame had remained undiminished all these years like some sticky and ineradicable residue? I studied my mother's face. She was beaming at me, in spite of my goofiness and fragility, loving me in spite of it, and loving that I had been taken into the embrace of Ella's family, her own Lakota family, knowing, as I did not that night, that I would always belong to them, and that forty years later I would be able to return, still loved.

I DROVE EAST from Pine Ridge across northern Nebraska to Macy, following the route that my mother often took in the 1950s, across a stale, melancholy landscape pocked with withering towns in places where towns should never have been put in the first place, most of them little more than a few rusting silos, an auto-repair shop, a luncheonette, and trailers stuck in among stunted cottonwoods. Horses grazed alongside the empty highway, and sometimes I could see a scrimshaw of black-haired cattle grazing on rolling yellow hills. Where there was water enough for farming, machine-baled rolls of hay lay like ancient tumuli. For a long time the only thing I could find on the radio was a report that went on for hours about how astronomy had to be reconciled with a literal reading of the Bible.

As I drove, I thought of my mother racing across these same dry plains, chainsmoking, pedal pressed close to the floor in one of the big Chevys that she liked to rent. Questions nagged at me: Was she really happier among the Indians than she was with us? Weren't we more important than whether the Cheyennes got back a piece of land,

or the Miccosukees got to continue living on their islets in the Everglades? I had to face the fact that, on some plane, we weren't. Yet I
also knew that she loved me with a terrific intensity. Nothing I found
out had given me any cause to doubt that. I could see it in the pictures that Ella Irving had given me; and, after all, she had taken me
with her on her trips, whatever the expense and the inconvenience.
"The only thing that bothered her when she traveled was that she
would be away from you," Sylvia Hermelin had told me. "When you
were old enough to go with her, then everything was all right." *But
if you really loved me that much, why didn't you take care of yourself? Why did you drive yourself into the ground like that? Didn't you
know that I needed you to stay alive?* Had she given up on the Indians, had she succumbed to frustration with the slow pace of change,
with obstructive government bureaucrats, with venal tribal politicians, with the endless petty tasks of organization, no one would have
blamed her. She might well still be alive today. Did I wish, then, that
she had abandoned the Indians and come home to us? Did I wish that
she had reached for less, demanded less of herself? Did I wish that she
had become *like everyone else?* This was the question that I was most
afraid to ask. Although I felt with all my heart that I would have
given anything for my mother to have lived, I knew that I could not
love her and then fail to love what she had believed in most, and the
sacrifice that she had made, and the life that she had chosen for herself and that had been the culmination of all that she had worked for
at least since her days with the War Relocation Administration and
probably before, perhaps even as far back as high school, when she
chose for her motto, "Justice is having and doing what is one's own."

The land finally began to come alive again east of the hundredth
meridian, which marked the end of the dry plains and the beginning
of the well-watered Midwest. There were farms now instead of
ranches, and thriving towns, and oceans of corn golden in the bright
autumn sun, and the car radio swarmed with high-school football
games and cowboy music. For a few remarkable minutes at sunset
everything—silos, cottonwoods, farmsteads—hovered eerily above
the earth in a strange vaporous light, and then it all went suddenly

black. In the darkness giant harvesters lighting their path with flood-lights continued to churn monstrously through the cornfields.

MACY LAY A SHORT DISTANCE off the state highway behind the steep bluffs that flank the Missouri River. As I drove along the dusty streets, through flurries of yellowing cottonwood leaves that fluttered gaily in the breeze like scraps of gold foil over the scrubby yards and rusting trailers and diminutive frame cottages, things seemed vividly familiar and, though still visibly poor, there was little of the obvious despondency and threat that I remembered from forty years before. The early promise of my mother's work had fallen short of her hopes here, too. As at Pine Ridge, unemployment was still high, too few students finished school, and alcoholism remained endemic. But there was a new clinic and nursing home that Pauline Tyndal had gotten built, and a new school where the Omaha language was taught, and a public swimming pool, and a new tribal office building, and a modern courthouse and police facility, the latter much more than merely symbolic in a place that forty years ago was virtually lawless, and they were all run by Omahas.

Of my mother's friends only Pauline was left. At eighty-one, she was now a pyramid of flesh in a voluminous scarlet dress, immense and grave, and crippled with diabetes. She moved only with great difficulty, with the aid of an aluminum walker. Her heart was also failing. She had already worn out three pacemakers and knew that she could not survive another operation. She told me that the last time she had nearly died on the operating table. Her round, walnut-colored face was pale, her eyes tired, melancholy, inward-turning. The light inside her neatly kept cottage was dim and aqueous even though it was mid-afternoon, and I had the sense, at times, that she was speaking to me from a great distance, as if she could already see death closing in around her. She would, in fact, die from heart failure a few months later.

"Your mom always seemed happy here," she said. "She brought life into our lives. People liked her and trusted her, and she became one of us. People loved her big hats and leather boots and the way she smoked. She'd sit there with a cigarette and laugh, and the kids would all run to her. After she left here, I don't know how many people smoked the way she did, with a cigarette dangling out of her mouth, just because she did it that way. As soon as she walked into a new situation it was like she had read a whole library on it. She could have been an Indian if she had wanted to be. She could talk to the street people, anybody. She was always interested in talking to you, always wanting to learn from you. She participated in our ceremonies. Anyone who worked with LaVerne was attacked. We were called Communists. Our cars were stopped by the state police. Our lives were threatened. One farmer who was leasing Indian land said, 'We're just going to shoot her.' But nothing scared your mother. She was never afraid."

Then Pauline told me a funny story about how once at a community meeting my mother, to everyone's horror, sat down next to a man everyone believed had the power of what the Omahas called "love medicine," which gave him the ability to have any woman he wanted, and would have my mother, too, if they didn't get her away from him and sitting safely among the women, and how, knowing that political power resided among the men, she refused to move, saying with a laugh that her own medicine was just as strong as his. Telling it, Pauline laughed, and then I did, too, both of us remembering my mother's grace and toughness, until Pauline's laughter choked away in a fit of coughing. As we talked in the dimness I felt even more than I had at Pine Ridge that I had come home, or had at least come back to a part of myself that I had long ago ceased to know. I told her what I had been thinking and worrying about on the drive from Pine Ridge.

"You have to understand what things were like," Pauline replied, in a voice that was suddenly youthful and clear, the voice of forty years ago. "The tribe was on the brink of extinction. We were like stray dogs living on a dump, scrounging something to live on. LaVerne gave us hope. Before she came here, we didn't think we could stand up to the people in power. No one had ever showed us what we could do to help ourselves. She taught us that we could speak out, that we didn't have to be the underdog unless we allowed ourselves to be. Little by little we began to come out of our shell. We have a better life today because of the things she did."

After my mother's death Pauline had gone on to become one of the most respected elders of the tribe. She had designed its health-care facility and had lobbied for it in Washington, and had invented a model for tribal health care that had been taken up by the BIA and replicated throughout Indian country. And she had herself become a model of commitment to public service, acknowledged as someone who in a community where fear of defeat was still a fact of life was undeterred by the difficulty of making things happen, as someone who got things done. "I was a born organizer but I didn't know it," Pauline said. "LaVerne brought me out into full bloom. Knowing her was one of the best experiences of my life."

Pauline was quiet for a long while after that. The shadow was so deep around her that I couldn't tell if her eyes were open or shut. She was silent so long that I supposed that she had fallen asleep. Then she said suddenly, "The last time I saw her, she brought all kinds of things with her, jars of pickles, hot dogs, and everything. We went down below the bluffs and built a fire and ate, and brewed coffee, and talked and talked into the middle of the night. She was really down, depressed. I hardly ever saw her like that. She was getting terrible pressure from the board because of her work out here. It was costing too much money. She knew she was going to have to withdraw from here. She said she wanted to stay here with us forever, but that this was probably the last time she'd be coming out here and be seeing us. I didn't know how much I loved her until she was gone. She was my best friend. When she was gone, I missed her like hell. I dreamed of her for years afterward."

I wanted to ask Pauline about the man in the motel room, the faint memory that hinted at a duplicitous life that my mother might possibly have lived and that I had, until now, avoided confronting. I started to ask and then left off, thinking that I wasn't so sure that I really wanted to know after all. Instead I got up and got myself a Dr

Pepper from the refrigerator. Then we talked for a while about Pauline's son Wayne and the courses he was teaching at the community college, and then about another son who was suing the tribal government for firing him from a job as a janitor, and then about a grandson who went away with a girl who treated him badly and had wound up on drugs in Saskatchewan and had hanged himself. Stories like these were so common on reservations that people reported them matter-of-factly, expecting neither commiseration nor shock. Then finally I told her what I remembered about the motel room after all and the peculiar atmosphere that I had felt in it, and what I thought about my mother and the man whom I knew at the time but whose face had remained a steadfast blank.

Pauline was silent again for some time. I thought she wasn't going to answer, and then she told me a name. I could see that it had cost her an effort. I remembered the man. I was startled. I knew that he had worked with my mother and that he was someone she respected for his political grit, but I remembered him as a hard, intimidating man, whose presence I shied away from when I could. It was difficult for me to picture my mother with him.

"She knew I knew," Pauline said evenly. "LaVerne was very polished about it. You never saw anything in public. But knowing what I knew and trying not to think about it was hard for me. It wasn't my way. I was always a one-man woman. But I loved LaVerne and I had a lot of respect for him, and in the end I thought, just let them be."

"How long did it go on?" I asked.

"Right until the end."

I saw now, of course, that leaving the Omahas meant leaving not only a community that she loved and to which she had committed her honor, but this man as well.

Even as I recognized that he must have made her happy in some way, I felt a bitter gust of the jealousy that I would have felt forty years earlier had I then discovered what I had just now learned. What Pauline said next made me feel a pity for my father that I had never felt before. "I never heard her mention your father," she said. "I knew he was there, but she never said anything about him, nothing.

Even when you weren't here with her she talked about you a lot, but never about him." Pauline continued to talk for a while about how you could understand how she "fell for" the man, how he was a "dignified" and "humble" man, qualities that had completely escaped my adolescent eye, an eye that even now I still imagined to have been precocious and discriminating but that had not seen so very much after all. I saw yet again how much of my mother's life—even that part of it that I thought I had witnessed—would forever lie beyond reach.

Circumstances and geography ensured that they could not have met very often. Still, their affair had gone on for years, Pauline said. It is possible, of course, that my dislike for this man was something raw and Oedipal that I was simply too young to understand. Where I saw hardness my mother knew there was tenderness, and where I saw harshness, dignity. I also understood that if I was really to understand this woman who was my mother, I would, however reluctantly, have to make room for this man in the charmed circle of her love. It was proof of something that, as an adult, should have needed no proof at all, but that the fourteen-year-old boy who still lived somewhere in me still found hard to swallow: that I was not enough for her after all, and that someone like him had made her happy in a way that I, of course, never could. Yet I was also glad for her, that in those last whirlwind years of ever-increasing work she had found someone to please her, to bring her the kind of happiness that, apparently, she could no longer find at home. Later I recognized the man in photographs in the Association's archives at Princeton. His face still seemed hard and unsympathetic to me. But I also saw something that startled me: in the face of this middle-aged Indian man of the Great Plains I saw, like fragments of an older hidden text, the same narrow "long-eyed" face that in her youth my mother had described over and over again in her poetry of the 1930s.

It had grown late. Outside the light was fading over the bluffs and the yellowing cottonwoods. I could see that Pauline was exhausted, and I felt that I had pressed her enough. I got up to leave. I was halfway out the door when she told me to wait.

"There is something else that I would never tell anyone," she said. "I promised her I wouldn't tell. But you should know this."

I stood holding open the screen door. Pauline had risen. She leaned heavily on her walker, steadying her weight. Her eyes were remote and unfocused. It occurred to me that probably she could barely see me.

We let the silence lengthen.

"She was a night person," Pauline said. "That was when she liked to talk and plan. I'd want to go to sleep. But she loved to sit up all night and talk into the early hours. Sometimes I'd fall asleep and wake up later and she'd still be talking. One night we were in a motel in South Dakota, lying there, and she started talking."

I let the screen door shut behind me. I felt the three of us coming together in the kitchen in the fading light. *You are coming to me now, coming to me on Pauline's lips.* The intensity of my mother's presence was almost insupportable. I felt an unaccountable impulse to flee, to make some kind of excuse for myself and run to the car and drive blindly away to Omaha or Sioux City, or just into the bright emptiness of the 7-Eleven at the gas station up in Homer, as if there were something urgent that waited for me anywhere but here. Then I thought, *I will never leave you.*

"She told me that one time she went out on a date with a boyfriend," Pauline said very slowly. "They went to some kind of party. Later they were out riding and this carload of boys came. The boys forced them to stop somehow. It had happened in some kind of park. They got her out of the car. She tried to get away. They gang-raped her. They made the boyfriend watch. She was devastated. She said it never went away.

"I was shocked," she said. "I was too horrified to ask her more about it. She hated those boys for what they did. It affected her life. She said so, but never said exactly how. She didn't dwell on it, but she was very angry."

Pauline thought she might have had an abortion. "I think she was told that she might never be able to have children." This was when she told Pauline that she wanted a baby so much that she dreamed of kidnapping someone else's. "It really scared her. She was afraid for a long time that she would really steal one."

I sat down numbly and went over again and again what Pauline remembered. She couldn't say where the thing had taken place, although she thought it was somewhere around New York, and someplace like a park, or when it had happened. "She was young," Pauline said. "I think she was a virgin." Pauline didn't know what happened to my mother afterward, or whether the boys were ever caught or what happened to them if they were. Unable to let go now, I tried to pull more out of her, anything at all, but that was all there was, just the one wisp of memory, gossamer and awful and reverberating.

Pauline said that later, when she could think clearly about it and was no longer so sickened by the thought of it that she feared to bring it up, she had tried to ask my mother more about it. But my mother refused to ever speak of it again.

Driving back from Macy to my hotel in Sioux City that night, I felt in my stomach the tidal rise and fall of the hills more than I actually seemed to see them through the image of my mother's rape that played incessantly in front of my eyes. I drove through Winnebago and then Homer, and then down onto the flat flood plain of the Missouri, where I could see, across the river, the multitudinous lights of an oil refinery shimmering like some bizarre parody of a fairy castle. Farms and clumps of trees flashed by in my headlights. Nothing seemed real except my mother's fear and pain, released now like ancient air from a long-sealed tomb. I was grateful for the too-brightly lit lobby of my hotel, the fatuous greetings of the desk clerks, the unmemorable whodunit that was playing on the old-movie channel on the TV. I double-locked the door as if it could shut out the images that swarmed unstoppably through my mind. I ordered a club sandwich from room service and then thought, *That's what I always ordered when I was alone with my mother in hotels long ago.*

I stayed awake a long time staring at the TV, boiling with rage and pity, in shock as if the thing had occurred only a few hours before. Again and again tears welled up in the corners of my eyes and I forced them back. *Don't worry*, I kept thinking, absurdly. *I'll find the boys, punish them. They won't get away*. My imagination relentlessly filled in details that I could never really know. I saw a wooded road and my mother—sometimes the open-faced girl I knew only from photographs, sometimes the grown-up mother of my childhood—in a Model A . . . with whom? A friend? A boyfriend? The square-jawed Frank O'Neill? Or Jimmy Phelan? *Three or four boys are standing on the roadside next to a broken-down car. You stop. The boys beg for a lift. 'Help them out,' you say. 'It's the right thing to do.' Soon there are innuendos, insinuating hands, a knife. Then smirks and leers, tearing at your clothes, horror in your eyes as you perceive that what you fear most is really going to happen. I see their bodies on top of you, one after the other.* Sometimes, in the fantasy, I reached for her and tore her away from their hands, clutched her to me and spirited her away to safety, did everything that I had failed to do that last morning of her life on the road in Vermont. I covered her ravaged body, cradled her in my arms, told her that things would be all right, that truly they would. *You will live. You will be loved. I swear it. You cannot know it now. But I know it.* Other times I was the friend pinioned by the leering boys, forced to watch as they took her one after the other. It went on and on, over and over.

9

CERTAIN PUZZLING MEMORIES now began to make sense. There was the curious incident that occurred one night in Vermont on our way back from the movies in Newport. We had just seen a Western about a black cavalryman unjustly accused of raping a white woman. The crime was handled so obliquely on screen that I don't think I even understood at the time just what had happened to the victim. The evening stuck in my mind only because of my mother's behavior afterward. On the way back to the lake, on an otherwise deserted stretch of road, we encountered four teenagers—two boys and two girls—who flagged us down and begged for a ride, saying that their car had broken down and that they'd be punished if they didn't get home before their curfew. I remember them as typical country kids, clean-cut and polite, but my mother tensed and ordered my father to roll up the window to a crack. She told him to say that we would take only one of them and no more. When they pleaded that they all needed to go, I said that we could make room somehow, thinking that it was the right thing to do and the thing that my mother would want. But she turned suddenly on me and told me to shut up, and told my father to drive on, and wouldn't say any more when I asked why.

And there were the words that Maddy had repeated incessantly in the months before she left—no, was sent away, exiled—to the nursing home where she died: "Poor LaVernie, poor LaVernie. What have they done to her? What have they done to my LaVernie?" I would say, lying, that she was fine, or that she was in South Dakota or Washington, that there was nothing to worry about, and pray that Maddy would shut up. *But she knew. She knew.* It would of course have been Maddy to whom my mother would have gone first to for help. I couldn't begin to imagine the shock that the rape must have given to Maddy's Catholic sensibilities, but she was a trained nurse who would have seen to it that my mother got medical attention, or would even have provided it herself in the house on Washington Street. She kept the secret coiled tightly in her memory for decades, kept it perfectly until senility finally sprang it loose and forced it to the surface. How ignorant I was. She wept, not, as I had supposed, because she had lost her memory, but because she remembered all too well.

I wasn't sure what to do next. Had I any right to pry further into something that my mother had deliberately kept secret all her life, confessing it finally only in the dead of night in a motel room far from home? I wished that I had never heard about the rape, but there was no evading it now. Gradually the raw anger began to subside and questions formed in its place like scabs. What had this terrible thing meant in my mother's life? How had she ever become the fearless woman whom everyone remembered? How much were her journeys into Indian country, along with so much else, a kind of testing, proving to herself over and over that she could survive as a woman alone, that she could overcome fear of danger and violation? How had she managed to wall it off from the rest of her life, from all our lives? However had she found the strength to go on?

I called my mother's childhood friend John McCaffrey, who had joined the Mount Vernon Police Force in 1936 and had risen to become chief of detectives, and asked him if he had ever heard any rumors about her having been raped. The department was a small one then, and had the rape of someone he knew been reported to it while he was there, he would surely have heard about it. He was shocked at the question as perhaps only a devout Irish Catholic of the just barely post-Victorian world could be at the fact that a man would even want to know such things about his dead mother. He hadn't. "That kind of crime was rare," he said thickly. "I don't even know if it happened here in Mount Vernon. We just didn't have reports of it." Then could it have happened while she was in high school? He replied, "If it had, the news would have been all over town." I could tell that he was forcing himself to respond. But I still wanted to know how a woman like my mother might have reacted to rape in the 1930s, what she was most likely to have done. "She'd want to forget it completely. It was the worst thing in the world. She'd be soiled." Pressing him further, I asked how the police would have responded to her if she reported it to them. The old man's forbearance finally collapsed. "Drop it," he said suddenly. "You're not going to accomplish anything good for your mother. My advice is, just forget it. Just say a prayer for her every day."

My best guess was that my mother was raped sometime between her graduation from high school and her marriage to Harold, probably in the early 1930s and perhaps not long before her graduation from NYU in 1934; it might, I thought, account for her surprising failure to show up for her yearbook picture or for the pictures for any of the several organizations to which she belonged. I also remembered something that had struck an off note in the interview that she had given to the *Mount Vernon Daily Argus* in August 1936. Toward the end of the interview the reporter had tacked on several items that didn't fit conveniently into the body of the piece: "She is fond of outdoor sports, but not in the competitive sense, she says; and she enjoys swimming especially. Her 'mania,' she declares, is anti crime. 'I hate war, but what good is peace if a country is unsafe to live in?' she queries." The vehemence of this statement was startling, all the more so since crime was at its nadir during the Depression. And in Mount Vernon there was no serious crime at all.

If the rape had occurred sometime before the summer of 1936, then why hadn't any allusions to it turned up in the stories and cycles of sonnets that she completed that year or not long before? Or had they? I went back and looked for clues. I didn't expect to find a literal description—in that era she would hardly have written openly about rape—but *something*. Little by little I began to see things, images mostly, that I had scarcely noticed before but that now took on new meaning. For instance, there was an arresting image of what appeared to be a ravaged body in a sonnet that she called "Scattered Agamemnon":

> *And strange marauders sack you at their ease*
> *And squabble for your rings, though you beseech,*
> *With eyes that see not, to be left in peace,*
> *And then the combers rake you down the beach*
> *And sort you from the waves and release*
> *What serves no purpose for the sun to bleach.*

Among the poems that I found in Catherine Ruth Smith's house there was another, untitled sonnet that at first reading appeared to be a romantic rendering of disappointed love, but which could just as easily describe a woman in a state of trauma:

> *Expelled from love, stripped bare and shunted out,*
> *My body lies for any mage to drag*
> *Back into life, while idlers crowd about*
> *With noisy nothings in their heads that wag*

And some will slap me on the ashen cheek;
Some watch the feather shake beneath my teeth;
Some thumb the pulse or hear the void heart speak;
And all will think I live because I breathe.
But they will do a grisly miracle
Who rob Golgotha of its lawful prize
And paint the lips and make the nostrils swell
And graft false brilliance on the nerveless eyes.
What man, however leprous, will espouse
A woman salvaged from a charnel house?

There was another very long poem—eighteen pages—that contained a more explicit, unsettling allusion to sex. It is based on an incident described by Herodotus in Book One of his History, occurring in a section that is devoted to classical rape myths: the abduction of Io, the ravishing of Europa, the rape of Helen by Paris, and others. In my mother's rendering, Candaules, the king of Lydia, is so cursed by dreams of his queen's magnificent beauty that he is incapable of actually possessing her in the flesh. In order to escape from this torment, Candaules hits on the idea of ordering his bodyguard, Gyges, to conceal himself in the royal bedchamber in order to watch the queen disrobe, although the law explicitly bars commoners from looking upon the unclothed bodies of their rulers. Candaules

> *Resolved at length that Gyges dream his dreams*
> *And he through Gyges be himself redeemed.*

Reluctantly Gyges agrees. Gyges's voyeuristic presence finally frees the impotent king to consummate the act of sex. Unknown to Candaules, however, the queen spies Gyges in the shadows. The next day she confronts Gyges and offers him a cruel alternative: he must either yield his own life as punishment for his crime or slay Candaules and take his place. Gyges chooses self-preservation over loyalty to his king. The queen orders him to conceal himself in the royal bedchamber as he had the night before. When Candaules is asleep Gyges creeps from behind the door and stabs him to death.

> *The king's lips parted to the breath of pain,*
> *And from them fled some indistinct, glad word,*
> *His last-dreamed thought, wrung out articulate*
> *In that wild fleeing of all things from death.*

Like my mother's companion on the night of her rape, the voyeur in the poem was also an unwilling witness, trapped in the bedchamber by his king's command as surely as if he were held by physical force. Gyges's presence also transformed the royal copulation into a violation by transference through the voyeur's eyes. Unlike my mother, however, the outraged queen would have her revenge upon the man responsible for her humiliation by transforming one night's helpless voyeur into the next night's avenger.

A RETIRED New York City detective I knew, Dennis O'Sullivan, introduced me to Linda Fairstein, the director of the Sexual Crimes Unit in the Manhattan District Attorney's office, and we talked for a long time one day in her office in lower Manhattan. She said that what had happened to my mother, sketchy as the apparent facts were, sounded like what police call a classic lover's-lane situation. "You have a couple parked in a secluded area. Suppose there are five guys. They catch people off guard. It begins as a robbery. Then one of the guys gets the idea to do something more. Maybe the girl is already necking or doing something more sexual. It becomes a matter of opportunism." Fairstein thought that there was at least a fifty-fifty chance that the rape had been reported. Until recent changes in the law abandoned the requirement that there be a corroborating witness in cases of rape, very few were reported, and even fewer were successfully prosecuted. As recently as 1970, of the more than one thousand men who were arrested for rape in New York City, only eighteen were convicted. But Fairstein made an obvious point about my mother's case. "Your mother had an eyewitness, a friend. These cases where a man is with a woman who is assaulted are relatively uncommon. It increases the chance that it was reported. A middle-class woman with a well-educated background would be better met at the police station where they reported it."

On Fairstein's advice I first contacted Mount Vernon Hospital to see if, perhaps, my mother had been treated there after the rape. A sympathetic clerk in the records office promised to help, but after several weeks of exchanging phone calls she told me that the hospital had apparently lost its records from the years in question. Then I began contacting police departments. The rape could have taken place in any one of dozens of jurisdictions anywhere in the New York area, including northern New Jersey or Long Island, or even Connecticut. I knew that because this was a rape case my mother's name would probably have been kept out of later court proceedings, but O'Sullivan told me that if she had reported the crime at all, her name would initially have been entered in the daybook of the police station where she reported it.

Trying to gain access to sixty-five-year-old files in dozens of station houses was manifestly futile. Systems of record keeping had changed, old records were often difficult to retrieve or had been misfiled, and even where they survived, access to them depended on the whim of the officials in each station house. However, I reasoned that if my mother had reported the rape to a police department anywhere in the area, it might well have been communicated to the Mount Vernon Police Department, since she was a resident of the city, a standard practice at the time. O'Sullivan arranged the cooperation of the Mount Vernon Police Department, which allowed me to spend days examining the old daybooks stored in the attic of its headquarters. Each of the ten- or twelve-pound books was heavily bound and thick with a half-century's dust that blackened my hands as I turned the thick, ruled pages, scanning the entries, thousands of them, from the late 1920s to 1940, each one meticulously written in the careful penmanship that was essential in an age when typewriting was still, to many, an arcane art. Each entry was dated by day and hour and head-

lined with a short description: "Boy injured when alighting from trolley car," "Dog bite on highway," "Grass fire," "Cat unmoved from
tree." In the summer, toddlers fell from open windows in distressing
numbers; in the winter, children were injured riding sleighs. Dead
dogs needed to be removed from gutters. People slipped off curbs and
twisted their ankles, a Depression-era ploy to make a little pocket
money, since people injured on city sidewalks could collect damages
of a few dollars from the city treasury. Murders, rapes, robberies,
drug dealing, and child abuse were almost completely absent. I read
thousands of pages. My mother's name was not there. It was possible, of course, that the local police where the rape occurred never
passed their report on to the MVPD. More likely, like the vast majority of rape victims, my mother never reported the incident at all.

Somewhere the truth existed. But it was beyond my reach. I
stared at the piles of dusty complaint books. What would I have done
if I had found the rapists' names and somehow managed to track
them down, the wild boys of sixty or more years ago now become old
men, so senile perhaps that they no longer even remembered what
they had done? What could I possibly say to them? I felt no mercy for
them, but I felt embarrassed at the image of myself standing over
some feeble man of eighty-five and accusing him of rape. I felt both
defeated and relieved. Stripping away uncertainty was my way of
coming to grips with things. But increasingly, as my anger cooled, I
began to feel that relentlessly pursuing the details of the rape was another kind of violation, a ripping away of the final veil from the one
thing that my mother had deliberately kept secret all her life. Would
she have wanted me to go on, to strip bare the complete truth of the
most shaming thing that had ever happened to her? For once her
ghost was silent. I was on my own. There were still other police departments to contact, other hospitals to approach, other archives to
ferret out. But I would leave her shame in peace. Still, it was hard to
let go, to accept that there was a place in my mother's life where I
could never go, a place that would forever remain a terra incognita,
and whose meaning would never come clear.

There was just one other thing, a couple of handwritten scraps that I found among my mother's papers, inside an old manila folder. They were notes for a novel that she probably never wrote. In this fragment, she is ostensibly speaking about her unnamed protagonist:

[She] *lived three times in her life. She lived the time of the fear, the time of the dog, and the time of the stranger.*
   The time of the fear—
      Rage at violence
      Animal canniness, avoiding death
      Submission—but crawling skin and stiff hair, knowing that
         death possible, likely
      Walked in dripping blood
      Afterward, waves of sorrow would break like waves on a
         shore
      Deliriously close to madness

This was the closest that I was likely to come to hearing my mother tell me in her own words how she felt about what had happened to her and to the raw place deep in herself that she had kept from sight for so many years. Clearly she had felt terror and the threat of imminent death and had come close to a mental breakdown. Somehow, "animal canniness," raw survival instinct, had enabled her to endure what was done to her. What did she mean? Perhaps the pretense of willing compliance, or just the decision not to fight back, the purchasing of life at the price of pain and humiliation. I pictured her afterward in the house on Washington Street, numbed, perhaps unable to speak, too frightened to go out, certain that she would never be able to live a normal life again.

   Therapy was no option for someone like my mother in the early 1930s, when psychiatry itself was still new and not well understood, and certainly not affordable by people already devastated by the Depression, and when the prospect of talking openly about rape was unthinkable. For my mother then, there was just Maddy, the two dogs Zero and Bunker, with their total and unjudging love and, finally, I think, the redemptive power of the sonnet. Poetry was her route back to sanity, her only proof that she could exert control over anything in a suddenly dangerous world in which even familiar trees and roads and cars harbored hidden terrors. The deliberate aestheticism distanced, transmuted, cleansed. The classical architecture of the sonnets provided structure where it no longer existed, a sense of strength, a kind of emotional musculature that gradually enabled her to rebuild her psyche, aestheticizing sexuality, and levering her up from the slough of shame and self-loathing, transforming the repellent things of the flesh into a form as cold as Grecian marble.

Women who have been raped describe prolonged feelings of extreme vulnerability, fear, rage, helplessness, and suicidal impulses. Nancy Venable Raine, who was raped in 1985 by a man who invaded her home, writes in *After Silence,* an account of her ordeal and its aftermath, of feeling as if a part of her had "split off" during the attack and remained like "a shadow self that perched above me like a sparrow, waiting for her dead mate on the sidewalk below to wake up." Even long after the event she notes, "The waking world as I had known it became nothing more than a thin permeable membrane that could not hold back this other world occupied by horrors. . . . I lived with sudden fear the way others live with cancer. The fear was always there, in warrens just below the surface of my skin, waiting." Raine experienced alternating periods of extreme exhaustion and shattering anxiety, along with a collapse of her self-confidence and intense shame, when she wondered whether she had been "a despicable coward" for caving in to the rapist's demands. She became a slave to her memory of the rape. "What the rapist did to my body was not in the past, as I had no past—because the memory of what happened did not feel like a memory. It felt here and now, in the present tense. The result of this peculiar predicament was an inner stupor. I began to feel that everything that had happened was happening now, or I felt nothing at all." She was terrified of being alone and for weeks followed her mother around the house as she had when she was an infant. Strange men seemed to radiate "bolts of menace," and for a long time, feeling "like prey," she found it almost physically impossible to sit near them. *Was that why you chose my father for a husband? Did*

*he even know that you had been raped, or did you keep it from him,
too? Was he the first man that you trusted afterward? You knew that
you would be safe with him, that he wouldn't hurt you. He was a decent man. He admired you. He made you laugh. And why else would
Maddy, who wanted a doctor for you and who dreamed of a restoration of her own gilded youth, have so easily given her blessing to this
man with an eighth-grade education who installed boilers for a living?*

It is possible, too, that the rape contributed to the apparent fearlessness that everyone who knew my mother describes, and to the
near-foolhardiness that she displayed during her travels around isolated reservations where there was little or no law and order, violence
was common, and women were considered fair game. Such behavior
is not uncommon among rape survivors as a kind of reaction to deep-
seated, lingering fear. Raine writes, "Somewhere was the vague
thought that if I paid attention to this fear, if I ever once said to myself that I wasn't going to do something because I was afraid of being
raped, that I would make the thing I feared happen." Another rape
victim who has written eloquently about the prolonged effects of her
experience, Martha Ramsey, notes, "I decided I was going to think of
the world as incapable of attacking me again, and of myself as invul-
nerable. I would cover up my fear with a mask of fearlessness. . . .
Later, walking alone on deserted city streets, I would summon up a
feeling of invincibility, of having paid my dues, given up what could
be taken." Freud observed that repression is an ongoing process and
that the object of repression exercises a "continuous straining in the
direction of consciousness" that requires a continuing expenditure of
energy. I knew that my mother's life could, of course, never be explained by a single event, however traumatic. Still, I couldn't help
wondering how much its subterranean repercussions might have contributed to the manic, self-destructive overwork and intolerance of
her own exhaustion that came to a head in the months just before her
death.

But knowing precisely what had happened to my mother on some
suburban road six or seven decades ago was ultimately less important

than understanding how she had survived—not only survived but triumphed—to become a woman of such remarkable generosity and courage. Her father's death had already destroyed the edifice of her Catholicism, an ordered universe in which everything was an expression of God's will and therefore good, or at least endowed with divine purpose. Now her self-confidence, her judgment of people, her intuition, her very identity had been shattered as well. After this she knew that death would always be at her side and that evil could exist anywhere, that a familiar stretch of road or a friend's car could be suddenly converted into a theater of cruelty. Yet she somehow discovered in herself a reservoir of strength and determination, not just to soldier on, but to live a life that was bolder and more engaged in the world than it had been before. From a somewhat precious poet and a scholar whose greatest pleasure lay in the decipherment of papyri she became someone who sought out conflict and controversy, and often provoked it, and challenged conventions of all sorts. The rape must always have been there in her mind, like a filmstrip forever flickering behind her thoughts, perhaps much the way her death cast its long shadow over my own life. But she refused to allow shame and fear to cripple her, refused to think of herself as a victim. Perhaps, I thought, her rape was the very medium that had enabled her to identify so viscerally with those—Japanese-Americans, Indians—who had been shamed and humiliated and made helpless and forced into silence. Although she couldn't speak about the memory that must have gnawed at her core, it enabled her to give voice to other people who couldn't speak, to articulate the rage they felt and then to transform it into a politics that insisted on justice rather than vengeance.

My mother was condemned to silence by the mores of her time. No woman could speak openly about rape then, and for her there was no alternative to stoic endurance. In 1936 she wrote in her critique of a character in one of Catherine Ruth Smith's plays, "If you persist in giving him unhappiness without the strength to bear it and weakness without the will to conquer it, you portray a neurotic instead of a strong, brave man in the grasp of a strange affinity. Don't mistake me. Both unhappiness and weakness are admirable qualities

in a hero, but only when he is man enough to keep still about them."
*So silence, too, was something that we unknowingly would share,
and pain, harbored within ourselves, as if it were something that we
wanted because we could do nothing else with it. Be a Viking, you
would tell me when I cried as a child. Be a Spartan. Wait until something really terrible happens. Wait until you know what pain really
is. In August 1962 I found out what it really was, but the only thing
I knew to do was, like you, to keep silent, to do what you had taught
me to do. Strange, then, how the spawn of this thing that happened
to you and that was never spoken of eventually became my own and
lived on in me, transformed, so that I, too, made silence heroic.*

Part Four

Return

And the end of all our exploring
Will be to arrive where we started
And know the place for the first time.

—T. S. ELIOT
"Little Gidding"

I T IS NIGHT in the Lyndon. At the shore water murmurs against the rocks like a susurrus of uneasy voices. Jean and Chloe went upstairs to bed long ago, leaving me alone by the fire, surrounded by my mother's last letters, final reports, scrawled memos. I sit on the same sofa where she worked during the last days of her life, legs tucked under her like a cat, night after night, free for a few hours from Maddy's logorrhea and my father's drinking and my importunate adolescence, writing on her long yellow legal pads, her mind rushing forward like the hasty slant of her script.

On March 8, 1962, there is an anxious letter from Guy Okakok in Alaska: "Dear LaVerne: This is not going to be easy battle because our opponents all train in College and we are don't [sic] much in the white man's language. But we have a [sic] very good friends and you are one of them, you know the language and I depend on you."

On May 9, Alfreda Janis writes from Pine Ridge: "Things are such a mess that I wonder what will come of everything as it's happening now. I wish you could come, Lord knows we need you."

A week later my mother is promising to visit the Mississippi Band of Choctaws in September. "Your people have been forgotten for too long, and we in this association are ashamed when we think of it. Please be patient with us. We promise to find a way to help."

On June 19 Pauline Tyndall writes from Nebraska that she is making my mother an Indian dress. "It is ribbon work etc. bright, and you will wear it to Montana, & Idaho. It will be called 'Summer Hunt.' "

Nearly every day that month she writes to LaFarge or the lawyers in Washington or someone on the Association's board, expressing worry about where money for the Alaska project is to come from. Finally, on June 22, she reports to LaFarge, with relief, "I feel reasonably sure that sooner or later I shall be able to get the Rockefeller Brothers Fund or some other foundation of that type to make a sizable grant. . . . I hope to write this presentation while I am on vacation in August."

On July 5 she is in Washington with Emma Willoya, an Eskimo from the Nome Skinsewers Association, helping her scour the offices of the Department of the Interior for technical assistance.

On July 12 she writes to Harry Forbes, "I have never felt as inadequate in my personal life as I have felt this past year. . . . My mother's condition has been growing worse for the past year. This is the first situation in which I ever found myself in which effort and determination could not bring improvement."

On July 19 she is in Washington again, testifying before the hostile House Subcommittee on Public Lands about a bill that would convert native villages in Alaska into townships, threatening to extinguish native claims against the government forever. "Almost universally," she admonishes the congressmen, "Alaska Natives . . . have been misinformed and led to believe that renunciation of their inheritance is a necessary step toward political and social equality with white Americans (who seldom renounce theirs)."

On August 2, replying to a letter from Guy Okakok in which he warned her that she is increasingly being attacked by the Alaska press for her defense of native rights, she writes, "I expect they will get even rougher with me before we win the fights. It does not matter to me. I am only a woman, but I am not a coward."

As I read these letters, it becomes difficult to breathe. I have an almost physical sensation of my mother's time seeping away. *You don't know. You don't know that these things will never happen. The presentation will never be written. You will never wear the dress that Pauline is sewing in Nebraska. You won't be there for the Choctaws in September. You will never write that proposal.*

On August 13 she is writing to Harry Forbes's wife Hildegard concerning Maddy: "My mother's sense of reality shows new deterioration every day. She chatters from morning until night—literally—so that it is impossible for anyone to escape the sad truth even for a moment. I have lived long enough to acquire a good supply of compassion, but my patience breaks once in a while. My need and desire to give my work the usual mental and physical attention is the thing that gives me a feeling of desperate urgency about finding a reasonably stable solution. The urgency is real, as you know. The desperation is hysterical and—thanks to a therapeutic Vermont—is abating somewhat. We are doing lots of horseback riding—the best thing I know for jiggling thoughts and bones back into place."

On August 19, two days before her death, she writes again to LaFarge, the last words that I have from her hand. She writes about her June trip to Alaska and about traveling across the Arctic with Guy Okakok from village to village, and dining on frozen raw caribou, and the intricacy of native feuds, and the complex relations between Inupiat whaling men and their *omealiks*, their bosses, and the historic if belated political coming together of the Eskimos. "It is not strange that they have to undergo this process. . . . The Irish—pardon the expression—were not a united people when their country was occupied, but became one under occupation." She ended, "We know what to do. I wonder whether we shall have the time to do it."

Upstairs I hear footsteps. Jean is moving from Chloe's room to ours, circling the stairwell to the same room where my parents slept that night, through the same door that I entered on my mother's last morning. I can see her now—my mother—asleep as if drugged, first rolling away from me, then finally reaching for the Winstons on the night table. . . .

Ghosts swarm around me in the night, no longer fended off by Chloe's laughter. Time has dissolved and turned fluid. We have all become part of the house now, as much a part of its fabric as the pinewood paneling and the sagging sofas and the ancient brass lamps and the creaking stairs: my mother with her flood of foolscap and crossword puzzles, my father weeping at the kitchen table, Maddy with her terrified eyes babbling about the Brooklyn of the 1890s, the boy on the veranda. I look out the window and I can see him, his feet propped on the veranda railing, reading hour after hour, dreaming of Shiloh and Chancellorsville and Gettysburg, unconscious of the catastrophe that is about to engulf him like implacable battalions. And here where I now sit, in her chair, thinking her thoughts, the last days and hours of his mother's life are trickling away. We have come together at last: I am simultaneously she and the child, the watched and the watcher, parent and child, idol and devotee, ghost and rememberer.

Here in this room in the stillness of the night I have become you at last. I lie here on the old couch, writing as you wrote, thinking far into the night about the Oglalas and Cheyennes and the Miccosukees and the Inupiat, as I now think about you, about that summer and that day that has become the measure of all summers and all days.

And then you get into the Buick and speed away into the night. I see you at the wheel hurtling through the blackness, driving fast on the narrow lakeside road, blue smoke curling from the cigarette in your fingers, your pale face eerily lit by the lights of the dashboard. Are you racing toward a decision of some kind, a new idea, a solution for villagers on the Arctic shore? Are you simply fleeing Maddy's logorrhea, the knowledge that she is disintegrating in front of your eyes, becoming not your mother at all, and that you will have to put her away? Or are you fleeing from all of us? Have you already left us and gone searching in the black night of your heart for some place of your own, some place free from all our importuning voices, and finally turn back only from exhaustion and guilt, knowing how much Maddy needs you, how much your son needs you, how much tribes scattered from Mississippi to Alaska need you, still knowing that you can't keep it up much longer and are already stretched to the breaking point, but that if you break things will fall apart and people will lose hope, and that after all there is no place for you all your own in the night? And so you drive hour after hour, piloting the Buick through the shrouded mountains, smoking and wishing there were some place to go but home.

It is almost dawn now as we move toward convergence, you and I. I can hear your voice in the silence, welling up from my own heart.

I do not hear the bedroom door open, do not hear my son's voice until it has become insistent and pleading, until I feel his hand on my arm, pulling me from sleep. I am helpless at the sound of his voice. I

cannot tell him where I have been, cannot confess to despair, cannot
say no. In an hour I shall not exist, shall be a ghost.

I wake, still on the couch, to a morning ripe with birdsong and
streaming sunshine splashing the maples and birches and spruce
against the sky. A motor is humming somewhere across the lake, and
a child's voice tinkles through the woods. Jean is already in the
kitchen, rummaging for breakfast. And soon Chloe is clattering
downstairs from the room where she sleeps, the room that was mine
as a boy, shouting for English muffins and bacon, and then begging
me to let her row by herself on the lake, barging into my solitude,
blundering among the ghosts, shattering them like shards of glass in
the sunlight.

JORGE LUIS BORGES once wrote, in the story "Tlön, Uqbar, Orbis Tertius": "already a fictitious past occupies in our memories the place of
another, a past of which we know nothing with certainty—not even
that it is false." In some ways my mother was now like this for me,
more of a mystery to me than ever. Like an archaeologist extrapolat-
ing a vanished form from a handful of potshards, I had fitted together
a few new pieces of information and come up with a shape that made
sense but that I knew was made up as much of speculation as it was
of the solid stuff of fact. I write, "My mother must have felt *this*" or
"She certainly believed *that*." But was it true? Did the rape of which
I have written really take place? There was no documented proof of
it. There were just ambiguous fragments of poetry, images that I had
cloaked in meanings that my mother may never have intended. Her
comment about violence to the reporter from the *Daily Argus* could
have meant almost anything. Even Pauline Tyndall's memory was
suspect: a dying old woman remembering a bit of conversation that
she had thirty-five years before. Perhaps I was simply imposing a pat-
tern that reflected my own need to make sense of a life that had
grown dim and irrecoverable more than it did the truth of what she
had lived. Perhaps, without intending it, I had created a story that
was as much a fiction as James Patrick Farrell's alleged exploits dur-

ing the Civil War. I had the awful sense of her real life flooding away from me in darkness, like the nighttime prairie beyond the headlamps of a speeding car, falling away beyond sight and beyond reach, lost utterly but for fleeting shadows across the pavement, leaving behind only the deep void of emptiness that exists where every life has once been. She had taken so many secrets away with her after all. They had trickled out of her that morning on that road in Vermont.

For that matter, had her death even happened the way I "remembered" it? Was this memory really any more trustworthy than any other? In the years that we had been coming back to Lake Willoughby now, staying each summer at the Lyndon, I had driven past the place where my mother and I had taken that last ride scores of times, sometimes several times a day on errands to Barton and back. I was both drawn to the road and frightened of it. There was a kind of reassurance in speed, in the illusion that in a few seconds I could safely leave the past behind. I often thought of stopping the car and walking the road, but each year I put it off until we were already packing and on our way home and there was no time left, and I drove away from the lake with mingled feelings of both relief and failure, and guilt that I had let down my mother once again and that I had caved in to fear.

One morning in August 1997 I sat with Chloe, who was now seven, on the boulder in front of the Lyndon. Her arms had grown strong enough now to row the Perkinses' skiff and, loving it, she was begging me to take her down to the lake and to let her row all the way to the lake's far shore, its dark side, where I at her age would never have ventured. Only half-listening, I was thinking of the road and what I feared there. Then I thought how for a long time I imagined that what I was frightened of was reliving what happened to my mother. But when I thought clearly about it, I could now see that what I was really frightened of was not her death at all, which I had relived so often, but my own ghost, the ghost of a boy so selfish that he had led his mother to her death and so helpless that he could not save her. What I feared, irrationally but potently, was that if I entered his domain he would recapture me, turn me back into himself and imprison me forever in that long-ago morning. I could tell none of this to Chloe. She knew that my mother had died nearby and knew that it sometimes cost me an effort to drive near that place. But I could not tell her how much I was afraid and how the thing that frightened me lived in the very place that had drawn me—and now us—back to it year after year, and that it was my own self that I feared most of all.

I told Chloe to go inside to her mother for a while, that we would row later, that there was something that I had to do. I drove north along the lake, past Nod Away and the Willoughvale, and out the Barton Road past farms that were mostly overgrown now and neglected, and past the field where my mother and I saw Wally that last morning. I could still see his sunburned face in the light drizzle, hear his crisp twang asking us if we didn't want to go home and come back tomorrow, and then myself goading my mother to go on. "*I want to ride.*" Filled with a strange mixture of dread and of the reawakened anticipation that I felt as we set out on that last morning's ride, I parked in the grass at the end of the Hunts' lane and began to walk north on the Barton Road. The road's ordinariness was unsettling. Very little had changed. The forest was a little denser perhaps, a little wilder than it used to be, and in places pines and birch trees had begun to grow up where there were disused fields. There were two or three modern houses tucked away on plots in the woods. Not much else. As I walked, I felt time falling away, collapsing around me. I felt the August morning of thirty-five years past close in around me like something alive. My heart was racing so fast that it was becoming difficult to breathe. I stopped and forced myself to breathe more slowly and to suck in the familiar, strangely soothing smell of loamy decay that had always been an impalpable backdrop to our rides and that still filled the air and that was still freighted with the ever clearer ring of my mother's laughter, the creak of leather and of horses' hooves, insistent and menacing.

She sits alongside me on Pepper, compact and erect and self-contained, her brain muzzy from lack of sleep, tense from cup after cup of Gertrude Hunt's strong coffee, her lungs aching from all the cigarettes she has already smoked this morning, tense with anxiety, with whatever it was that had taken her away in the Buick in the night. I chatter on about how the sky is clearing and how smart we are to come riding after all. Of the three or four horses she could have ridden she has picked headstrong Pepper, the horse that she loves most, that she loves for his independence, for what in him is most like herself, and that will in a few minutes' time be her undoing.

It took me only fifteen minutes to walk the three-tenths of a mile from the Hunts' lane to the corner of Fiske Road. I was walking no faster than a horse, probably a little slower. That meant that everything that happened that morning, from leaving Wally's to my mother's fall, probably took no more than twenty or twenty-five minutes. I turned right on Fiske Road. Its surface, as it was in 1962, was still hard-packed earth, good to feel underfoot, and easy on horses' hooves. Almost immediately the land began to slope upward. I didn't remember that. (Could any detail at all have slipped my memory? But, then, I would of course scarcely have noticed the incline from horseback.) After that the land flattened out again, unfolding to the east into the familiar panorama of mown fields, copses of pines and maple trees, and beyond them the silver roofs of barns and steep rolling hills. So serene was the landscape that the sight of it now tried to refute my memory, arguing that no death could ever have occurred here, that what I remembered could only be my imagination.

Up to this point my mother and I had been walking our horses alongside Wally and the two New Jersey women. Here where I stood now she had abruptly spurred Pepper into a trot and then a canter. *Why? Why did you do this? Were you still worrying about whatever it was that made you drive away into the night? Were you still thinking of the Cheyenne warrior-woman on her fleet-footed white horse? Did you just want to feel the wind in your face? Or to escape even for a moment from the rest of us, from me? No, not that. You called to me, told me to follow. "Let's gallop!" you said. (Didn't you?)* I "remember" that I followed her, kicking General into a trot and then a canter because, like her, I loved speed, too, and the quickening wind and the animal muscles rippling beneath me, the way she did. But it isn't true. Speed frightened me. And I sensed the danger that lay in the animal's power, and I had nothing like her confidence that I could keep my horse under control. I followed because I didn't want her to leave me behind, because I didn't want to disappoint, didn't want her to see that I was afraid.

Where the road angles slightly to the west the others must have lost sight of us. Had we looked back from our horses, we would have seen the bold knob of Haystack Mountain that anchors the landscape to the south. But we didn't even think of it. We were galloping now. What we saw instead was hardly landscape at all, but rather the smallest fraction of it—a patch of hard-packed earth, a glimpse of electrified fence—infinitely and continuously subdivided to the yard and foot and inch as we gathered speed. I could still see her as I walked, as I have always seen her, tiny and blond and erect on the roan horse, filled with all the magnificent freight of her life—crafter of sonnets, decipherer of papyri, sometime Communist, voice of the voiceless, friend of Miccosukees and Omahas and Inupiat, mother of a selfish and devoted son—pulling away from me on the road, hurtling farther and farther beyond my reach.

My mother is losing control now and beginning to panic. Here I spur forward in my hopeless effort to save her, failing and failing again as Pepper gathers speed. Pepper knew—all the horses knew—this route well. Sometimes he followed it several times a day. He knew that the corner of Spiller Road, just ahead, was the halfway point, that when he turned it he would be heading home to oats and the barn. All the horses knew that. They often quickened their pace a little. We knew it too. We had ridden this route many times before. Pepper must have sensed that my mother hadn't the strength to hold him back, and he began to run flat out for the barn.

She is bent over his neck, clinging helplessly to him with her short legs. Had she simply held on, Pepper must either have tired or have carried her back to the barn. Later some people said that one of the stirrups had broken, that Wally hadn't checked it properly before sending her out. But it wasn't so. Fear got the better of her.

For some distance—thirty or forty yards? here where the land breaks away to the east—I struggle to catch up, to reach for her reins. Could I have saved her here? Caught up to Pepper, grabbed the reins, pulled him to a halt? I play these scenes through my mind without believing them. I lacked the skill. General may even have lacked the speed. Or at least I did not know how to get it out of him. So instead I slow down, shouting to my mother—this has happened before, with other, more compliant horses—that maybe Pepper will, too. That is what I do. I slow down, letting the distance between us widen, never to close.

You are shouting my name, then shouting for help, shouting that you can't stop. These are the last words that you speak to me. It is the end. From now on when I speak to you, it will be to ghostly memory, to my fiction, to the mother whom I have made up, who lives only through my force of will, who is indestructible, like someone on a printed page.

It was a five minutes' walk to Spiller Road from where we began to gallop. Galloping, it could have taken two minutes at most. Here by the second telephone pole from the corner my mother went off her horse. I can see her rising in the saddle, swinging her right leg over Pepper's back, standing for a moment in the stirrup and then stepping away. After that I see nothing until I see her on the ground with blood at the corner of her mouth. In a moment I was already past her, and then turning around, never expecting to see her motionless on the road, but instead shaking herself off, brushing away dust, swearing with embarrassment at losing her mount. Her forehead must have hit the ground with terrific impact. Yet still I see something very different, as if a photographic negative, a second image as real as anything on film might seem to be, had been laid over the first, over the true fact: in this image I see General's forelegs stepping on my mother's fallen body. It cannot have happened this way: General did not break his stride as he galloped past my falling mother, and there was nothing like the mark of a horse's hoof on my mother's bruised skin. But for thirty-five years, "memory" has told me unequivocally that I rode my horse over my mother where she lay on the ground. I can now recognize this as a distortion, the interior distillation of everything that happened that morning, of all the selfishness and mistakes of judgment that brought us to my mother's last terrible moment.

I stared at the road, instinctively searching it for her bloodstains, as if they had soaked indelibly into the earth where I stood. Here at my feet the images of great pinioned wings and of long dark eyes and of the Dakota prairie and the snow-blown tundra, all her certainties of a better future, all her unshared secrets, all her vast reservoir of unspent love finally trickled away. Here, at last, her beautiful, overcharged mind finally shut down. Her sheer *goneness* was like a rock inside my chest pressing against my lungs. *Why did I run for help that never came? Why didn't I stay with you? Wouldn't a kiss or the touch of my hand, a cradling arm, have brought you back? Why didn't I tell you I loved you? Why didn't I beg you to come back so that you heard me? How could you have refused?* Would any of this really have made a difference? Even as I looked down at her she may already have been dead.

I know that my mother bore some of the responsibility for what happened that morning. She was exhausted, and perhaps close to a nervous breakdown. We Shake Hands was in trouble. Alaska was in crisis. Her marriage had failed. Her lover was lost to her. Maddy was disintegrating in front of her eyes. In a month she would be fifty. Her two lives, public and private, were tearing at each other, tearing at her. She should never have listened to me when I begged her to get up, should never have agreed to go on when Wally tried to send us home, should never have gotten on a horse that day, and certainly not Pepper. She should never have broken into a gallop, should never have tried to climb off. She wanted a few minutes' peace and she found it in speed, on a horse that she couldn't control. All that was true enough. It was possible for me to see her death as pure accident, without any meaning at all, and without moral implications of any kind. I knew that if I wanted to I could blame what happened on her state of mind, bad judgment, and bad luck. I was free to let myself off the hook. But I couldn't do it. The truth no longer terrified me as it had for so long, but it was no less the truth. I did not kill her. But I was not innocent of her death. We were collaborators in the final scene of her life.

I have read that there will soon be medications that will suppress the recurrent memories characteristic of trauma. There was a time in my life when I would have given anything for a drug that would flush the scene of my mother's death and all its consequences from my brain like suds down the drain. I felt grateful now that I never had such a choice and that my efforts to cauterize the past had failed. I was no longer frightened of what had happened here. I accepted responsibility for my part in it: it was the moral core of the last experience that my mother and I shared. That was the last thing that I could give to her. Loving her, I would love even the sight of her on this road. I would love her last cries for help, love even the last terrible, foolish thing that she did, trying to climb off Pepper in midgallop, because they were the last things that she bequeathed to me. I would reject nothing, forget nothing until my memory was beyond repair.

I WALKED BACK to the car the way I had come. A few minutes later I was back at the lake. A few hardy bathers were inching with jerky, stoical steps into the frigid water. Children were building sand castles on the beach. There was not much warmth to the sun, but the air was crisp and clear, and the mountains at the far end of the lake rose like live, ripe things that drew their sustenance from the glistening water. I parked in the small lot across the road from the beach and looked in vain for the tiny blond figure that so often I saw slicing vigorously through the water, oblivious to the cold.

For most of my life I had lived with a ghost, ever present, restless, beloved, observing, inspiring, never satisfied, always just beyond reach. The ghost was gone now. She had been replaced by someone who only resembled the woman that I remembered as my mother. I knew things about her that I had never known while she lived. But I would probably never feel her—or at least the fiction that I had called "my mother"—close to me in quite the same way again. I used to think that my mother believed she was indestructible. But this wasn't true. She was perfectly aware of the price that she was liable to pay for the way she lived. Safety, I think, she saw as a kind of moral surrender, an illusion in what she knew to be a fundamentally dangerous world. I still wished until I ached that she had taken better care of herself, shouldered less responsibility, been less ambitious, smoked less, slept more, thought more about the consequences of the risks she took for those of us she left behind. I wished that she had *played it safe*. At the same time, and with equal passion, I wanted her no other way than the fierce, brilliant woman who was, in the end, my true mother. Although I wished that she could know me now, and know that I had found a partner I loved, a woman with a fine mind, an uprightness, and a gentleness of spirit that she would admire, but without her hellbent self-disregard, and could know her granddaughter, in whom I could see flashes of tenacious independence so like her own. I was grateful in a way that I had never seen her grow old, never seen her eyes dull, her flesh sag, her memory disintegrate, her optimism falter. In my memory she remained, and would remain, ever hopeful, ever confident, ever engaged upon some urgent mission to some place with a mysterious name. I did not know much of her in the short span of years that we were together, but I think that I knew the best part of her, the part that I suspect she would have wanted me to know if she had any inkling of how much I respected and loved all that she was.

CHLOE AND JEAN had made gingerbread while I was away, and when I got back to the Lyndon we put on sweaters and sat on the veranda eating it and drinking tea, looking down through the gap in the trees toward the lake and talking about driving tomorrow or the next day to Quebec, and how we would practice our French and eat croissants better than the ones we could get at home.

Jean watched me warily, wondering what my walk had cost me but waiting in her patient way for me to say what I thought I needed to say.

"It was okay," I said, feeling that it was necessary to reassure, saying nothing more, knowing that she would accept silence, for now.

When we had eaten enough gingerbread, the three of us walked down to the shore and Jean and Chloe pushed the lightest of the rowboats off the small beach next to the boathouse and I sat in the shade on a lawn chair watching them row out into the lake, my daughter's tiny figure tugging heroically at the oars. Once, I thought, memory had seemed to me a triumph over loss and death. I felt that I was diminished by everything that I forgot, fearing that I would be marooned from my past, from what I loved, from my mother. But I could see now that remembering was no great trick at all. It was forgetting that took real talent, knowing how to let go of things and how to clear room in my heart for what was alive, missing nothing of the fleeting present as it rushed ruthlessly past, never to be slowed.

Along the far shore several small sailboats glided like blown feathers. Soon a motorboat broke the silence, roaring from around the point, pulling two gaily shrieking girls wobbling behind it on water skis. Watching Chloe negotiate the motorboat's wake I felt a sudden pang of fear at the terrible fragility of her innocence and at my helplessness to protect her from my death. I fought away the thought of her someday staring at my body on a road and of its meanings rippling away through all the years of her life. As she rowed, her little arms revealed a strength that I had never imagined and her tanned face a mixture of joy and determination. The lake had become hers now, along with its ghosts. She would never see them at all, for they were not hers, but would instead remember, as I now did again, sparkling days and icy lakewater, and mountains that were like green sleeping lions, and that her father watched her unwaveringly while she rowed out across the lake. She was still too young to understand that her joy here every summer had given it back to me, had made it possible for me to return and, finally, to repeople the ghostly landscape of memory with the living, ourselves.

In the softening light the figures of the two water skiers became dancing dragonflies that flitted and swooped over the surface of the water. I could hear Chloe's oars now, growing louder as she neared the shore. I snapped pictures of her as she approached. She was shouting something that I couldn't understand.

Finally her tiny piping voice came to me.

"Look how strong I am, Daddy! Look how strong!"

And I began to cry.

Acknowledgments

IN ADDITION TO those who have already been mentioned, this book has benefited in ways large and small from the assistance of many people whom I met in the course of my research. Nancy Smith, the secretary of the Classics Department at New York University, led me to the surviving members of the department in the 1930s. Prof. Naphtali Lewis and Virginia and Prof. Martin Bernstein shared many interesting memories of the university in that period. Henry Foner, John Toland, Nora North, Mervyn Jones, Vic Teich, and Jean Bornstein Agulay provided valuable insights into left wing activity at NYU. Doris Grumbach helped me to understand her—and my mother's—former professor Margaret Schlauch. Prof. Joseph Burns showed me the way to a fascinating collection of Schlauch's correspondence.

The families of Ella Irving and Pauline Tyndall were overwhelming in their hospitality on my trips to South Dakota and Nebraska. Richard Schifter, Arthur Lazarus, Prof. Robert Hecht, Don Mitchell, Leo Vocu, Earl Dyer, Betty Clark, Buffalo Tiger, Harold Mantell, Pen LaFarge, and Corinna Locker were generous with their time and thoughts about my mother's work with the Association on Indian Affairs. I was, as ever, challenged by Elizabeth Clark Rosenthal's incisive analyses of the Association's policies, and inspired by her many crisp and affectionate memories of my mother. Ben Primer and his staff at Seelye G. Mudd Manuscript Library were unfailingly helpful; the Association's archives are now a pleasure to work with, thanks particularly to the work of John Weeren, whose superb reorganization of them is the gold standard of library sicence.

Lt. John Roland of the Mount Vernon Police Department kindly made it possible for me to examine records dating from the 1920s and 1930s. Dr. Prem Peter was always available to answer questions on medical issues.

Jack Barschi, Craig and Pat McKay, Ben LaFarge, Tom Dardis, Ellen Ervin, Buzz and Peg Gummere, and David Lipton all read parts of the manuscript. Their thoughts have improved it in more ways than I can count. Roger Scholl, my editor at Doubleday, was enthusiastic about this book from the start; I am deeply grateful for that. My agent, Carl D. Brandt, was, as always, a constant source of encouragement.

No one, however, has contributed more than my wife, Jean, and my daughter, Chloe, whose love, support, and patience have been a far more powerful retort to the claims of the past than mere prose is ever likely to be.

About the Author

FERGUS M. BORDEWICH is the author of the critically acclaimed books *Killing the White Man's Indian* and *Cathay: A Journey in Search of Old China*, and the general editor of *Children of the Dragon*, an anthology of eyewitness accounts of the Tiananmen Massacre. His articles have appeared in many national publications, including *American Heritage, Smithsonian Magazine, The Atlantic Monthly, The New York Times Magazine, Reader's Digest*, and others. He lives with his family in New York's Hudson Valley.